KAISER BILL!

Blaine Taylor (*b.* 1946) is the author of fourteen histories with illustrations on war, politics, automotives, biography, engineering, architecture, medicine, photography, and aviation.

The well-read historian is a former Vietnam War soldier and Military Policeman of the US Army's elite 199th Light Infantry Brigade under enemy Communist Viet Cong fire during 1966–67 in South Vietnam. He was awarded twelve medals and decorations, including the coveted Combat Infantryman's Badge/CIB. A later crime and political newspaper reporter, Taylor is also an award-winning medical journalist, international magazine writer, and the winner of four political campaigns as press secretary for county, state, and US Presidential elections, 1974–92.

During 1991–92, he served as a US Congressional aide and press secretary on Capitol Hill, Washington, DC. Blaine lives at Towson, MD/USA.

Previously Published books by Blaine Taylor

Guarding the Fuhrer: Sepp Dietrich, Johann Rattenhuber, and the Protection of Adolf Hitler (1993)
Fascist Eagle: Italy's Air Marshal Italo Balbo (1996)
Mercedes-Benz Parade and Staff Cars of the Third Reich (1999)
Volkswagen Military Vehicles of the Third Reich (2004)
Hitler's Headquarters from Beer Hall to Bunker 1920–45 (2006)
Apex of Glory: Benz, Daimler, & Mercedes-Benz 1885–1955 (2006)
Hitler's Chariots Volume 1: Mercedes-Benz G-4 Cross-Country Touring Car (2009)
Hitler's Chariots Volume 2: Mercedes-Benz 770K Grosser Parade Car (2010)
Hitler's Engineers: Fritz Todt and Albert Speer/Master Builders of the Third Reich (2010)
Hitler's Chariots Volume 3: Volkswagen from Nazi People's Car to New Beetle (2011)
Mrs Adolf Hitler: The Eva Braun Photograph Albums 1912–45 (2013)
Dallas Fifty Years On: The Murder of John F. Kennedy—A New Look at an Old Crime, 22 November 1963–2013 (2013)
Guarding the Fuhrer: Sepp Dietrich & Adolf Hitler (2014)
Hermann Goering in the First World War: The Personal Photograph Albums of Hermann Goering (2014)

KAISER BILL!

A NEW LOOK AT GERMANY'S LAST EMPEROR
WILHELM II 1859-1941

BLAINE TAYLOR

FONTHILL

Fonthill Media Language Policy

Fonthill Media publishes in the international English language market. One language edition is published worldwide. As there are minor differences in spelling and presentation, especially with regard to American English and British English, a policy is necessary to define which form of English to use. The Fonthill Policy is to use the form of English native to the author. Blaine Taylor was born in the US and educated at Towson University, and now lives at Towson, MD/USA, therefore American English has been adopted in this publication.

Fonthill Media Limited
Fonthill Media LLC
www.fonthillmedia.com
office@fonthillmedia.com

First published in the United Kingdom
and the United States of America 2014

ISBN 978–1–78155-001-4

Typeset in 10pt on 13pt Minion Pro
Printed and bound by CPI Group (UK) Ltd, Croydon, CR) 4YY

Contents

Foreword   7

Dedication   8

Acknowledgments   8

Chronology   9

Preface: Just Who *Was* Wilhelm II?   19

PART 1: PRUSSIAN PRINCE & GERMAN CROWN PRINCE 1859–1888   25

1   The Advent of Brandenburg-Prussia 1618–1797   27

2   The Modern Military Kings of Prussia and German Kaisers 1797– 1888   30

3   The Medical Case Files of the Imperial Triad 1797–1888   43

PART 2: KING OF PRUSSIA & GERMAN KAISER/EMPEROR 1888–1914   59

4   "Dropping the Pilot:" Firing Bismarck 1888–1890   61

5   "Kaiser Bill" 1890–1914   72

6   Navies, Merchant Marines, and Ocean Liners of Kings & Kaisers 1701–1914   84

7   The German Overseas Colonial Empire 1883–1914   106

PART 3: SUPREME WAR LORD IN THE GREAT WAR 1914–1918   109

8   In the West   111

9   In the East and Middle East   117

10   In Africa   124

11   In the Air and on the Sea   125

12   At Berlin & Spa, Autumn 1918   131

PART 4: KAISER-IN-WAITING AND EXILED MEMOIR AUTHOR 1918–1941   139

13   The Kaiser in Holland 1918   141

14   At Doorn, Holland 1920–41   143

Bibliography   154

Foreword

The Great War of 1914–1918 cost a reported two million dead and six million wounded, both sides inclusive. Of these, the very last man to die was Henry Gunther of Baltimore, at 10:59 a.m., one minute before the Armistice came into effect at 11 a.m. on the 11th day of the 11th month of 1918.

Baltimore has another notable connection to the man known—among other epithets—as *Bully Billie* and *Sheikh Billy of Potsdam and the Berlin–Baghdad Railway*—in the person of the late *Sunpapers'* editor and columnist, H. L. Mencken.

Of German extraction, Mencken was forced by the *Sun* to take a leave of absence during all of both World Wars because he favored the cause of Germany over that of the Allies.

Some decades ago, I visited the home of the *Bard of Baltimore* in a row house on Union Square on its west side. At the top of the stairs of the second floor, I found an autographed photo of Kaiser Wilhelm II.

Dedication

To my friend, colleague, and computer specialist Frank White of Phoenix, MD/USA, who helps make it all possible.

Remembering the Dearly Departed.

Fellow Maryland author and politician/surgeon Ross Z. Pierpont, MD; Baltimore *Sun* Book Page editor James Bready, who reviewed all of my books.

Ritz Camera Store owner William Seim; Cecil County, MD/USA Sheriff and US Marine Jack DeWitt; and political advisor Frank Furst Daily, Jr. Gone, but not forgotten! RIP.

Acknowledgments

Anne S. K. Brown Military Collection, Brown University, Providence, Rhode Island/USA, Curator Peter Harrington; Towson State College history teachers Dr Armin Mruck and Dr Herbert Andrews, as well as TSC Political Science teacher Dr Gerd Ehrlich; Baltimore County Public Library, Towson, MD/USA, Mrs Joan Lattanzi, Inter-Library Loan Department; Enoch Pratt Free Library Periodicals Department, Baltimore, Ms. Margaret Gers; ace researcher Curtis Mason, formerly of Towson Copy Center, Towson, MD/USA.

Photographic Assistance: Stan Piet, Bel Air, MD; The Kelmscott Book Shop, Baltimore, Mrs Susannah Horrom.

German translations, Mrs Erika Burke, Pearland, TX.

Peter Bernotas, President of International Historic Films, Inc.; Chicago, for stills and other materials from *The Dismissal*, 1942, and manager Ron Ocumbo and Katherine Mandue for stocking my books at Barnes & Noble, Towson, MD.

Photo/art research by the author and publisher Alan Sutton.

Chronology

1640–1688: Rule of Great Elector Frederick Wilhelm of Brandenburg and Duke of East Prussia.

1688–1701: Rule of son Elector and Duke Frederick III, 1701: Brandenburg–Prussia becomes a Kingdom, with Frederick III taking the title of King *in* Prussia Frederick I.

1713–1740: Frederick Wilhelm I becomes King *of* Brandenburg–Prussia and builds a powerful army.

1740–1786: His son Frederick II (the Great) reigns as King of Brandenburg–Prussia, using the army to seize the former Austrian Province of Silesia and hold it in the series of Silesian Wars of 1740–1745.

1756–1763: Frederick wages the Seven Years' War with Sweden, Russia, Bohemia, Austria, Saxony, and France.

1772, 1793, and 1795: Trio of Partitions of Poland among Prussia, Russia, and Austria.

1778–1779: War of the Bavarian Succession to prevent Austria from seizing Bavaria

1785: Frederick forms the *Fürstenbund/Princes' League* of North German States.

1786–1797: Frederick Wilhelm II succeeds Frederick the Great as King.

1797–1840: Reign of King Frederick Wilhelm III.

1806: Napoleon I defeats Prussian Army at twin Battles of Jena–Auerstadt.

1807: Prussia humiliated at the Tilsit Conference between Napoleon and Tsar Alexander I of Russia.

1813: Prussia leads German states in War of Liberation to defeat Napoleon at the Battle of Leipzig.

1814: Prussian Army helps defeat Napoleon in France; Paris taken.

1815: Prussian Army helps defeat Napoleon during the Waterloo campaign; Paris falls.

1840–1861: Reign of King Frederick IV.

1848–1849: Revolts in Prussia and across Europe occur and are suppressed by armies.

27 January 1859: Birth of Prince Wilhelm of Prussia, later King of Prussia and German Kaiser; also in the line of succession to be King of England.

June 1858: Prince Wilhelm of Prussia (born 1797) named Regent for his ill brother.

1861–1888: Wilhelm I as King upon the death of his older brother.

1862: Otto von Bismarck named Prime Minister of Prussia by King Wilhelm I.

1864: Prussia and Austria jointly seize Province of Schleswig-Holstein from Denmark.

1866: In the Seven Weeks' War, Prussia defeats Austria, forming the North German Confederation.

1870–1871: German states defeat Imperial France of Napoleon III during the Franco-Prussian War.

1871–1888: King Wilhelm I reigns also as the German *Kaiser*/Emperor.

March–15 June 1888: Kaiser Frederick III rules for but 99 days.

15 June 1888-November 1918: Reign of Kaiser Wilhelm II.

March 1890: Kaiser Wilhelm II dismisses Bismarck as Imperial Chancellor.

1890–1894: General Leo von Caprivi Chancellorship.

1894–1900: Prince Chlodwig von Hohenlohe Chancellorship.

1900–1909: Bernhard von Bülow Chancellorship.

1909–1917: Theobald von Bethmann-Hollwegg Chancellorship.

1917–1918: Dr Georg Michaelis and Count Georg von Hertling Chancellorships.

October–November 1918: Prince Max of Baden Chancellorship.

The Great War of 1914–18

1914

28 June 1914: Assassination at Sarajevo of Austrian Archduke Franz Ferdinand.

28 July 1914: Austria declares war on Serbia.

29 July 1914: Russia mobilizes its army.

1 August 1914: Germany declares war on Russia; France mobilizes its army.

2 August 1914: Germany invades Belgium and Luxembourg.

3 August 1914: France declares war on Germany.

4 August 1914: Great Britain declares war on Germany.

7 August 1914: First British Expeditionary Forces (BEF) land at Ostend, Belgium, and also at Calais and Dunkirk, France.

8 August 1914: Serbia at war with Germany.

12 August 1914: France and Great Britain at war with Austria-Hungary; Montenegro at war with Germany.

17 August 1914: German Army takes Liège, Belgium forts and city.

20 August 1914: Brussels falls to Germans.

21 August 1914: Battle of Charleroi between Germans and French.

23 August 1914: First fight ever between Germans and British at Battle of Mons, followed by a second Reich victory at Battle of Le Cateau.

24 August 1914: Germans invade France at Lille.

26 August 1914: Germany wins the Battle of the Frontiers versus France and Belgium.

28 August 1914: Austria-Hungary declares war on Belgium.

29 August 1914: Russian Army takes Königsberg, East Prussia.

30 August 1914: Germans take Amiens, France.

31 August 1914: Hindenburg and Ludendorff's 8th Army defeats Russians at Battle of Tannenberg in East Prussia.

4 September 1914: Germans take Rheims, France.

6–10 September 1914: German 1st Army defeated by the French Army and British Expeditionary Force at the First Battle of the Marne River; general retreat of the German Armies to the Soissons-Rheims Line.

14 September 1914: French Army retakes Amiens and Rheims; von Moltke tells the Kaiser that the war is lost.

29 September 1914: Germans bombard Antwerp, Belgium.

2 October 1914: British Royal Navy mines North Sea, starting naval blockade of Germany, 1914–1920

9 October 1914: Antwerp surrenders, and Belgian government relocates to Ostend.

13 October 1914: British Expeditionary Force takes Ypres.

14 October 1914: Canadian Expeditionary Force/CEF lands 32,000 men at Plymouth, UK; First Battle of Champagne, France.

15 October 1914: Germans take Ostend, and Belgian government moves to Le Havre, France.

16 October 1914: Germans bomb Hartlepool, Scarborough, and Whitby on English east coast.

November 1914: Turkey enters the war on the side of Germany and Austria-Hungary.

Mid-September–December 1914: War of maneuver devolves into stalemate trench warfare.

24–25 December 1914: Christmas Truce.

1915

10 February 1915: Germans defeat Russians at the Battle of the Masurian Lakes.

18 February 1915: German Navy declares blockade of British Isles.

19–20 February 1915: First German *Zeppelin* airship raid on England.

10 March 1915: British Expeditionary Force takes Neuve-Chapelle in Flanders, Belgium.

22 April 1915: At Second Battle of Ypres, Germans use poison gas to attack CEF.

7 May 1915: German Navy U-boat submarine sinks liner *Lusitania* off Ireland.

23 May 1915: Italy declares war on Austria, and on Germany three months later, both former allies since 1882.

31 May 1915: *Zeppelin LZ 38* bombs London.

4–6 June 1915: German aircraft bombs English towns.

15 June 1915: Allied planes bomb Karlsruhe, Germany.

31 July 1915: French Air Force bombs Baden, Germany.

25 September 1915: Allies take Lens in Artois Offensive.

12 October 1915: English nurse Edith Cavell shot by Germans for helping British POWs escape from Belgium.

13 October 1915: *Zeppelins* bomb London, with 55 dead and 114 wounded.

14 October 1915: Bulgaria joins Central Powers of Germany, Austria-Hungary, and Turkey, and invades Serbia.

15 October 1915: Great Britain declares war on Bulgaria.

17 October 1915: France declares war on Bulgaria.

19 October 1915: Italy and Russia declare war on Bulgaria.

1916

29–31 January 1916: *Zeppelins* bomb Paris, and also English towns.

21 February 1916: Battle of Verdun begins in France; Germans take Haumont.

25 February 1916: Verdun's Fort Douaumont taken by Germans.

9 March 1916: Germany declares war on Portugal.

15 March 1916: Austria-Hungary declares war on Portugal.

31 March 1916: Melancourt at Verdun taken by Germans.

14 April 1916: British Royal Naval Air Service bombs both Constantinople and Adrianople in Turkey.

20 April 1916: Russian troops land at Marseilles for service on Western Front.

15 May 1916: British Expeditionary Force takes Vimy Ridge.

31 May 1916: Battle of Jutland fought between German and Royal Navies, with heavy losses on both sides; Germans win a narrow edge victory, but never sortie out in strength again.

6 June 1916: German Army takes French Fort Vaux at Verdun.

July 1916: Hindenburg succeeds von Falkenhayn as Chief of the German General Staff with Ludendorff as First Quartermaster General.

1 July 1916: British Expeditionary Force and French attack north and south of Somme River, and RFC gains air control.

14 July 1916: British Expeditionary Force cavalry breaches German lines.

15 July 1916: British Expeditionary Force takes Longueval.

25 July 1916: British Expeditionary Force takes Pozières.

30 July 1916: British Expeditionary Force and French advance between Delville Wood and Somme River; British RAF and French Army of the Air conduct first joint aerial operations against the Imperial German Flying Corps.

3 August 1916: French Army recaptures Fleury.

27 August 1916: Rumania declares war on Austria-Hungary.

28 August 1916: Italy declares war on Germany, and the latter on Rumania.

31 August 1916: Bulgaria and Turkey declare war on Rumania.

2–3 September 1916: First *Zeppelin* shot down over UK.

15 September 1916: British Expeditionary Force takes Flers-Courcelette and other positions on Western Front using tanks directed by aircraft.

26 September 1916: British Expeditionary Force and French take Combles and Thiepval.

24 October 1916: Verdun's Fort Douaumont retaken by French.

2 November 1916: Germans evacuate Verdun's Fort Vaux.

13 November 1916: British Expeditionary Force advances along Ancre River.

22 November 1916: Emperor Franz Josef I of Austria-Hungary dies, and is succeeded by Kaiser Karl I

23 November 1916: German Navy bombards English coast.

28 November 1916: First German daylight air raid on London.

15 December 1916: French Army wins attrition Battle of Verdun.

18 December 1916: President Wilson issues first peace offer to both sides; rejected.

1917

22 January 1917: Wilson suggests a "peace without victory".

31 January 1917: Germany resumes unrestricted submarine warfare against neutrals.

3 February 1917: US breaks diplomatic relations with Germany, and German Ambassador returns home.

17 February 1917: British Expeditionary Force wins Battle of Ancre River.

28 February 1917: Zimmermann Telegram scandal breaks, in which Germany secretly offers both Mexico and Japan a wartime alliance against the US with US territory to be ceded in Far West.

3 March 1917: British Expeditionary Force advances on Bapaume.

4 March 1917: German Army withdraws to rear defensive line.

14 March 1917: China breaks with Germany.

15 March 1917: Abdication of Tsar and Tsarevich in Russia, but Russia stays in the war.

17 March 1917: British Expeditionary Force takes Bapaume, as French capture Roye and Lassigny.

18 March 1917: Germans retreat on an 85-mile-long front, giving up Péronne, Chaulnes, Nesle, and Noyon.

26–31 March 1917: Battle of Cambrai between British Expeditionary Force and Germans.

6 April 1917: US declares war on Germany.

7 April 1917: Cuba and Panama declare war on Germany.

8 April 1917: Austria-Hungary breaks diplomatic relations with US.

9 April 1917: Germans defeated by British Expeditionary Force at Battle of Arras, and Bolivia severs diplomatic relations with Germany.

13 April 1917: Canadians take Vimy, Givenchy, Bailleul, and Lens from German Army.

20 April 1917: Turkey ends diplomatic relations with the US.

7 May 1917: German *Gotha* bombers make first London night raid.

9 May 1917: Liberia breaks with Germany.

16 May 1917: British Expeditionary Force takes Bullecourt during Battle of Arras aftermath.

17 May 1917: Honduras breaks with Germany.

19 May 1917: Nicaragua breaks with Germany.

25 May 1917: 21 heavy German *Gotha* bombers make first mass daylight attack on UK.

7 June 1917: British Expeditionary Force takes Messines-Wyschaete Ridge.

8 June 1917: US General John J. Pershing arrives in UK *en route* to France.

13 June 1917: First mass daylight 14 *Gotha* bomber raid on London with 588 casualties.

18 June 1917: Haiti breaks with Germany.

1 July 1917: Kerensky Offensive by Russian Army in Galicia starts.

3 July 1917: First American Expeditionary Forces/AEF arrives in France.

10 July 1917: Fall of Imperial Chancellor Theobald von Bethmann-Hollwegg, succeeded by Dr Georg Michaelis.

16–23 July 1917: Russian Army beaten by Germans, and retreats on a 155-mile-long front.

22 July 1917: Siam declares war on Germany and Austria-Hungary.

7 August 1917: Liberia declares war on Germany.

14 August 1917: China declares war on Germany and Austria-Hungary.

15 August 1917: CEF takes Hill 70 overlooking Lens.

22 August 1917: Final German daylight bombing of UK.

16 September 1917: Kerensky proclaims Republic of Russia

20 September 1917: Costa Rica breaks with Germany.

26 September 1917: During Battle of Ypres, British Expeditionary Force takes Zonnebeke, Polygon Wood, and Tower Hamlets.

6 October 1917: Peru and Uruguay break with Reich.

9 October 1917: British Expeditionary Force and French take Poelcapelle.

23 October 1917: AEF fires first shots in trench warfare, and French Army advances northeast of Soissons.

26 October 1917: Brazil declares war on Germany.

1 November 1917: German Army abandons Chemins des Dames position.

6 November 1917: Canadians take Passchendaele.

7 November 1917: Reds under Lenin depose Kerensky in Russia.

9 November 1917: Italian Army retreats to Piave River.

20 November 1917: Battle of Cambrai.

21 November 1917: British Expeditionary Force takes Ribécourt, Flesquires, Havrincourt, and Marcoing

23 November 1917: Italians repulse Germans from Asiago Plateu to Brenta River

24 November 1917: During on-going Battle of Cambrai, British Expeditionary Force tanks capture Bourlon Wood.

1 December 1917: German East Africa falls to Allies.

3 December 1917: Russian Reds ask for armistice with Germans.

5 December 1917: British Expeditionary Force retreats from Bourlon Wood and Graincourt west of Cambrai.

7 December 1917: Finland declares independence from Russia under German aegis.

8 December 1917: Jerusalem lost by Turks after 673 years to British General Allenby, and Ecuador breaks with Germany.

10 December 1917: Panama declares war on Austria-Hungary.

11 December 1917: US declares war on Austria-Hungary.

15 December 1917: Germany and Russia sign an armistice at Brest-Litovsk, Poland.

1918

8 January 1918: Wilson proclaims his 14 Points for peace.

19 January 1918: AEF takes over sector NE of Toul, France.

1 February 1918: Argentina recalls military attachés from Berlin and Vienna.

18 February 1918: AEF in Chemin des Dames sector.

1 March 1918: AEF wins a victory in salient north of Toul.

3 March 1918: Russia and Germany sign peace Treaty of Brest-Litovsk, Poland.

4 March 1918: Treaty signed between Reich and Finland.

5 March 1918: Preliminary peace treaty signed between defeated Rumania and Central

Powers.

9 March 1918: Reds move Russian capital from Petrograd to Moscow.

21 March 1918: Germans launch *Kaiser's Battle/Michael Offensive* against Allies on the Western Front to win the war on 50-mile front from Arras to La Fère, including a bombardment of Paris from a long-range gun 76 miles distant.

24 March 1918: German Army takes Péronne, Ham, and Chauny.

25 March 1918: Bapaume and Nesle fall to Germans again.

9 April 1918: Germans start second drive in Flanders, Belgium.

10 April 1918: First German drive halted at Amiens after an advance of 35 miles.

15 April 1918: Second German drive stopped at Ypres after a 10-mile advance.

21 April 1918: Guatemala declares war on Germany; Richthofen killed in combat.

23 April 1918: Royal Navy raids German submarine base at Zeebrugge, Belgium, blocking its access channel.

7 May 1918: Nicaragua declares war on all Central Powers.

19–20 May 1918: Final German bomber raid on UK in which there are casualties.

24 May 1918: Costa Rica declares war on Central Powers.

27 May 1918: Third German drive starts on Aisne-Marne River front of 30 miles between Soissons and Rheims, France in Second Battle of the Marne.

28 May 1918: Germans sweep past Chemin des Dames, crossing the Vesle River at Fismes, while AEF takes Cantigny.

29 May 1918: French Army gives up Soissons.

31 May 1918: Germans cross Marne River, reaching Château Thierry, 40 miles from Paris, but lose the Second Battle of the Marne River.

3–6 June 1918: US Marines and Army halt German advance at Château Thierry and Neuilly after an advance of 32 miles, as US cooperation with Allies begins on large scale.

5 June 1918: Strategic bombing of Germany by British bombers starts.

9–14 June 1918: German Army halted on Western Front.

15–24 June 1918: Austrians defeated by Italian Army.

30 June 1918: AEF numbers 1,019,115 soldiers in France; US Marines engage the German Army at Belleau Wood, and recognized as saving Paris.

1 July 1918: AEF takes Vaux.

15 July 1918: Haiti declares war on Germany, and AEF halts renewed German drive on Paris.

18 July 1918: French Army and AEF launch joint offensive on Marne-Aisne Rivers front.

23 July 1918: French seize Oulchy-le-Château, driving the Germans back 10 miles between Aisne and Marne Rivers.

30 July 1918: Allies on the Ourcq River, with Germans in full retreat to the Vesle River.

1 August 1918: French Army retakes Soissons.

3 August 1918: Wilson agrees to joint Allied Expeditionary Force with UK, Japan, and France to Murmansk, Archangel, and Vladivostok.

3 August 1918: Allies push past Rheims and Soissons, capturing German Fismes base as well as the entire Aisne-Vesle Rivers front.

5 August 1918: Final *Zeppelin* air raid on England.

7 August 1918: French and AEF cross the Vesle River.

8 August 1918: British Expeditionary Force drive starts in Picardy, advancing 14 miles; "Black Day of the German Army," according to Ludendorff.

10 August 1918: Allies retake Montdidier.

13 August 1918: Mt. Lassigny taken by French.

15 August 1918: CEF captures Damery and Parvillers NW of Roye.

21 August 1918: Battle of Bapaume.

26 August 1918: Battle of the Scarpe.

28 August 1918: Renewed Battle of the Somme River.

29 August 1918: Allies retake Noyon and Bapaume.

1 September 1918: Australian Army takes Peronne; AEF fights in Belgium for the first time, capturing Voormezeele.

11 September 1918: German Army driven back to Hindenburg Line of November 1917.

13 September 1918: AEF starts St Mihiel offensive on a 40-mile front.

14 September 1918: St Mihiel recaptured from Germans, with 150 square miles of France liberated from German occupation since 1914.

19–20 September 1918: British Royal Air Force destroys Turkish 7th Army in Palestine from the air.

21 September 1918: Turkish Army loses 40,000 prisoners to the British in Palestine.

27 September 1918: French and AEF take 30,000 POWs in drive from Rheims to Verdun, attacking the Hindenburg Line.

28 September 1918: Belgian Army assaults Germans from Ypres to the North Sea, advancing four miles.

29 September 1918: Bulgaria surrenders to the French Army.

30 September 1918: British-Belgian Army advance reaches Roulers.

October 1918: Marines defeat Germans at Battle of Blanc Mont/White Mountain Ridge.

1 October 1918: Allies capture Hindenburg Line cornerstone of St Quentin, Damascus taken by British Army during Palestine campaign.

2 October 1918: Germans retreat from Lens.

3 October 1918: Italians clear Austrian Army from Albania.

4 October 1918: King Ferdinand of Bulgaria abdicates, succeeded as King by son Crown Prince Boris.

5 October 1918: German Imperial Chancellor Prince Max of Baden asks for Allied Armistice terms from President Wilson.

7 October 1918: French Army takes Berry-au-Bac.

9 October 1918: Allies take Cambrai.

11 October 1918: AEF advances in Meuse-Argonne Forest.

12 October 1918: German Foreign Minister Solf states Germany will give up all occupied territory.

13 October 1918: Germans retreat from Laon and La Fère; AEF takes Grandpré after four-day battle.

14 October 1918: Wilson refers Germans to French Marshal Foch for Armistice terms.

16 October 1918: British Expeditionary Force enters Lille.

17 October 1918: German submarine base at Ostend, Belgium taken by Allied amphibious

attack; Allies take Douai, former GAF base.

19 October 1918: Belgian cities of Bruges and Zeebrugge fall to Belgian Army and British Expeditionary Force.

25 October 1918: First five days of Italian Army offensive gains 50,000 POWs.

28 October 1918: Kaiser fires Ludendorff as First Quartermaster General, replacing him with General Wilhelm Groener; Hindenburg remains as Chief of the General Staff.

30 October 1918: Austria-Hungary and Bulgaria desert Germany by leaving the war.

31 October 1918: Turkey surrenders, and Dardanelles Straits open to shipping.

1 November 1918: US 1st Army takes Cléry-le-Grand.

3 November 1918: AEF sweeps ahead on 50-mile front above Verdun, with Germans in full retreat; German Fleet mutinies at Kiel.

4 November 1918: AEF strikes at Sedan; Italians win Battle of Vittorio Veneto.

7 November 1918: AEF enters Sedan.

8 November 1918: Sedan heights taken by AEF.

9 November 1918: Allies take Maubeuge; Kaiser Wilhelm II decides to abdicate.

10 November 1918: CEF takes Mons; Kaiser flees General Headquarters at Spa, Belgium and crosses Dutch frontier at Eysden, Holland.

11 November 1918: Germans and Allies sign the Armistice, effectively ending the First World War; Kaiser receives shelter at Amerongen, Holland.

28 November 1918: Wilhelm II abdicates as German Emperor and King of Prussia; Crown Prince Wilhelm abdicates his offices on 1 December 1918.

1919

11 February 1919: Friedrich Ebert elected civilian German President.

21 June 1919: German High Seas Fleet scuttles itself at Scapa Flow, Scotland.

28 June 1919: Versailles Peace Treaty signed by Republican Germany.

1920: Kaiser Wilhelm II moves from Amerongen to Doorn, Holland, residing there into 1941.

1921–1980

4 April 1921: Death of Kaiserin August Viktoria at Doorn after 40 years of marriage

5 November 1922: Kaiser Wilhelm II, 62, marries Princess Hermine Caroline of Schönaich-Carolath, 34, under title of Empress Hermine.

1923: Former Crown Prince Wilhelm allowed home to Germany after five years of Dutch exile.

1925: Hindenburg elected President of Germany.

1929: Death of Kaiser's younger brother, Prince Heinrich.

1931–32: Hermann Göring visits Doorn to see the Kaiser; Hindenburg elected to second term as President.

2 August 1934: Death of von Hindenburg; Adolf Hitler succeeds him.

5 June 1941: Death of Kaiser Wilhelm II at age 82.

1947: Death of Kaiserin Hermine.

1951: Death of former Crown Prince Wilhelm.

1980: Death of Kaiser's only daughter, Victoria Luise.

Preface
Just Who *Was* Wilhelm II?

"I am the Supreme War Lord! I don't decide, I *command*! In war, I will be my own chief of staff!"

So trumpeted boastful German Kaiser Wilhelm II, the last man to hold the twin titles of King of Prussia and German Emperor. Many past authors and persons who knew him well have asserted that the reality was far different, however. We shall see in this new, independent biographical examination.

On the winter afternoon of 27 January 1859—amidst the firing of a 101 artillery salute—Prussian Field Marshal Friedrich Graf F. H. E. von Wrangel threw open a window of the Royal Palace on Unter den Linden in Berlin, and shouted to the expectant crowd of people assembled below, "Children, it is a Prince, and a stout recruit, too!"

Thus was born the future and final German Emperor, Kaiser Wilhelm II, the man whom many historians continue to blame for the outbreak of the Great War, of 1914–1918, now in its Centennial worldwide.

In recent decades, however, the former, absolute sanctity of this dictum and harsh judgment has been modified by authors both German and Allied. Thrilled since he was but a small boy by warfare as an exciting game where one wore splendid uniforms, as a ruler, the Kaiser prompted his cousin Tsar Nicholas II to fight the Russo-Japanese War of 1904-05 in far-off Manchuria that ended in a humiliating Russian defeat. As a person half-English himself, Wilhelm II took a deep interest in England's Boer War in South Africa, and in his typical over-the-top fashion had his own military draft winning campaigns for *both* sides, claiming in 1908 that it was his plan adopted by Lord Roberts that eventually beat the Boers, no less. When he came to visit actual battlefields himself during the Great War of 1914-18, the stark reality of misery, suffering, and slaughter made him heartsick—too late! To the end of his long life, however, the Kaiser delighted in dressing up in fancy uniforms and headgear.

The world today remembers him for the constant saber rattling across the three decades of his reign, yet he declared himself be the "Peace Kaiser," and maintained that status for the first quarter century of his rule, much to the chaffed chagrin of his Prussian officer corps that agreed with this self-assessment. They wanted him to be more like a Teutonic Mars, the God of War.

A play actor at heart, in reality Wilhelm II wanted Napoleon's victories without Napoleon's battles, yet was still buried in uniform in exile at Doorn, Holland, on 5 June 1941, where, indeed, his mortal remains still reside today.

In school, the young Prince's favorite subject was always history, and he wasn't much interested in any games that didn't feature war in some form. In both pursuits, he was acutely aware that—as Bonaparte had allegedly asserted—"Prussia was a state hatched from a cannonball!"—*and* that his mighty dynastic House of Hohenzollern had helped defeat Napoleonic France—twice. This was particularly true at the June 1815 Battle of Waterloo in Belgium, where his paternal grandfather had seen action. His own father—Crown Prince Frederick (later Kaiser Frederick III)—had taken part in the glorious Franco-Prussian War of 1870–1871, was present at the creation of the German Empire, and had been awarded a coveted Field Marshal's baton for his valorous military service in the full trio of Prussian wars that helped unite Germany.

Wilhelm himself in 1900 would also receive an unearned baton from the hands of the Imperial Army, as well as the martial staff of one of his later wartime partners, Bulgaria. He was as well an honorary British Field Marshal, presented to him by his Royal uncle and rival, King Edward VII of Great Britain, on the Kaiser's 42nd birthday, 27 January 1901.

The King's sister—and Wilhelm's mother—was the former Princess Royal of Great Britain, the eldest child of the United Kingdom's revered Queen Victoria, who was thus also his maternal grandmother, he being her first born grandchild.

Queen Victoria died in Wilhelm's arms in January 1901, and his own mother in August that same year.

Commissioned at age 10 as a second lieutenant in the uniform of the 1st Prussian Foot Guards, Prince Wilhelm was also awarded the Order of the Black Eagle, and on 2 May 1869, when he attended his very first military parade.

The following year, his father and grandfather went off to the third and last of Prussian Chancellor Otto von Bismarck's fabled "wars of unification" that concluded with the German capture of the French capital of Paris and the proclamation as well of the German Empire in the Hall of Mirrors at the Palace of Versailles of France's famed "Sun King," Louis XIV. His revered grandfather took the title of German Emperor that he would also one day inherit by birth and succession.

These were understandably heady events for the young Prince, and he always believed that he, too, would some day lead his own troops on horseback down the broad boulevards of the French capital, conquered anew by *him*.

It was not to be, however, although he did get to see the fabulous "City of Light" in 1878 as a young student traveling incognito.

The young officer reveled in the camaraderie of Prussian Army life, and then and later was much influenced by the fellow officers he met during this period. A later Chief of General Staff when Wilhelm II was Emperor—Field Marshal Count Alfred von Waldersee—habitually had to bail out the Prince from his indiscretions with prostitutes across Europe during this same time of male maturation, reportedly.

Prince Wilhelm was no mental lightweight, however, and some thought that he might have become a successful journalist had he not been born and thus destined to reign as monarch over the Second German Reich.

Indeed, the Prince found time to read a 14-volume naval history that was the genesis of his creation of a German surface fleet that he felt would command greater respect from what he saw as a haughty British Lion across the adjacent North Sea. He also saw the new Imperial German High Seas Fleet that he built as being an instrument to advance his far-reaching plans for an overseas German colonial empire in Africa and across the vast Pacific Ocean.

Promoted to Army captain at age 21, Wilhelm was married to his first wife—the future Kaiserin Augusta Victoria of Schleswig-Holstein (nicknamed Dona)—on 27 February 1881, a marital union that lasted 40 years until her death. She bore him six sons (five soldiers and a sailor), and also a daughter, whose memoirs are one of the best source books extant on the Wilhelminian Reich.

Named to the Hussar cavalry in 1882, Prince Wilhelm became a battalion commander in the 1st Foot Guards the following year, and in 1885 was being touted by his own circle of toadying subordinates as a second Frederick the Great.

The Iron Chancellor's son—Prince Herbert von Bismarck—called the young Prince, "Cold as a dog's nose … heartless, superficial, and vain," a characterization shared by his mother, and a reputation that seemed to be borne out over succeeding decades as he disposed of both friends and ministers who outlasted their value to him.

Unfortunately for history's sake—and ours!—Wilhelm's paternal grandfather forbade him to take a desired tour to see British India, China, Australia, and the United States. Had he been allowed to do so, he might have hesitated still more before becoming engaged in the First World War. Instead, on 27 January 1888, the aged Kaiser Wilhelm I promoted his beloved grandson yet again, to the rank of Army major general.

By the tenth year of his reign in 1898, His Majesty boasted 300 German regimental uniforms alone, plus those of conelcies and several Field Marshals' batons, including one from the British Army that he renounced upon Britain's declaration of war upon Imperial Germany in 1914. The martial kits he wore on State occasions when welcoming visiting foreign Royals and other statesmen.

In addition, he held honorary commands over a trio of Austro-Hungarian Army regiments, plus of three more in the Imperial Russian Army of the Tsars, and was also an Admiral in the navies of Great Britain, Sweden, Russia, Norway, and Denmark, as well as being a Grand Admiral commanding his own, the Imperial German High Seas Fleet, that he is credited rightly by history as having created.

At the deaths of both his grandfather and father in 1888, Wilhelm skipped an entire generation and became Kaiser at the age of 29. His military household alone totaled 20 officers, a figure that doubled by the final year of his reign in 1918.

The German Emperor was served by a trio of Imperial Cabinets: civil, military, and naval, having created the last himself in 1889. All reported directly and solely to him, as did the Chief of the Great German General Staff.

Most of these officers were of the age group of his father's generation, and one—Army General Hans von Plessen—had served during 1864–1918 under *all three* Kaisers, from Wilhelm to William. By 1890, however, former longtime Prince Wilhelm fan, von Waldersee, sourly noted that, "His Majesty no longer has the slightest desire to work"—preferring constant travel, speechmaking, ribbon-cutting, reviews of parades, and hunting instead. During 1888–1914, the Kaiser had five Imperial yachts in all, a train that shunted him back and forth across Continental Europe, and a fleet of expensive Daimler and Benz touring cars.

Meanwhile, His Majesty's Imperial Army consisted of 18 corps and a 30,000-man personal Guard.

Constantly afraid of the Red revolt that did, in fact, break out, the Kaiser talked of having loopholes drilled into the walls of his Berlin Palace to shoot down German Socialists and others who were inimical to his "personal rule by the Divine Right of Kings from the Middle Ages." When it duly came in the autumn of 1918, he was, however, more than ready to personally lead the Army back from the defeat on the Western Front, only to be told by all his responsible ministers and generals that the Army would no longer follow him.

No one ever accused Wilhelm II of personal cowardice, though. The unkindest cut of all came when the ordinary sailors of his own creation—the Imperial German High Seas Battle Fleet—mutinied in their home ports and refused to make what they saw as suicidal final sorties against the British Royal Navy at the war's end.

Wilhelm's diplomacy has been roundly criticized by most historians, yet his two pre-war trips to Istanbul helped to bring Turkey into the Great War as a German partner, and then maintain her in the Central Powers alliance until the very end—a feat that should be noted. If Kaiser Wilhelm II is deserving of blame, he also must be given at least some of the credit for Germany's successful war effort up until and even including the final crisis year of 1918.

The man who thought that the best briefing was the shortest, also believed that the Great War would inevitably come in 1916—as did the Russians—and not earlier, as it did. He hoped instead to put it off until 1920, when he felt that his fleet would be built up enough to serve as a valid deterrent to that of his English cousins.

At the Imperial Crown Council of 8 December 1912—an event that some historians today cite as "proof" that the Kaiser "plotted" the outbreak of the World War—he was told by his military advisors that at all costs he must delay it until the summer of 1914, when the Kiel Canal would be finished, giving the Reich thereby an internal opening by water to the North Sea opposite Great Britain.

Meanwhile, his generals and courtiers were becoming ever more aware that their Sovereign was not a man of decisiveness and resolve to suit their purposes, no matter the bellicose tenor and frequency of his public utterances.

"When the situation gets critical," said one, "His Majesty can't see it through," regarding plunging the Reich into war.

When the World War finally came to Germany on 4 August 1914—despite the Kaiser's protestations of ultimate victory—Wilhelm privately believed that it would be the ruination of his own reign and dynastic House as well.

Thereafter, he shunted back and forth to his and the German High Command's various headquarters on both the Eastern and Western Fronts in his ornate cream, gold, and sky blue Imperial train, attending briefings, inspecting troops, and handing out batches of Iron Crosses. Ironically, the man who had proclaimed himself the "All-Highest" and the "Supreme Warlord" left the actual, daily running of the war to the professional soldiers, deferring to their stolid—and many times wrong— judgments. Kaiser Wilhelm intervened against them only on the occasions when they and his political statesmen could not resolve a particularly thorny issue, such as the start and stoppage of unrestricted submarine warfare against Allied and neutral maritime shipping. His Majesty felt that in the end it would bring the United

States into the war against Imperial Germany, and he turned out to be right.

A few days after the War began, Wilhelm visited the grave site of his father, who had died 25 years earlier of throat cancer, and was ambivalent to the war from the very start. In March 1918—during the famed "Kaiser's Battle" or *Michael* offensive that was supposed to be a last-ditch attempt by the Reich to win the war on the embattled Western Front—the German Emperor had occasion to visit and talk with a group of British POW Tommies. One of them later recalled that he:

> Had kindly features; he was benevolent, nothing like all the caricatures as we had seen in the newspapers. He said, "There is no need for you to be ashamed of being prisoners." He congratulated us on the tremendous fight we'd put up, but said, "my victorious troops are advancing everywhere, and you'll soon be home with your families once more."

On 8 August 1918, the Kaiser was informed bluntly by the High Command that the war was irretrievably lost, and that—although there were no enemy troops yet on German soil—it was high time that peace talks begin. His Majesty agreed to this, firing First Quartermaster General Erich Ludendorff—whom he despised—on 26 October 1918, and refusing to give up his throne under pressure, asserting, "A successor to Frederick the Great doesn't abdicate!" The debate over this pressing question continued. On 4 November 1918, Allied bombs fell near his train, prompting him to call for its arming with machineguns. Recalling the example of his cousin Tsar Nicholas II's murder by Red Army soldiers but a few months before, the Emperor mused aloud, "I have no desire to be strung up by some eager fellows!" He also noted that the Kaiserin was herself under armed Red Guard troops in Berlin. Might not she, too, be murdered, as had Tsarina Alexandra and all the other members of her family as well?

Later foes of Wilhelm charged him with having "run away" to neutral Holland at the moment of maximum crisis, but who could really blame him? Like Napoleon in 1814, the Kaiser was anxious to avoid a bloody civil war at home, and as an historian, he knew full well that had occurred in France in 1871 after the fall of Napoleon III. Thus, he took perhaps the most controversial decision of his life and left the Reich, but only after his "abdication" had been officially, falsely, and prematurely announced for him by his greatest domestic enemies, the German Independent Socialists in the Reichstag in Berlin.

In any event, a Red–White civil war ensued afterwards anyway, one that was brutally suppressed in the end by the forces of the right and the new German Republic in an uneasy, fragile alliance that would collapse at last in 1933 under the Nazis.

After the war, the former Emperor blamed the Jews, the Social Democrats, Communists, and the home front in general for the loss of the war, while also castigating Great Britain for starting it, and German Field Marshal Paul von Hindenburg in particular for causing him to abdicate in 1918, and thus for costing him and his dynasty as well their hereditary throne.

From exile in Holland during 1918–1941, the ex-Kaiser published a number of interesting and well-written memoirs telling his side of the long saga of his life. These encompassed the following: *The Kaiser's Memoirs/Wilhelm II Emperor of Germany 1888–1918,* that covered the entirety of his reign, published in 1922. *My Early Life by William II ex-Emperor of Germany* concerned the period from his birth in 1859 to his accession to the throne on 15 June 1888, published in 1926. *My Ancestors by William II* was a history of the House of Hohenzollern from its beginnings up through the death of his father—Kaiser Frederick III—on 15 June 1888. Thus, His Majesty himself wrote about the entirety not only of his own life and reign, but also that of all his earlier forebears.

Nor was that all! In addition, there was published in 1904 the all-inclusive work, *The German Emperor's Speeches: Being a Selection from the Speeches, Edicts, Letters, and Telegrams of the Emperor William II*. A decade later—in 1914—there appeared in print, *The War Lord: A Character Study of Kaiser William II, by Means of His Speeches, Letters, and Telegrams Compiled by J. M. Kennedy*. In 1920, this was followed also by, *The Kaiser's Letters to the Tsar Copied from the Government Archives in Petrograd, and Brought from Russia by Isaac Don Levine*, found at Ekaterinburg by the Communists in July 1918 after they murdered the Tsar and his family.

Then there are the memoirs of his son and Heir, the German Crown Prince Wilhelm and his wife, Crown Princess Cecilie; His Majesty's second wife, Empress Hermine, Princess of Schönaich-Carolath; and the Kaiser's only daughter, Her Royal Highness Victoria Luise, Princess of Prussia; as well as the major Imperial Chancellor of his reign, Prince Bernhard von Bülow, among many others.

Finally, there are many accounts of others who knew the Kaiser personally, long, and well. My intent has been to tell this tale primarily in their words, and only secondarily in those of the historians of the enemy powers that defeated him, primarily British and—later— Americans.

Is the life of this monarch of almost a century ago still relevant in today's world? I have attempted to craft a brief overview life of this man, one that will both introduce him to first-time readers who may then want to learn more, as well as to bring to light various aspects that may be new to older readers more familiar with his era.

At Doorn, the Kaiser himself plaintively asked his "official" biographer—former Imperial German Army officer Joachim von Kürenberg—"Was *everything* wrong?"

I do not believe it was, and in the following pages, you the reader will be the judge.

Blaine Taylor
Berkshires at Town Center
Towson, MD/USA
1 August 2014
Centennial of the Great War 2014-2018

PART 1

Prussian Prince and German Crown Prince
1859–1888

Laying their heads together.

A political cartoon from 1871. A caricature of Kaiser Wilhelm I of Germany and Otto von Bismarck smoking and drinking, with the description "Laying their heads together." (*Nast, Publisher Archive*)

The Advent of Brandenburg-Prussia
1618–1797

The original Margravate of Brandenburg was the Seat of the main branch of the Hohenzollern Dynasty whose members had been since 1415 Prince-Electors within the Austrian-dominated Holy Roman Empire/HRE. The Duchy of Prussia was established by the 1525 Treaty of Krakow (Poland), via a partial secularization of the religious State of the Teutonic Order of Knights.

At first, it was a vassal state of the Kingdom of Poland, led by Duke Albrecht of Prussia, a member of the House of Hohenzollern. Brandenburg-Prussia evolved from the marriage of Margrave of Brandenburg John Sigismund to Duchess Anna of Prussia. The 1603 Treaty of Gera established the precedent that the lands ruled by the House of Hohenzollern were not to be internally split up in future, and thus were to remain as a single, unitary realm.

When Elector Albrecht Frederick died in 1618, the Brandenburg Electors inherited the Prussian Duchy, but it remained also as a fief under the Polish Crown until 1656–57. Brandenburg-Prussia was the first realm ruled by the Brandenburgian Hohenzollern family during 1618–1701, founded on the Imperial Electorate of Brandenburg, the major branch of the family that intermarried with the Duchy of Prussia.

Elector Georg Wilhelm, 1619–1640

Also incorporated via intermarriage were the Lower Rhine Principalities of Cleves, Mark, and Ravensburg under the 1614 Treaty of Xanten. During 1619–1640, Elector Georg Wilhelm was also Duke of Prussia, and during the calamitous Thirty Years' War, he was forced to join by the Treaty of Königsberg in 1627 the Catholic-Imperial coalition, and even to accept garrisons on his lands.

When the Swedish Army under King Gustavus Adolphus invaded Brandenburg, Georg Wilhelm was pressured to join the King as an ally, this being enforced by occupation of part of the Electorate, including a Swedish Army outside Berlin itself. The Elector resisted an actual alliance with Sweden, but did grant her army transit rights, a pair of forts, and money.

As a result, "Roman Catholic armies repeatedly ravaged Brandenburg and other Hohenzollern lands" during the Thirty Years' War.

Great Elector Frederick Wilhelm, 1640–1688

When the Elector died in 1640, he was duly succeeded by Frederick Wilhelm, aged 20, who later became famous in Hohenzollern hagiography as "the *Great* Elector," who—like Russian Tsar Peter the Great—had a long stay in the Dutch Republic during his educational grand tour of Europe. In Pomerania, he also met his uncle, none other than King Gustavus Adolphus of Sweden.

At first, the new, young Elector "retired" the Brandenburgian Army, only to revive it during 1643–1644. When the 1648 Peace of Westphalia ended the Thirty Years' War, Brandenburg was given both Minden and Halberstadt. The Electorate of Brandenburg had been the most destroyed of all the Prussian lands by the war, it consuming a reported 60 towns, 48 castles, and fully 5,000 villages; moreover, half of the population had been killed, and in some areas, but 10 percent still lived.

In summer 1651, Frederick Wilhelm invaded Julich-Berg that was on his frontier of Cleves-Mark on the Lower Rhine River. Because his forces stole cattle, it became known as the Cow War. Farther Pomerania was incorporated in 1653 under the Treaty of Stettin. That same year—by a decree of 26 July 1653—the Elector established a standing Prussian Army that grew from an initial force of 8,000 men to 30,000 professional soldiers by his death in 1688. It won notable field victories at Warsaw in 1656 and against the Swedes at the Battle of Fehrbellin in 1675, as well as during the Great Sleigh Drive of 1678, in which Frederick Wilhelm chased retreating Swedish forces over the frozen Curonian Lagoon.

By 1688, the Prussian Army's cost was half the entire State annual budget, or 1,500,000 thalers. The Great Elector saw the Prussian Army as the only way to establish Prussia as a powerful state.

When the 1657 Treaty of Bromberg ended the Second Northern War, Brandenbrug's Electors ceased being Polish vassals, and the Prussian Duchy also received both Lauenberg-Bütow and Draheim. In 1679, Brandenburg's Pomerania was expanded to include the Lower Oder River area, and the following year added the Duchy of Magdeburg to its overall holdings as well.

The later Kaiser Wilhelm II's favorite ancestor was, indeed, Great Elector Frederick Wilhelm, who founded not only the first Prussian Navy, but also the initial German colonies along the Brandenburger Gold Coast in Africa. In addition, he opened Prussia to Protestant religious emigration from other European lands, especially the Huguenots, via the Edict of Potsdam. Another highlight of the Great Elector's rule was the centralization of his civil administration to reduce the power of the landed estate owners, later known as the *Junkers,* of which the Bismarcks were but one of many families. He died in 1688, and was succeeded by Elector Frederick III, who became King Frederick I in 1701.

King IN Prussia, 1701

In 1701, then Elector Frederick III of Brandenburg (1657–1713) succeeded in allowing himself to be titled "King *in* Prussia," a feat accomplished via the Duchy of Prussia's being a sovereign state outside the Holy Roman Empire of Germany, approved by the very Austrian Habsburg

Emperors who would later be both Prussia's enemy *and* ally in several different wars over a trio of centuries, 1700–1945.

Notes one source, "Great Britain and the Dutch Republic … accepted Frederick's elevation prior to the coronation. On 17 January 1701, Frederick dedicated the Royal Coat of Arms—the famed Prussian Black Eagle—and a motto, *Suum cuique/To each his own.* The next day, he crowned himself and also his wife Queen Sophie Charlotte in a baroque ceremony at Königsberg Castle, the location of all future such events. Neither the Teutonic Order of Knights nor the Pope accepted it, however, until 1787. The Poles had grudgingly accepted the new Kingdom in 1764.

As Prussia took part in several succeeding European military alliances during the War of the Spanish Succession and the Great Northern War—the latter between Russia and Sweden—Brandenburg-Prussia became referred to as the "Kingdom *of* Prussia," or just Prussia.

Over time, the Prussian State welded its diverse and geographically scattered provinces and other areas into a common land ruled from Berlin, the Kingdom's capital. Due to Frederick Wilhelm's reforms, the State income increased threefold during his reign, and the tax burden per subject reached a level twice as high as in France, a far larger Kingdom.

Frederick Wilhelm I: "The Soldier King" and His "Long Fellows" 1713–1740

Frederick Wilhelm I, the famed "Soldier King"—abandoned the Prussian Navy in favor of building up the Prussian Army instead. He was especially noted for a regiment of tall soldiers—the famed *Lange Kerl [Long Fellows]*—that was disbanded by his son Frederick II as being militarily impractical for the pitched battles that he had in mind. Ironically, the choleric and violent tempered King Frederick Wilhelm I never committed his army to war—that remained for his son and successor to do.

King Frederick II the Great, 1740–1786

Within the first year of his coming to the Prussian throne, the Soldier King's successor seized the Austrian Province of Silesia, and then waged a series of Silesian Wars to keep it, fighting both superior French and Russian armies as well, even losing his capital Berlin to Russian Army occupation during the Seven Years' War of 1756–1763.

Known as "the Great" during his own lifetime, Frederick's famous dazzling martial victories and comebacks against seemingly invincible odds put him into the ranks of such Great Captains as Napoleon, Wellington, and Lee. He died in 1786, but his successors ruled more as civilian monarchs than as Prussian soldiers.

The Modern Military Kings of Prussia and German Kaisers
1797–1888

Wilhelm: Prince, Vice Regent, Regent, King of Prussia, and German Kaiser

Wilhelm I was an accidental King of Prussia who also became a reluctant German Emperor in the triad of Bismarck's Unification Wars. In October 1806—four days after Napoleon had crushed the Prussian Army of the revered King Frederick the Great's era at the Twin Battles of Jena-Auerstadt—his eventual successor's wife, Queen Louise, met with their two sons at Castle Schwedt. She asserted tearfully, that:

> Prussia is no more ... We are overthrown and demolished. Our national glory is departed! Strive to rescue your people from the disgrace of this hour, from the burden of humiliation under which this nation is now groaning. Aspire to re-conquer from the French the glory of your forefathers ... in the same way as your ancestor, the Great Elector, avenged his father's shame and humiliation upon the Swedes at Fehrbellin...

The two boys were the eleven-year-old Crown Prince—the future king Frederick Wilhelm IV—and his younger brother, Prince Wilhelm, nine. The latter never forgot how the French had devastated the nation of *Der Alte Fritz* by humbling its beaten army, and how Napoleon the following year by the 1807 Treaty of Tilsit with Russian Tsar Alexander I brought low their own father, king Frederick Wilhelm III.

As a boy, the younger Prince was weak and sickly, but by the time he was seven, he was drilled daily under a Prussian Guards sergeant to toughen his body. He was duly commissioned a lieutenant in the elite Guards at the age of ten, like all Hohenzollerns to the very end of the House's Dynasty in 1918 under his own later grandson, our subject. Unlike his more volatile, romantic, and intellectual elder brother, Prince Wilhelm was seen by his mother to be simple, straightforward, and sensible—attributes that would later endear him to his people, first in Prussia, and then in Imperial Germany as a whole. Since his older brother was set to be King, Prince Wilhelm planned his own career as a professional soldier; ironically, he became both, as well as becoming an unwilling German Emperor.

From the age of eleven he kept a diary and—like both his son and grandson later—became fascinated with military uniforms and their accoutrements.

Prussia began the War of Liberation against Napoleon in 1813, and the young Prince made his first cavalry charge with the allied Russians at the Battle of Bar-sur-Aube in France the following year. He also took part in the 1815 Waterloo Campaign, and met the famed British Army's Duke of Wellington before visiting London in triumph, as well as surrendered Paris three times: 1814 and '15, and then 1871.

Returning home a hero to Berlin, Prussia's capital, Prince Wilhelm continued his military training under the remainder of the reign of his beloved father King Frederick Wilhelm II, who died in 1840, when his elder brother ascended the throne.

The Revolution of 1848: Wilhelm Becomes "The Cartridge Prince"

The new King—Frederick Wilhelm IV—being childless, named his younger brother Heir Presumptive, a role that Wilhelm had never expected to have. When the Revolution of 1848 occurred, the Prince was serving as Governor of Pomerania, and was regarded by the powerful *Junker* land-owning conservatives in Prussia as one of their own.

As the 1848 "Springtime of Peoples" got underway, Wilhelm's cousin—Tsar Nicholas I of Imperial Russia, the younger brother of the abdicated Alexander I who had also fought the Great Napoleon—shouted to his officers, "Saddle your horses, gentlemen! A republic has been declared in France!"

All expected a great revolutionary crisis over Europe, as one of the French Little Corporal's greatest opponents—Prince Clemens von Metternich, Chancellor of Imperial Austria—was overthrown, and, indeed, it happened. Almost all of the ancient capitals of anti-Bonapartist, absolutist, archconservative Old Europe were in political ferment within just a few weeks. Only Spain and Portugal from the former Peninsular Wars seemed to be immune.

The reasons were all left over from the suddenly concluded Napoleonic Wars of 1815. These were nationalism, personal and political liberties, ethnic minorities, and what the rulers of that era euphemistically called, "the social question"—i.e., the poverty that ultimately brought on the even greater (and successful) revolts of 1917–1919.

Asserted Alexis de Tocqueville, "We are sleeping on a volcano." Indeed, once the red-hot lava of political liberalism started gushing forth, the Austrian Kaiser Ferdinand was replaced by 18-year-old Franz Josef I, who remained on the throne until 1916. Meanwhile, in reactionary Berlin, King Frederick Wilhelm IV sympathized with the rioting republican minded mobs besieging the Royal Palace. The political issues at hand were for a British-style constitutional monarchy with an elected assembly, with Prussia to lead the long desired unification of fragmented Germany along democratic lines, freedom of the press, and the abolition of German customs barriers.

The rebuilt Prussian Army was ordered out of Berlin by the King, who also recalled his younger brother Prince Wilhelm to the embattled Prussian capital. Upon his return, the Prince found a mob ready, it was felt, to storm the Royal Palace.   Remaining troops were ordered out and shots fired into the mob: 18 soldiers and 183 civilians were killed in one day alone, with Wilhelm, 50, bitterly tagged by an angry populace with the nickname of, "*The Cartridge Prince.*"

By now, he was commanding a 14-hour-long battle between the people of Berlin on one side and 2,500 soldiers on the other, with cannonballs and grapeshot hurtling into the raging mob.

The Prince himself commanded an artillery battery, and seemed to relish this role. Order was restored after the troops were pulled back and a Civil Guard people's militia was formed to protect the King and safeguard the revolt.

Prince Wilhelm was blamed for the bloodshed, and was forced to flee for his life. Angrily, he threw down his cavalry saber in disgust, fled in disguise first to one of Berlin's river islands, and then across Europe to seek political asylum in Victorian London, which was granted. He had barely escaped with his life. As he later told his grandson and namesake, he never forgot this humiliation.

As the infamous "Riot Act" was read in London and the Chartists were routed there, the 1830 July Monarchy in France of the Orleanist Dynasty King Louis Philippe (creator of the renowned French Foreign Legion) was overthrown in Paris, and his throne burned by the mob, in 1848.

France was called the only country where the Revolution destroys the monarchy, as accurately lamented by the Prussian Reaction; it seemed that the French model might also be repeated at Berlin.

Alarmed, the various dynastic Houses asked alike—with memories of Jacobins and "Bonaparte" rising in their fevered brains—"What will it bring: the French, new battles? Murder? The Guillotine?"

Despite this, however, the initial response of those in power—just as in Berlin—was conciliation and compromise, and this would also recur in 1917–1919 anew across a Europe embroiled as well in the First World War during Wilhelm's II's star-crossed reign.

The Reaction of 1849

Eventually, the Berlin revolt failed, the Prussian King retained his throne with his pledge to try for a united Reich, and even Prince Wilhelm was allowed to return home if he swore to uphild the new Constitution; did so under his breath, but stayed silent at the popular demand that he renounce all future claim to the throne, and in time sat on it as one of the most revered men on Earth.

In the spring of 1849, the reactionary forces all across Europe regained their composure, and marshaled their "forest of bayonets" and "hot lead of counter-revolution" to defeat all of the revolts except that in France, mainly because of the division within the leaders themselves in all the various national, liberal-leftist uprisings.

Thus, Austria suborned Northern Italy and separatist Budapest in Hungary, French Marshal Oudinot suppressed dissent in Rome, and the threat of Russian military intervention helped subdue both Germany and Poland.

All the Great Powers set their policies to avoid a general, Napoleonic-style European war, and this helped cause the failure of the Polish national movement of 1848, with no Poland as such becoming a reality until the Treaty of Versailles in 1919, over seven decades later.

Intially, the Second French Republic was duly recognized by all the other Great Powers, with no martial intervention, such as had occurred in 1792 when the Prussian Army had been defeated by the French at the Battle of Valmy by Revolutionary France. This time, however, the interventions of 1789–1793 were not repeated, and this even despite the "French Alarm" of a renewed Bonapartist expansion under a future "Napoleon III" that indeed came to pass during 1852–1871.

Chanting, "Long live the Emperor!" from a bygone but now restored age, Emperor Louis Napoleon III became the new political and military reality facing the Kingdom of Prussia in Germany. His crowning was a lasting result, therefore, of the scattered 1848 uprisings. Prussian Berlin, meanwhile, was secured by its army, and under its martial leadership in time, this Second French Empire, too, would fall, as had the First, but not yet. Until it did, though, the threat of French military intervention in affairs German and Prussian was ever present.

Requiem for Prussian King Frederick Wilhelm IV, 1857–1861

In the late spring of 1857, His Majesty was said to be suffering from nervous exhaustion, and the following summer, he had a stroke. Within months, his doctors diagnosed the King with softening of the brain and incurable insanity, in effect, with being an imbecile.

Prince Wilhelm, therefore, became Vice Regent for a trio of succeeding 90-day terms beginning in October 1857, and in September 1858, was made full Regent when the King his brother signed the Act of Abdication, the first—but not the last—Hohenzollern to do so.

When King Frederick Wilhelm IV died in 1861, his younger brother thus became his successor as King of Prussia at the age of 64, when most others retire.

King Wilhelm I of Prussia and the Advent of Otto von Bismarck (1815–1898)

The following year—during a Constitutional crisis involving parliamentary financing for the Prussian Army—there arrived on the scene Otto von Bismarck, a land-owning *Junker* who became the King's Prime Minister. Together, they would rule for the next 26 years. Bismarck became known in German history as the "Blood and Iron" Chancellor who would unite Germany and its various cities, states, and principalities around the hard core of steel of the Prussian Kingdom and its well-trained army. This was accomplished in a series of three wars. The first came in 1864 when the Prussians and Austrians jointly took the Danish Duchies of Schleswig and Holstein. King Wilhelm allowed himself to be talked into the war at age 67, and dispatched General Count (later Field Marshal) Friedrich von Wrangel (1784–1877) to lead the joint Austro-Prussian expedition to invade the twin territories.

Outnumbered by the German armies opposite them by six to one, the hardy Danes fought well, but surrendered, with an Armistice proclaimed. By the Treaty of Vienna of 30 October 1864, the two former Danish Provinces as well as Lauenberg were to be jointly administered by Prussia and Austria, until Bismarck ended this dual arrangement with his second war, of 1866.

Thus, the first step had been taken on the road to the future German Empire, or Reich.

Imperial Austria as the Next Bismarckian Stumbling Block, 1864–1866

Ever since the beginning of modern German history following the fall of the ancient Roman Empire—particularly during the era of its later successor, the Holy Roman Empire, and then during the Napoleonic Wars—the Empire of Austria had played a predominant role in the affairs of the splintered German-speaking lands of central Europe. Bismarck saw clearly that this influence must be ended if Prussia were ever to unite Germany around it.

It had, however, to be accomplished in such a way that an overly embittered Austria (and, in 1867, Austria-Hungary) would remain an ally of the new German Reich after the conclusion of a war between the two major German states. This became his second diplomatic and military stroke, via the Austro-Prussian or Seven Weeks' War of 1866, one that almost nobody in Prussia (including the King) wanted except for the Prime Minister himself.

Austria's policy was to uphold the 1815 Congress of Vienna-imposed German Confederation of the 39 separate states, while Bismarck wanted a unitary state over the loose-knit Confederation that would be bound together at and by Berlin.

In June 1866, Austria—Prussia's former ally of already several decades past—declared war on her for administrative encroachments in Schleswig-Holstein allegedly, that were in reality, to improve Bismarck's German unification under Prussian domination, and also Austrian exclusion thereby.

The Seven Weeks' Austro-Prussian War of 1866

Austria attacked on twin fronts: in Bohemia against the Prussians and in Venetia against Prussia's Italian allies. Overall, the Austrians had an army of 400,000 men to fight the Prussian forces of 300,000 soldiers and the Italians of 200,000.

Still angered by the late Frederick the Great's earlier wars that had taken the rich Province of Silesia from Austria, Kaiser Franz Josef I planned to partition Prussia and seize its treasure once the expected military victory was obtained.

He failed to fully understand, however, the reforms made in the Prussian Army sanctioned by the King, funded by the Royal Chancellor, and carried out by the Prussian Chief of the General Staff, General Helmuth von Moltke the Elder (1800–91.)

These included streamlining the old Prussian *Landwehr*, tripling the active duty strength of the Regular Army, establishing permanent Army Corps to speed up mobilization of forces, and adapting both railways and telegraph lines to modern warfare. These were all lessons gleaned from the just-completed American Civil War in the United States that had defeated the Rebel Confederacy in 1865.

The greatest innovation, though, was von Moltke's adaptation of the new, breach-loading needle gun rifle that could fire six shots to the enemy's one. The Austrians were still using muzzle-loading weapons of bygone days to preserve ammunition, as well as tactical battalion-sized unit columns in field combat. Von Moltke used his rapid fire to devastate Austria's massed columns to good effect at the Battles of Skalice, Jičín, and Königgrätz-Sadowa that were all resounding victories for Prussian arms.

At Königgrätz alone, the Austrians lost 44,000 men to the Prussians' 9,000.

King Wilhelm was ecstatic, and it was all that both Bismarck—and the monarch's own son, Crown Prince Frederick (1857–1888)—could do to persuade him *not* to stage a triumphal entry into Vienna, much less not to occupy any new Austrian territory. Rather, on 22 July 1866—in what was called the Seven Weeks' War (but was really decided in the opening three)—the Austrian Kaiser acceded to all of the Prussian Prime Minister's political demands. These included: the dissolution of the former German Confederation, the Prussian annexation of Austria's beaten ally, Hanover; the establishment of a Berlin-run North German Confederation, and the withdrawal of Austria from any future say in German affairs.

Bismarck's Third and Final Armed Struggle: the Franco-Prussian War, 1870–1871

Bismarck was now ready for the third and final of his Unification Wars, but again his obstinate monarch King Wilhelm I had to be maneuvered into it against "His Royal Cousin," Napoleon III, Emperor of the French, whom the Prussian King both knew and even liked.

It came about in a strange way when the throne of Spain became vacant, and a Hohenzollern Prince was almost selected to occupy it. This alarmed Imperial France, since Napoleon did not want a Hohenzollern ruler on both his German and Spanish frontiers at the same time. The nomination was rescinded, but the elderly King Wilhelm I was offended at Ems when he was asked by the French Ambassador never again to even allow there to be a Hohenzollern candidate for the Madrid post.

His Majesty refused this on the spot, and sent Bismarck a telegram informing him of the action taken. Hoping to instigate a war from this matter, Bismarck edited the telegram and published it in the German press in such a way to make it appear that his venerable master had been summarily insulted by the haughty French.

This became known as the celebrated *Ems Dispatch,* and before the damage could be corrected, there was nationalist, jingoistic war fever on both sides, with the French Emperor unable to contain his ministers from rushing an ill-prepared Imperial France into the Franco-Prussian War of 1870–1871 that July.

On paper, the French Imperial war machine looked formidable, having weathered past conflicts in the Russian Crimea, Italy, Mexico, and Algeria in North Africa, but it had also suffered therefrom as well.

The French were, nevertheless, overconfident, and declared war on Prussia on 15 July 1870, without allies, while Prussia marched off to hostilities with the North German Confederation as well as the Kingdom of Bavaria in South Germany behind her. As before, in 1866, both Great Britain and the Russian Empire stayed neutral, another huge advantage for Prussia and the planned result of Bismarck's careful diplomacy beforehand. The war was basically won within the first 30 days, with victories at Metz and Sedan among others. The King—already a Prussian Army Field Marshal himself—promoted his son Crown Prince Frederick Wilhelm and his military rival cousin, Prussian Prince Frederick Karl, with their own batons as well.

Captured, Napoleon III became an Imperial Prisoner-of-War at Sedan, and a revolution began at home in Paris that overthrew the Second Bonaparte Dynasty. A Communist Red revolt broke out in the capital between their Paris Commune and the French Army in a bloody civil war while the Prussian and German Armies looked on from outside during protracted peace negotiations.

It was a scene all too familiar to the former "Cartridge Prince" of 1848. A new debate arose: to bombard Paris with artillery or not? The King opted for bombardment, believing that it would hasten a French surrender, and thus it began on 5 January 1871, but it proved to be ineffectual, only inducing the French to attack again, but ultimately to no avail.

An armistice was duly signed on 23 January 1871, and for the third time in the King's life, a French Napoleonic Empire had fallen.

His Majesty Becomes German Emperor, 18 January 1871

On 18 January 1871, however—in the Hall of Mirrors at Versailles—his own had begun with the proclamation by the assembled German Princes of a new German Empire, with Wilhelm himself named as German Emperor, and not as Emperor of Germany, a territorial title.

The first implied that the Prussian King was merely the first among equals of the other German Princes, a difference that he disdained. Stepping down from the dais amidst cheers ringing in his ears, the new Emperor or Kaiser (German for *Caesar,* as Tsar is the Russian form) refused to shake his new Reich Chancellor's hand, and would not speak to him for several more days, since he would rather have remained King of Prussia alone instead.

Nevertheless, both his son and grandson warmed to the new title, and it made the new Imperial Germany the preeminent land power on the Continent of Europe as well, foreshadowing the Great War of the next generation of his successor and namesake, Kaiser Wilhelm II.

Ironically, Bismarck—made a Prince and still later also a Duke and Prussian Army Field Marshal—would retain the coveted Austrian alliance that he prized, but it would prove to be just this that would in the end drag his new Germany into the First World War.

The year 1888 is called in Germany the, "Year of the Three Kaisers," since the Old Kaiser—Wilhelm I—died at 91 that March, followed by his son and heir at 57 in June, both then being succeeded by the "last" Emperor, Wilhelm II.

Thus was entirely skipped by a full generation a reign that might have led to a more liberal era of peace and modernity.

In the glorious 1871 Victory Parade at Berlin, however, all this was in the very far, dim future, as the Kaiser and King Wilhelm I, 74, kept his pledge to his long dead mother, Queen Louise, and had the captured French Army Napoleonic eagle standards and flags thrown into a heap at the foot of his late father, King Frederick Wilhelm III of both 1806 and 1813–1815. The wheel of history, had, indeed, turned full circle, from abject defeat to glorious victory.

Also riding horseback in His Majesty's Berlin Victory Parade was his son and Heir, now Imperial Crown Prince Frederick—the future Kaiser Frederick III—and his son and heir, Prince Wilhelm of Prussia, at eleven riding a small pony behind his now sainted grandpapa and Field Marshal father, all to the lusty cheers of the Berliners.

Frederick: Prince, Crown Prince, and Prussian King–German Kaiser

(1831–1888)

Remembered today as the ruler who reigned as German Emperor for but 99 days and who died of cancer of the larynx, Kaiser Frederick III earned his Marshal's baton as the hero of three wars and also fathered our subject, Wilhelm II.

The speaker is a much-vexed Napoleon III. Slamming his hand down on a table, he vented his spleen over the recent Prussian victories in their Seven Weeks' War with Austria in the summer of 1866.

The particular object of his wrath was the Hohenzollern Crown Prince of Prussia and Prussian Army commander, Frederick, as His Majesty exclaimed excitedly, "The future King a good general, too! That is the last straw!"

Ironically, in 1856—at the very apex of the French Emperor's reign—his own Empress Eugenie penned this portrait of the future German Kaiser in a letter to a friend:

> The Prince is a tall, handsome man, almost a head taller than the Emperor. He is slim and fair, with a light yellow moustache—in fact, a Teuton such as Tacitus describes them. He is chivalrously polite and with a touch of Hamlet about him.

During an 1868 visit to Savoyard Italy for the wedding of the Italian Royal Heir Apparent Prince Humberto to Princess Margherita, a fellow dancer stepped on her gown and tore off its trim. With a small pair of scissors from a case in his pocket, the Prussian Crown Prince cut off the torn trim, pressed it to his heart, folded it, and put it into his pocket, leading the romantic onlookers—particularly the women—to gasp, "He is a true knight!" One wonders what his wife thought about this episode!

On the other side of the ledger, however, one of his son's more recent biographers, Macdonough, asserts that Crown Prince Frederick returned from the 1869 opening of the Suez Canal as Prussia's representative with a case of venereal disease caught from a Cairo prostitute.

Like most of his Hohenzollern forbears, "Fritz" treated his own son and Heir somewhat shabbily, and was also jealous of him—an emotion that was returned. Like him as well, he—and his wife, the future Empress Frederick, the daughter of Queen Victoria and Princess Royal of Great Britain—were, reportedly, overly fond of the trappings of office and power. This included especially gaudy, resplendent uniforms, again ala their first-born son.

Unquestionably, the future Kaiser Frederick III was the most accomplished in his own right of all three of the German Emperors who purported to be Soldier Kings. He was also the only one of them to truly deserve his Field Marshal's baton won as the actual hero of the trio of Wars of German Unification fomented by his political rival and bane, Bismarck. Neither had an overly high opinion of the other. Lamented the Crown Prince, "Bismarck has made us great and powerful, but he has robbed us of our friends," while in turn the Iron Chancellor opined, "The Crown Prince is the dumbest and vainest of men! He's crazed again by the 'Kaiser madness,'" i.e., to gain a more glorious title than his own father's prized King of Prussia.

The soldier who would later write his wife, "I detest this butchery! May this be the last war," was born on 18 October 1831 at Potsdam some 16 miles southwest of Berlin on the Havel River. He was the son of Prince Wilhelm of Prussia and his wife Princess (later Queen and

Kaiserin) Augusta.

When his Royal father became King of Prussia on 18 January 1861, the 30-year-old Fritz automatically became Crown Prince of Prussia. Exactly a decade later, his title was expanded to Crown Prince of the German Reich, or Imperial Germany, as well.

Young Fritz

Like other Hohenzollern princes, Fritz was required to take up crafts of the common people, and he selected printing, bookbinding, and carpentry. In 1849, young Fritz was promoted to first lieutenant in the Prussian Army, having been commissioned a second lieutenant at age ten in 1841.

In 1851, he was again promoted, to captain, commanding a company of the elite 1st Guards Regiment of Foot/Infantry. He was also a member of both Austrian and Russian regiments, thus attending field maneuvers of all three armies.

In 1853, Fritz was promoted to major, and also appointed a battalion commander the following year, having seen service by now as well with the artillery, dragoons, and militia, plus the infantry. This duly gave the future Crown Prince a thorough grounding in all branches of the Royal Prussian Army, something that would prove of inestimable value in the trio of conflicts ahead.

In 1859, Fritz missed a chance to become a full divisional commander during the war between France and Austria—the latter then Prussia's ally—when the Emperors of those two warring dynasties decided to make peace and end their war in Italy.

Fritz in 1864

In the 1864 Austro-Prussian war against tiny Denmark, however, Fritz was appointed to the staff of the aged Field Marshal von Wrangel.

Because of the Marshal's inability to lead the 2nd Army himself, the Prussian Crown Prince in effect became the co-commander, and thus its real leader.

By now, Fritz was a lieutenant general, a grade that he attained by earning it a full 28 years before becoming Kaiser. It was largely due to his decisive influence that the final Danish Fortress of Düppel was taken by frontal assault on 18 April 1864, leading his father the King to name the Crown Prince's own regiment that had taken it for his son and Royal Heir, a signal honor.

Fritz was in addition given the prestigious *Order of the Red Eagle* to add to his previously awarded *Order of the Black Eagle* and the *Hohenzollern Order.*

After the successful conclusion of the war and the Peace Treaty of London, Prussia in time annexed the two provinces.

Fritz in 1866

In 1866, the Crown Prince was promoted to General of Infantry, and also named supreme commander of the 2nd Army, as well as being Military Governor of Silesia, with headquarters at Pommern.

His great military rival—his cousin Hohenzollern Prince Frederick Karl—was named Commander-in-Chief of the Royal Prussian Army, a post that he himself had deeply coveted. When war was declared by Austria on Prussia, Crown Prince Frederick was given as his Chief of Staff General Count Leonhard von Blumenthal, who would remain with him through the campaigns of 1870–1871, too. During the 1866 fighting, the pair directed together the 2nd Army in the Battles of Nachod, Trautenau, Skalitz, Soor, Schweinschaedel, Koniginhof, Gradkitz, and Tobitschau before making an arduous trek through mountainous terrain to arrive just in time to help the Prussians defeat the main Austrian Army at the climactic Battle of Königgrätz-Sadowa.

For this glorious feat of arms, His Majesty the King awarded his son the *Pour le Merite*, taking off his own such medal and draping it around the neck of the Crown Prince on the battlefield itself. Hero Fritz also received the Italian Gold Metal of Bravery from Prussia's ally. Following the war, the King named his son to an Army Commission to examine the military lessons learned from the just completed campaigns.

Fritz During 1870–1871

On 18 July 1870—as the war with France broke out—the Prussian Crown Prince was given the command of the 3rd Army that included the Army of the South German Kingdom of Bavaria, the second largest Kingdom and force in Germany.

The British Army military observer attached to Fritz both in 1866 and 1870–1871—Col. Charles Walker—described him thus:

Cool, thoughtful, considerate of the opinion of others, ready to give them free hand in the first instance and full credit afterwards, without a spark of jealousy. A noble fellow, and a future blessing to his country.

Leading his men into the invasion of French Alsace, Fritz assaulted the Fortress of Weissenburg on the Lauter River northeast of Strasbourg, leading Col. Walker to exult that it was:

A brilliantly conducted affair … I've never seen anything more perfect than the Prussian advance to take the heights.

In all, the Crown Prince's 3rd Army would take part in the Battles of Worth, Sedan, Villiers-sur-Marne, Mont Valérien, Stonne, Raucourt, Remilly-sur-Meuse, Valenton, Dame-Rose, Villejuif, Châttillon, Malmaison, Chevilly, and Choissy-le-Roi, as well as the later Siege of Paris that ended the war. For his great services in the war, the Crown Prince was awarded his Field Marshal's baton, the Iron Cross 1st and 2nd Class, and the Great Crosses of both Saxony and Bavaria, among other medals and honors. In 1871, the new Imperial German Crown Prince was named by His Majesty the German Emperor as well to the post of Inspector-

General of the new Imperial German Army.

Even the beaten French praised the magnanimity of their Teutonic foe, the gallant Fritz, as one enemy journalist wrote thus:

> The Crown Prince has left the memory of countless traits of kindness and humanity in the land that he fought against … When he was present, no excess remain unpunished … No human life was uselessly or lightly sacrificed, and no oppression was permitted … Versailles owes to him in great measure the order observed during the period of occupation.

Noted wife Vicky to mother-in-law Queen Victoria in her voluminous correspondence that was later published while her son was in his Dutch exile in 1929, the popularity of Fritz was nowhere greater than in the Army.

"The soldiers adore him…When they get sight of him, there is always a burst of enthusiasm," and they took to calling him *Unsere Fritz [Our Fred]*, after what previous generations of Prussians had called Frederick the Great, *Der Alte Fritz [The Old Fred]*.

For his part, this most successful warrior-monarch since the Great Frederick hoped—like Wellington post-Waterloo—that he had seen his last battle; he had, indeed, at least of a military nature, that is.

Fritz Triumphant

During the 15 June 1871 victory parade in Berlin, his father the German Emperor drew his own saber and rode past his son in salute, an unheard of honor in Prussian military history, both before and since. Like Bismarck, however, the 27 years after 1871 were for Fritz both unfulfilled and anti-climactic. For both of them, "the great things" had already been done, and were thus behind them. The Imperial Chancellor lamented, "I'm bored! The German Empire is accomplished," and Fritz couldn't have agreed more, but for a different reason: he was ready to rule, but could not. His elderly Sovereign and parent seemed capable of living on forever, thus denying him the throne, and with it the chance to rule in his own right.

The Crown Prince's Lament

Moreover, the liberal policies that he and his wife espoused were at odds with those of his father, his own son and Heir, the Prussian ruling *Junker* class, and many others in the country and Empire at large, too. But, in the later 37 volumes of his lifetime diaries that were published after his death, there was not a single suggestion as to what Kaiser Frederick III might have done had he been given the 30-year-long reign inherited instead by his vainglorious son, Wilhelm II.

It was thus assumed that he would have followed the lead of his wife in all things political, this view being challenged, though, in 1995 by Kollander's biography.

Most historians then and now, however, believe that this made the monarch a weak-willed man, but he might just have *agreed* with her, as he did admire the English Constitutional form of monarchy from his earliest years.

In addition, it turned out, rightly, that he also felt that *some* change and reform was ultimately necessary to prevent the collapse of the dynasty and the Second Reich that duly occurred in 1918, three decades after his demise.

Since a speech that he had given contradicting his father's military budgeting process while stationed at Danzig in 1863 had provoked a crisis, the Crown Prince had been forbidden by His Majesty from ever again participating in partisan politics, a stance that he adhered to until he became Kaiser himself 25 years later. Still, he remained a man of his own strong views.

The tale is told from Fritz's youth when he saw a mule in Babelsberg pulling a loaded cart up a hill that was too heavy for it. The driver was beating the animal, causing the young Prince to call out in anger, "If this was any of my business, I would put you in front of the cart and make *you* pull it!"

Once, when the Austrians intercepted a letter from General von Blumenthal to his wife intimating that *he* was, in fact, responsible for the military victories attributed instead to the Crown Prince, it was characteristic of the noble Fritz that he put his arm around the shoulders of his Chief of Staff and told him not to worry about it.

Later—during his brief, doomed reign as Kaiser—one of his last acts was to name his former deputy to the military grade equal to his, that of Field Marshal.

Most past and even some present authors on the House of Hohenzollern harp on the estrangements between its various fathers and sons, but this gives unequal weight to what was in fact the true situation. Despite their many differences, each generation supported the others in terms of shoring up the institution of monarchical rule. Indeed, in 1871, a grateful Kaiser Wilhelm I wrote to the Crown Prince, "I have found in you a crutch to lean on, and a true help." In particular, he appreciated his son's military reports to him as Inspector General of the Army that he considered to be written with extreme clarity.

In 1878—when the old Kaiser was the victim of an assassination attempt—his son and Heir stood in for him during his father's several months of hospitalization. Diplomatically, the Crown Prince was also instrumental in 1882 in getting the Russian Tsar Alexander III to renew Prince Bismarck's Three Kaiser Pact that included Germany and Austria. Moreover, the Crown Prince was named protector of all German museums, created the new National Portrait Gallery in Berlin, founded the Hohenzollern Museum, and published the papers of the dynasty's historic forebear, Frederick Wilhelm, the Great Elector.

What he might have achieved as Kaiser had he but lived longer is today as moot a point of speculation as at the time of his death, but he may well have kept Germany out of the World War, if, indeed, there even was one at all.

Fritz's Long Goodbye

In 1887, Fritz's father the Kaiser turned 91, and clearly his days were at last numbered, but so were those by then of his future successor, who had been diagnosed with cancer of the larynx that same year. All Germany and Europe wondered who would die first, the aged Kaiser or his critically ill Heir. Because of medical disputes between a team of English doctors sponsored by his British-born wife and a German team favored by the two Wilhelms, his case was fatally botched from the start. When his father died in March 1888, the new German Emperor and King of Prussia whispered hoarsely, "I stand with one foot in the grave. The future belongs to my son," who led his Infantry Guards in a parade by His Majesty on 24 May 1888, the one and only such review that Kaiser Frederick III ever saw. He died at age 57 on 15 June 1888 at the New Palace at Potsdam where he had been born. His widow—Kaiserin Victoria, or the Empress Frederick—followed him in death in August 1901, of spinal cancer, aged but 60.

The Family of the Fredericks

Prince Wilhelm was born on 27 January 1859, and in 1881, he married Princess Augusta of Schleswig-Holstein-Sonderburg-Augustenberg (1858–1921.) The couple had six sons and a daughter. Sister Princess Charlotte was born 24 July 1860, and in 1878 married Prince Bernard of Saxe-Meiningen (1851–1928). The couple had a daughter. She died 1 October 1919.

Brother Prince Heinrich—the famed "Sailor Prince"—was born 14 August 1862, and in May 1888, married Princess Irene of Hesse (1866–1953). The couple had three sons. Prince Heinrich was also a famous German racecar driver in his own right, and died on 20 April 1929. Brother Prince Sigismund was born 11 September 1864, and died 18 June 1866, while his father was away fighting the Austrians.

Sister Princess Victoria—named for her mother and grandmother—was born on 12 April 1866, just before that war. She married Prince Adolf of Schaumburg-Lippe (1859–1916), and was remarried to Alexander Zubkov (1900–36.) There were no children of either union. She died on 13 November 1929, having begun divorce proceedings against her second husband.

Brother Prince Waldemar was born 10 February 1868 and died 27 March 1879.

Sister Princess Sophie was born 14 June 1870, just prior to the start of that year's war, and married Crown Prince Constantine of the Hellenes (1858–1923), who reigned as King during 1913–1917 with her as Queen. He was forced by wartime, pro-Allied Greek politics to abdicate in the third year of the Great War, but was returned to the throne during 1920–1922, while his brother-in-law former Kaiser Wilhelm II was in Holland. The couple had a trio of sons, all of whom also ascended the Greek throne, plus three daughters. Queen Sophie of Greece died on 13 January 1932. Thus, His Majesty the Kaiser and King Wilhelm II as first-born of his parents also outlived all of his brothers and sisters, except one: this was sister Princess Margaret, born 22 April 1872. In 1893, she married Prince Frederick Karl (1868–1940), who later became the Landgrave of Hesse. The couple had six sons and these included a double pair of twins. She died on 21 January 1954.

3

The Medical Case Files of the Imperial Triad 1797–1888

Health in History

As we have seen, between 6 March and 15 June of 1888, the then German Reich or Empire witnessed a trio of rulers sit upon the ancient Hohenzollern throne in Berlin. Following an exalted reign of 27 years and eight European wars, Kaiser Wilhelm I died at age 91, being followed to the grave by his successor, Kaiser Frederick III, 57, who was then succeeded in turn by *his* son, the Old Kaiser's brash 29-year-old grandson, the youngest crowned head on the Continent of Europe, Wilhelm II.

The grandson chose his grandfather's illustrious name as that under which he would also reign, rather than that of his father. Thus, the entire "liberal Germany of the 19th Century" represented by his father, Kaiser Frederick III, was simply skipped over, with the former militarism of the 18th of Kaiser Wilhelm I being merged into that of the 20th of Wilhelm II. Liberal Germany ruled briefly during 1919-33, and again starting in 1955 to the present era.

The Hohenzollerns' Generation Gap

Kaiser Wilhelm I did not agree politically with his son Crown Prince Frederick, who in turn disliked his own son, Wilhelm II, who then could not abide *his* first born, the last German *Kronprinzen,* also named Wilhelm.

Hohenzollern Sex

The Old Kaiser was unhappily married, having been forced to give up his "true love" to marry his wife Augusta. Both his son and grandson were reportedly happily married, and both also had large families.

The second Kaiser Wilhelm's son Wilhelm, however, reportedly carried on extra-marital affairs during the entirety of his long marriage to Crown Princess Cecilie. A notorious playboy all his life, at his death at age 69 in 1951, a mistress was present, but not his wife.

The Most Famous Disabled Left Arm in History

Willy was born in 1859 with a paralyzed left arm, a lifelong infirmity that many authors feel determined much of the rest of his life and actions.

As he grew up, the malformed Prince came also to side with the politics of his revered grandfather and Bismarck over the more liberal views of his own parents, this costing him their love and respect, resulting in a deep estrangement that outlived them.

The Old Kaiser, Wilhelm I

In 1877, Kaiser and King Wilhelm I turned 80, when most men his age had long since retired. Still, he mounted his horse every morning at six, and got only five hours sleep nightly. His subordinates stood in awe of his stamina, and many claimed it was due to his midnight supper of lobster that he always ate.

Eyewitnesses describe his appearance as:

> Splendid looking … He certainly looked an emperor, every inch of him: so tall, upright, and correctly dressed, he was dignified without ever looking pompous.

His Majesty survived a trio of assassination attempts. In 1861, a student had fired a bullet that wounded the King's neck after first shredding his collar and necktie. The final two attempts occurred in 1878 within a few weeks of each other. While the Kaiser was on a drive on 11 May with his daughter, a deranged mechanic fired four missed shots before being apprehended. On 2 June, Dr Karl Nobiling fired a load of swan shot from a building at the Emperor, who was, again, riding in his carriage.

States one report:

> This time, William was hit; anywhere from 18–30 pellets entered his head, face, arms, and back. The Emperor, streaming blood, was raced back to the palace, where physicians began to remove the swan shot wherever they could find it. It was later said that he carried some of it in his body to his grave almost 10 years later.

The Kaiser at 90

He turned 90 in 1887, and up to his dying day remained a man of simple, unostentatious habits, even sleeping on an old army camp bed in the palace. Although he was always meticulous about his uniforms, he often refused to wear his good trousers to the theater. Courteous and on time at official ceremonies, the Old Kaiser's speech was difficult to follow due to both his deafness and poor dental work. It was also hard for his listeners to determine even in which language he was speaking. Still, he appeared every inch the monarch, tall, proud, handsome, and dignified without appearing vain and pompous, as did his namesake and grandson later.

Even during his many birthday celebrations, his courtiers—worried about his declining health and advanced age—asked themselves in whispers, "How much longer—and what will happen afterwards?"

The Problem of Fritz and Vicky

On 24 April 1916—during the very height of the slaughter of the Great War on the Western Front in Europe—German Navy Admiral Georg von Müller, Chief of the Kaiser's Naval Cabinet, wrote in his diary at His Majesty's Kaiser Headquarters at Charleville in German-occupied France the following entry:

> This evening—while we were standing about after dinner—the Kaiser told us some unpleasant details of his relationship with his parents during his father's illness. The Empress Frederick emerged in an exceedingly bad light.

This notation—made about events that occurred 28 years earlier—concerned the death from throat cancer of the unfortunate Kaiser Frederick III. Unlike most Hohenzollern princes, Fritz had received a university education in addition to his martial training, arranged for by his liberal mother, Queen Augusta. Physically, Fritz has been described like his father as magnificent, well-built and tall, but also having a golden mane of hair and fascinating blue eyes.

In the summer of 1855 at 24, Fritz visited in Scotland Queen Victoria and her husband, Prince Consort Albert. The following September, Fritz asked to marry their eldest daughter, Vicky, then 15, and the wedding took place early in 1858, when the groom was 27 and the bride 18. Under the influence of his mother, wife, college education, and parents-in-law, Fritz came to admire the English system of government of checks and balances as a model that his own country might follow someday under his reign. The Crown Prince and his new English wife were frank at the Prussian Court with their criticisms, and soon the Old Kaiser—led on by Bismarck—was estranged from his son and daughter-in-law, a situation that endured throughout the entirety of their marriage until the old man's death 30 years later. At a vigorous 40 as Crown Prince in 1871, Fritz added a full beard and moustache of blond hair that made him look more majestic than ever, but as his military career ended the same year, he found himself with little to do except perform ceremonial functions in place of his father.

By age 55 in 1886, the years of waiting for his throne had taken their toll on him: he'd lost weight, looked pale, and was tired. Had he been able to rule for even 15 years, it has been speculated by some authors that he might have converted the reactionary House of Hohenzollern into a more modern dynasty along English lines.

Being human, Fritz had his downside characteristics as well, as a worrier with a quick, sharp temper; pride married to deep depressions, too little drive and lack of stamina, and fear of challenging his father the King and Emperor.

In addition to that—and as attested to by many spiteful observers and foes—Fritz was allegedly completely dominated by his wife, Vicky. This trait more than any other was loathed by most Prussian and German males, and none more so than by his own son and Heir, Prince Wilhelm.

The Difficult Birth of Prince Willy

The future Kaiser Wilhelm II was born on 27 January 1859 as Prince Frederick Wilhelm Victor Albert, in a difficult birth to say the least. His left shoulder socket was badly injured and the left elbow joint dislocated, with both his left hand and arm—though perfectly formed—paralyzed and virtually useless. At adulthood, the left arm was shorter than the left, with its hand just reaching his pocket, where he generally placed it.

In addition, Willy's left leg was never as good as his right, he suffered from chronic pains in the left ear as well as on the left side of his head. At one point during his reign, it was even feared that this might force a medical abdication, but then subsided.

In Benson's 1936 study, he names the doctor as the Englishman Sir James Clark. The baby's neck was also injured, with the head being tilted too far to the left and the cervical nerve plexus injured. Reportedly, it took anywhere from three days to a full month to notice that the little Prince was, indeed, badly injured, hard as that might be to believe.

A Medical Look at the Birth of Kaiser Wilhelm II, 27 January 1859

An excellent treatise on the birth of Kaiser Wilhelm II—and the subsequent controversy over it—appeared in *The Maryland State Medical Journal's* edition of November 1972. Entitled *Three Deliveries That Changed the History of the World*, it was written by a physician, Louis M. Hellman, MD, then Deputy Assistant for Population Affairs of the US Department of Health, Education, and Welfare in Washington, DC. He wrote:

> Kaiser Wilhelm II … sustained an injury to the left brachial plexus during his birth on 27 January 1859. The resultant withering of his arm was for many years the subject of speculation and gossip.
>
> Some of the rumors were undoubtedly initiated by the Royal midwife who was offended when her role was taken over by male obstetricians. Others stem from efforts to attribute to the Kaiser's impulsive behavior [his love of the military and his belief in the Divine Right of Kings] to a physical deformity.
>
> There can be little doubt that Prussian militarism looked with disdain on *any* physical weakness. The Kaiser was sensitive about his deformity and overreacted to it. The psychological impact of this birth injury, occurring in a ruler of a nation convinced that it had been deprived of its share of the world's goods by the major powers—and in a nation already committed to military might—could've provided an impetus to the First World War.

The interesting account was published under the title of: "The true story of the birth of Wilhelm II has received scant attention."

In light of its historic importance, the following documents from Dr Eduard Martin, the obstetrician—and his son, Dr A. Martin—were made available to us from the Archives of the Prussian Royal House and have been translated into English by Dr Ralph M. Wynn.

HM T St #1494/31, Berlin-Schoneberg, December 1928, Baron von Stein St 2

Your Majesty!

May I be permitted to submit the following?

My father—Privy Medical Councillor Prof. Dr Eduard Martin, from 1858–75 Specialist in Obstetrics at the University of Berlin—was honored to be permitted to assist Your Majesty's mother at Your Majesty's birth.

There are all kinds of rumors going around in the press and literature about this action of my father, reproaching him in a most offending manner. All these rumors—irresponsibly exploited and expanded by authors without any authentic basis—are only too likely to slander my father's memory.

I have until now remained silent to all criticisms in the belief that these untrue and disparaging reports would cease by themselves. I was, furthermore, also reluctant to publish my father's report, which he wrote on the basis of his diary 12 days after Your Majesty's birth.

In view, however, of the attacks upon my father—which keep reappearing in the literature concerned with Your Majesty—I feel the cogent obligation to counter the malevolent and totally unjustified abuses against my father with the publication of the authentic material.

At stake is the honor of a scholar of high repute, a highly esteemed representative of the University of Berlin in the worldwide circles of those who were entrusted to his care.

Before publishing the herewith attached material, I ask Your Majesty for a gracious communication indicating whether Your Majesty has any objections. As Your Majesty will see from my report, it limits itself entirely to the essential facts. I have consistently avoided any polemics.

Knowing that my father throughout his career as an obstetrician enjoyed high and frequently shown appreciation in Your Majesty's family, I do not believe that I am making an inappropriate request in asking for Your Majesty's consent to the publication of the herewith attached statements in order to safeguard my father's memory against further unqualified insults.

Your Majesty's most humble, /S/ A. Martin.

There is no record that this request was ever granted, and it is assumed that the following material was never published until 1972 in medical article format, and now—in 2014, for the very first time—in book form, here.

Report of Dr Eduard Martin on the Delivery of the Empress (*sic*), 9 February 1859, and Supplementary Report of Prof. A. Martin of 28 April 1931:
REPORT on the Delivery of Her Royal Highness the Princess Frederick Wilhelm, Princess Royal of Great Britain.
The undersigned was summoned to the Palace at 10 o'clock, after labor was started in the early hours of 27 January and the membranes had ruptured allegedly between 5–6 AM.
At 10:30 AM, I found the cervical os dilated to about 1½ inches in diameter but tight, and

the right buttock of the fetus in it, the anus to the left and backward. The labor—though very painful— was not very effective; the pulse rate between contractions was 8–9 in 5 seconds, and it increased to 12–13 during contractions, indicating spastic, dysfunctional labor.

The illustrious parturient was therefore given one grain ipecacuanha at about 11 AM, which caused her to vomit once. Labor appeared to have improved, but was still very painful. I therefore recommended moderate inhalation of chloroform, which soon alleviated the great agitation of the Princess.

Her Royal Highness complained of unusually violent pains, however, whenever the moderate anesthesia subsided, asking most touchingly for sympathy and apologizing for her loud complaints.

Around 1 PM, the dilatation of the cervical os increased, and the protruding buttocks descended in appropriate later position in the pelvic passages. As the buttocks finally appeared between the labia—at about 2 PM, while contractions though frequent did not seem sufficiently forceful and sustained—there was reason to suspect inadequate uterine activity during the expulsion of the child as well as faulty contraction afterwards.

I therefore recommended administering secale cornutum as I had always done most successfully in similar circumstances. (Among others—even on the preceding as well as on the same day—were two primiparae in the Royal Institute of Obstetrics, one a woman of 47 and the other one of 20, whose babies similarly presented as breeches and, like their mothers, were kept in good condition by means of the same procedure.)

The secale cornutum repeated three times, 10 grains each time, had the desired effect that the illustratius parturient was no longer harassed so frequently by contractions, which—on the other hand—increased in strength and expulsive efficiency.

Thus, the buttocks emerged from the vulva at 2:45 PM with the Prince's legs folded upwards on his abdomen and chest. When, at this point, I felt the pulse in the umbilical cord weaken, slow down, and even become intermittent, the manipulation that had become necessary had to be made safe.

To this end, deeper chloroform anesthesia was administered and, thus, the indispensable total quiet and analgesia of the illustrious parturient was effected. I carefully raised the Prince's legs—which were folded upwards—and, since his life was seriously endangered, I immediately guided his arm, which was stretched upwards and backwards alongside his head, downwards, according to the correct procedure.

It involved considerable effort, as is understandable in view of the narrow genital passages, while I used the arm—according to the tested precepts of obstetric art—to turn the child's body around. Then I released the right arm—which was also stretched upwards— and finally the head, turning (according to Smellie's wise rule) the face back toward the hollow of the sacrum and bringing it out carefully.

As the weakening pulse in the umbilical cord had already indicated—when only the buttocks had been delivered—the Prince appeared quite lifeless, but the usual means of resuscitation sufficed to initiate his breathing even before I brought him to the bath that was kept ready, and he opened his eyes.

After thorough consideration of all circumstances and use of my wide experience, I am still convinced that the Prince would've lost his life had the procedure been different.

Her Royal Highness the Princess awoke after about a quarter of an hour, highly pleased with the painlessly completed, happy delivery, when she heard the Prince's cries from the next room. Her gratitude for the help I had given was as pleasant as it was moving.

The uterus had contracted very well, and about half an hour later, the placenta lay in the vagina, whence I removed it without causing the Princess any pain, while she carried on a conversation with Dr Schonlein.

The further course of the puerperium was normal, more so than might be expected of a primara.

Berlin, 9 February 1859
Dr Eduard Martin
Medical Privy Counsel Prof. Aug. Martin, Berlin

From January 1859 to the present time, the most malevolent reproaches against my father have been leveled in the press on the basis of statements made by the midwife on duty and by ladies of the Court.

These statements have been repeatedly expanded by writers, biographers, and historians, without any authentic, official statements at their disposal. The criticisms raised against Professor Martin were:

1) He had not responded immediately to the call for obstetric assistance; 2) He injured the child during birth; 3) He caused the apparently dead child to be put aside, considering its resuscitation impossible.

To 1), After repeated discussions with my father, I state that he answered the call with particular promptness, since it reached him just as he was about to enter the opened door of his coach in the street in front of his apartment en route to the Charite and thereafter [the famous Berlin hospital] where he was to give a lecture.

On 26 January 1859 in the family of Prince Friedrich Wilhelm [later Emperor Frederick III], the father, then Prince Regent [later Emperor Wilhelm I], insisted that—in addition to the English obstetrician whom the Queen of England had requested for the occasion and to the staff physician assigned to the Prince, the consultant of Berlin University—Professor Martin—be called in.

The invitation to Prof. Martin was sent in a letter by City mail on the evening of 26 January! This letter arrived at 5 Dorotheenstrasse/Street, then the Gynecological Clinic of the University, in the morning mail on 27 January.

It was handed to my father, who'd already entered the rooms of the Clinic at 8 o'clock for his daily rounds, along with the rest of the incoming mail, as he was about to leave, at 10 o'clock, for his lecture at the Charite.

At that moment, a lackey of the Crown Prince came running to ask whether the Professor wouldn't want to come? My father immediately directed his carriage to the Palace.

To 2), The two consulting obstetricians—as mentioned above—had not the previous evening made the diagnosis that the child was presenting by the breech. The report for the Queen of England shows that my father conducted the delivery in exemplary fashion.

The delivery was complicated by a disturbance called 'spastic labor' by obstetricians. With this complication the uterus contracts, becoming as hard as wood, while pains continue.

The illustrious parturient had been suffering throughout the night with great patience. The drugs administered by my father eliminated this spastic condition with appropriate speed, thus making possible a normal course of the delivery.

The family physician of the Royal House—the very famous Prof. Privy Counsel Schonlein of Berlin— had joined in the observation of the delivery. The report shows that—in addition to the obstetrician—the other physicians present observed the infant continuously without noticing any bodily abnormalities.

Special importance must be attached to this connection to the judgment of Privy Counsellor Schonlein—at the time the most famous physician and scholar in Berlin, and intimate family physician of the Royal House—who had meanwhile also come to the Palace.

Schonlein congratulated my father most cordially on his artfully accomplished assistance.

When—upon the birth of the buttocks—the child's heart tones disappeared and the umbilical pulse weakened, my father expertly delivered the body, legs, arms, and head. Notwithstanding the narrowness of the pelvic passages, he fulfilled this task without injury to the soft parts or to the child, as the physicians present stated with vigorous appreciation.

To 3) The report to the Queen shows that it was my father who personally made the efforts to resuscitate the deeply comatose infant. Through continuous rubbing of the infant's body, pouring cold water over the child in the warm bath, and short, strong slaps on the buttocks, my father induced the child to breathe.

Only after about half an hour of eventually successful efforts did he with his own hands place the infant into the hands of the midwife on duty. The child appeared to be quite normally developed; there was no thought of disfigurement of any part of his body, or of a bony fracture or anything of the kind.

The first cries found a lively welcome among the persons present, who were greatly relieved. All congratulated the successful obstetrician, especially the Royal grandfather, who heartily shook my father's hand and remarked: 'But this is not the way to beat Prussian Princes!'

The physicians present—especially Dr Schonlein—having examined the infant, expressed their appreciation repeatedly to my father. Only three-four days later was it noticed that the child's left arm was limp. Treatment was entrusted to appropriate specialists, not to the obstetrician.

Having no reason to assume that my father—the highest authority among his colleagues at the time—and Dr Schonlein could've overlooked an injury to the bone or joint during inspection and palpation of the infant, I consider the developing change in the left shoulder and the left arm a result of the pressure exerted by the arms, hands, and feet, which were folded upward during birth, upon the nerve plexus of the neck, which influences motion and development of the arm (now called 'Duchenne-Erb paralysis').

The premature rupture of the membranes and the long-lasting, very violent, spastic contractions of the uterus certainly played their fateful part.

The very happy mother was especially grateful to my father. The first manual work she was permitted to perform was the preparation of paper spills for my father, who was not a smoker.

The parents also later remained graciously thankful to my father, who was again in contact with Their Highnesses for weeks while staying in the New Palace in Potsdam in 1860, waiting for the second delivery. Title and decoration were, of course, awarded before long.

April 1931
A. Martin.

Dr Hellman rejoined:

Skillful as Dr E. Martin undoubtedly was, there can be little doubt that the brachial plexus was injured during the partial breech extraction. Dr Martin's report is not sufficiently detailed to fix the precise moment of the accident.

Apparently, however, the left arm was extracted with difficulty. The fetus lay, originally, with his back to the mother's left and his left arm anterior, inasmuch as the left arm was extracted first, the injury must've occurred either when the anterior shoulder was pulled beneath the symphysis, during the extraction, or when the arm was used to turn the fetus.

Dr Martin was faced with the serious obstetrical complication of having to perform a partial breech extraction on a primigravida with a contracted pelvis. The bilateral nuchal arms compounded the difficulty; they're not uncommon in such cases.

Modern obstetrical practice frequently suggests that extraction of the posterior arm first is easier than the procedure performed by Dr Martin. Certainly an episiotomy simplifies the operation.

Martin, however, followed standard teachings of his time, and in this respect his conduct of the labor was exemplary. The accident was more inherent in the circumstances than in the obstetrician ... Few obstetricians are placed in positions similar to those presented to ... Martin ... Each birth alters history in its own way. No man is an island, no birth is without its influence on the individual, and thus many people, occasionally on history.

In this respect, the responsibility of the obstetrician is without parallel in medicine.

It is interesting to note that 41 years elapsed between 1931–72 and the original publication of this article in *The Maryland State Medical Journal,* and now 42 more have elapsed to its book publication herein.

The Arm: What Effect?

All of Wilhelm's previous biographers have wrestled with the physical and psychological meanings of his lifeless left arm on his character and development and—beyond those—on what the injury meant in historical terms as well.

At age eight, Willy was taught to ride horseback without stirrups, lost his balance often, and fell crying to the ground time after time.

From the BBC TV dramatization, *Fall of Eagles*:

> Such treatment was brutal, and it confirmed in him that suppressed and humiliating sense that boys much smaller than himself could do with ease what he—for no fault of his—found so cruelly hard.
>
> In spite of all treatment, no power could be restored to his paralyzed limb and—in modern psychological terms (1936) there developed in him a deep rooted inferiority complex.

The crippled left arm received very painful electric shock treatment causing much extreme torture, but in time, he supported his left arm in his belt or pocket.

As again, depicted in *Fall of Eagles*:

> … to let the reins slip into his left hand from his normal right one … but in this way, the right arm became overdeveloped and heavy that frequently, when riding, it caused him to lose his balance, and slide off on that side.

By 1876, however—when Willy was 17—he could ride well, swim, fence, skate, and shoot, but had difficulty in running, climbing, and jumping, and walked somewhat awkwardly. As much as was possible, Willy overcame his infirmity as best he could. A specially designed, combined knife-and-fork was used by him to eat, and in her postwar memoirs, the English born Daisy Princess of Pless in Germany recalled cutting up the Kaiser's food for him at mealtimes at her castle dining table.

He refused to surrender to his infirmity, and also silently heard charges that a one-armed man should never rule the Second Reich as Emperor from his envious German cousins and uncles. During his long reign, His Imperial Majesty seemed oblivious to the condition that had bedeviled his trying youth.

When he was three, his mother wrote of him:

> William has inflamed eyes and is shut up in his room, which makes him look like a cheese. His eyes discharge a good deal of matter and are swollen; he had this before (five months previously, but it was only one eye then, and now it is both.) Wegner says it proceeds from cold.

Early in his life, a tendency toward violence and brutality manifested itself in Willy. At age four, he threatened an English uncle with a knife, and then bit him in the leg, and he used to shake hands so hard with English ladies in later life that they winced in pain. Like his father and son, Willy was commissioned at age ten in the infantry, but went on as well to win riding honors as a cavalry officer. Like his grandfather, young Willy loved military life.

Still, his parents reportedly behaved in a cold, distant fashion to him, preferring their other, younger children first. Both also thought him brash, headstrong, and immature as he reached adulthood, despite the fact that—most of his earlier biographers concur— he inherited many of their own traits and characteristics, especially those of his mother, with whom he had a love-hate relationship from his late teenaged years until her death in 1901.

First Marriage, 1881–1921

In February 1881, at 22, Prince Wilhelm married Princess Augusta Victoria (1858–1921) of the previously annexed Schleswig-Holstein, it being seen as a political healing of that prior event. Nicknamed Dona, some authors have seen her marriage to the Prince as being the final breaking point between him and his parents.

Most of Prince Wilhelm's previous biographers stress that she fulfilled all his sexual desires, providing him with six sons and a daughter. They were: German Crown Prince Wilhelm/Little Willy (1882–1951), who married Duchess Cecilie of Mecklenburg-Schwerin; Prince Eitel Frederick (1883–1942), who wed Duchess Sophia Charlotte of Oldenburg; Prince Adalbert (1884–1948), betrothed to Princess Adelaide of Saxe-Meiningen; Prince August Wilhelm [Auwi] (1887–1949), married Princess Alexandra Victoria of Schleswig-Holstein-Sonderburg-Glücksburg; Prince Oscar (1888–1958), wed Countess Ina Marie von Bassewitz; Prince Joachim (1890–1920) married Princess Marie-Auguste of Anhalt; and Princess Victoria Luise (1892–1980), married Duke of Brunswick, Ernst Augustus.

The "smart set" women at Court—the liberals like Vicky and also the English-born Daisy Princess of Pless—thought of Dona as "the stupid cow," good only for breeding, while those who knew her better adored her as "The Mother of the Nation." This included all her children and at least one daughter-in-law, Crown Princess Cecilie.

In 1999, biographer van der Kiste asserted that within a year of his marriage, Prince Wilhelm had a threesome with two paid Austrian girls, causing a scandal known to the police and Crown Prince Rudolf there, as well as to Bismarck in the Reich.

From the evidence available there is the distinct possibility that Wilhelm was bisexual, taking Prince Eulenburg and possibly other members of the latter's Biebenberg Circle as lovers for as long as, perhaps, 20 years, until the 1904 homosexual scandal engineered by a fired and bitter Holstein with the German Jewish journalist Maximilian Harden led to public trials for sodomy. Fearing for his crown and throne, His Majesty abandoned all these former lovers at once, and never saw Prince Eulenburg again, either, but remembered him fondly in his post-war memoirs nonetheless. Reich Chancellor Prince Bernhard von Bülow was allegedly linked to asserted gay lovers Eulenberg and Holstein, and within their clique, His Majesty was referred to as *The Darling*.

Demise of Kaiser Wilhelm I

The Old Kaiser would have turned 91 on 22 March 1888, but it was a birthday that he never lived to see, dying at 8:20 a.m. on 9 March that same year. He passed away surrounded by his wife, his grandson, and Prince Bismarck, but not the Fredericks, who were at San Remo, Italy, where the new Kaiser was trying vainly to regain his shattered health. Lying on his narrow soldier's cot in his sparsely furnished bedroom, the Old Gentleman—wearing a white jacket and a red neck scarf—told his grandson, "Always keep on good terms with Russia!" sound advice that he later failed to follow, alas.

Return of the Shadow Kaiser

On 11 March 1888, the new Kaiser Frederick III arrived in Berlin from Italy. His father was buried in an elaborate state funeral with the grandson standing in as chief mourner five days later amidst a Berlin snowfall, as depicted in the superb 1942 Nazi propaganda film, *Die Endlassung [The Dismissal].*

The brisk wind had prevented His Majesty Kaiser Frederick from meeting various arriving dignitaries at the main Berlin train station, but he did see them indoors at Charlottenburg Palace during his public debut as German Emperor, however, as described by the new German Kaiserin, Vicky, the Empress Frederick:

> "In full uniform with quick steps—dignified and upright as usual—he went to meet everyone," who were, "astonished to see him like that after all they had heard."

"That is where I ought to be now," he scribbled, as Fritz saw the proudly strutting figure of his son—the new German Crown Prince Wilhelm—walking behind the hearse, as it passed through Berlin's Tiergarten Park. His father Kaiser Frederick III was forced to watch the grim procession from a window at the Berlin Castle, silently raising his bejeweled Field Marshal's baton in reverent salute. Three months later, the "Shadow Emperor" himself would be buried, but with far less solemnity, and in too hasty bad taste as well.

The 99 Days' Reign

Frederick's rule was as tragic as it was short-lived. Bereft of strength and confidence in himself, His Majesty saw no course but to retain his late father's chief minister, Prince Bismarck, in office, and did. Aside from his son's growing arrogance and repeated proclamations to all that he would be Kaiser in a short time, the Shadow Emperor also had to endure the almost literal sight of *his* courtiers rubbing their hands with glee at the thought of his own coming demise.

While Fritz made a few deceptively good public appearances that spring of 1888—in a drug-induced stupor caused by Vicky, their enemies whispered—she meanwhile was in fact considering a Regency for herself after her husband's death that her eldest and second sons both promptly rejected as being against the Imperial Constitution, backed up by its legal executor, the Imperial Chancellor Prince Bismarck.

Death of Frederick III and the Accession of Wilhelm II

His Majesty aged 57 died on 15 June 1888, immediately succeeded by his son the Crown

Prince, who took the name Kaiser Wilhelm II, in honor of his late grandfather, whom he now took to calling Wilhelm the Great, but it never caught on, either at Court nor with the public at large. As soon as his father died, Wilhelm had the New Palace at Potsdam surrounded by soldiers, and an order was issued that no one—especially the doctors—could write to anyone outside, nor could any leave, or they would be arrested.

In addition, His Majesty's soldiers were trying to find his late father's personal papers—but to no avail—as they had already been smuggled out to England by the newly widowed Dowager Empress, former Kaiserin Victoria, the new Kaiser's mother. This scene is ably shown in the 1974 BBC series, *Fall of Eagles,* with the new Kaiser seen wearing red Hussar's uniform and jacket, telling the ex-Kaiserin, "Mama, go to your room!"

That was not all: disregarding both the wishes of his mother and late father, Wilhelm ordered an autopsy on the deceased Emperor to prove that Frederick had had the fatal cancer from the very start of his illness, as was, indeed, thus confirmed. The British Dr Sir Morell Mackenzie had been wrong.

Kaiser Frederick III was buried with scant respect or ceremony on 18 June 1888. Present was the new Emperor's maternal uncle—the elder brother of the former Kaiserin's siblings—the British Prince of Wales and heir to the throne of Great Britain, Edward. It was this shabby event, reportedly, that cemented forever Uncle Bertie's disdain for his vainglorious nephew. The new Kaiser thus began his reign under a moral cloud, but hastened to issue a trio of Imperial and Royal Proclamations at the outset: to the Army, his People, and—for the first time—to the nascent German Navy, a portent of things to come.

Widowhood of "The Englishwoman," the Empress Frederick, 1888–1901

During the next 12 years—the first of the new reign of her son—the widowed Empress Frederick lived a shadow existence herself. In 1898—a decade after her husband's death and at his exact age of 57—it was discovered that Vicky had cancer of the larynx as well. Although told that an operation—performed early—might be successful, she rejected it, "Swore the doctor to secrecy and gave out that she was suffering from lumbago" instead. By late 1900, at 60, Vicky herself began a macabre replay of Fritz's race with death with her mother, Queen Victoria, 80. Again, all Europe wondered: who will die first?

The *Faery Queen* Victoria died on 22 January 1901, followed by her daughter on 5 August 1901. The Old Queen's grandson had hurried to England straightaway to be present when his grandmother died and, indeed, held her in his arms for two and a half hours hours before he and the new King Edward VII lifted her into her coffin. In gratitude, Uncle Bertie commissioned his nephew a Field Marshal in the British Army, an honor he relished for the next 13 years.

Kaiser Wilhelm's Own Hoarse Throat, Autumn 1903

In Fall 1903—after being on the Imperial throne for over 15 years, the Kaiser suddenly complained of hoarseness. In March 1901, a growth was diagnosed on one of his own vocal chords, just as had his late father earlier in the very same location and with the exact symptoms. Also like Fritz, Wilhelm carried on government affairs in silence via notes, as all awaited the outcome of tests that had been taken. They proved benign, and thus not the malignant cancer that had been feared, and that had slain his father. All praised the silent courage that Wilhelm II had displayed during one of the most trying times of his life.

What irony! What would have happened if: 1) Wilhelm II had died in 1903, rather than almost four decades later? 2) He had abdicated the throne, instead of in 1918 when he actually did, in order not to be a "voiceless Emperor" himself? The World War might never have occurred under his son and successor, a projected Kaiser Wilhelm III. On the other hand, it might have come sooner, under an inexperienced new ruler then but 21 years old. The danger passed, but there were other disturbing medical signs.

Wilhelm II's Temperament

Most of the Kaiser's previous biographers agree that His Majesty had an extremely nervous temperament, a rude sense of humor at other people's expense, and was full of bluster, bombast, and conceit.

Once—when his doctor told him he had "a little cough," the 5′ 6″ tall Emperor retorted, "A *great* cough! I am great in everything!" It was not enough for him to be an Emperor. In May 1900, he allowed himself to be appointed a Field Marshal of the German Army, complete with an unearned baton.

The First Abdication Crisis Fall 1908

In November 1908—after a storm of public protest both in Germany and England over some intemperate remarks the Kaiser made in a published interview in the *Daily Telegraph* newspaper that had first been approved by his own Imperial Chancellor—Wilhelm II suffered a temporary nervous breakdown and took to his bed. He summoned his own Crown Prince Wilhelm, 26, and seemed ready to abdicate after two decades on the throne. He did not however, and, indeed, remained another decade. Was the Kaiser, possibly, an undiagnosed patient suffering from bipolar depression? Whatever, he always recovered from these attacks. The experience of his first bout with loud public criticism, affected a change in his psychological makeup according to all his previous biographers.

Described as a completely broken man without any self-confidence and afraid to rule, His Majesty within but four months entirely regained his psychological equilibrium, and reigned for another full decade as if nothing had happened.

The Kaiser went on to not only build the Imperial High Seas Fleet, but also to serve as Supreme Warlord during the First World War of four years' duration. Nor was he "broken" by losing his country, crown, homes, and wife. Rather, he survived all that as well, going on to publish several outstanding volumes of personal memoirs, some still in print today, almost a century later.

That there was a collapse has, however, been debated by both historians and even the Kaiser's own successive Imperial Chancellors of 1908–1918. A Dr Renvers told Chancellor Bernhard von Bülow in February 1909:

If the Kaiser were an ordinary patient, I should diagnose *Pseudologia phastastica,* a tendency to live in fantasy, or—putting it bluntly—to lie.

Such tendencies are common enough in all neurasthenic patients, and do not prevent their living to a ripe old age, displaying great activity and real talent in certain fields, since such infirmities are entirely compatible with unusual, even brilliant gifts.

Remedy? Bodily and mental quiet, composure, self-discipline.

This was exactly the kind of life that the former Kaiser would, in fact, live in Holland during 1918–1941. Indeed, Dr Renvers' assessment of the Kaiser was startlingly accurate: he did live to a "ripe old age," and his enforced exile in 1918 gave him "bodily and mental quiet," producing a serenity he'd never known in his decades of worldly pomp and power.

Not a Warmonger?

Despite all his pre-war martial gesturing and flamboyant speeches, the Kaiser shrank from war's actuality. In 1912—when war broke out in the Balkans— His Majesty did his best to keep Germany out of it, and succeeded, too.

The same was almost true again in August 1914, but then he failed. The Second, Wilhelmine Reich was on the fateful path to war, defeat, Hitlerism, and a second, even more catastrophic downfall, what author Nowak termed in 1932, *Germany's Road to Ruin.*

PART 2

King of Prussia and German Kaiser
1888–1914

One of the most famous political cartoons in European history, from *Punch*, 29 March 1890, entitled, *Dropping the Pilot*. (*Library of Congress*)

4

Dropping the Pilot
Firing Bismarck 1888–1890

Bismarck at High Tide, 1871–1888

On 15 June 1888—as the new and third Kaiser ascended his throne—Prince Otto von Bismarck was 73. Since 1862, he had been Prussian Premier and Minister for Foreign Affairs. In 1867, he became Federal Chancellor of the Prussian-dominated North German Confederation, and—with the founding of the German Empire in 1871—he was named the first Imperial Chancellor of the German Reich.

When the future Kaiser was born, Bismarck was already fully 44 years old, and serving as Prussian Ambassador to the Court of the Tsar at St Petersburg, one of the regime's top diplomatic postings of the Foreign Office. Thus, as Prince of Prussia, young Willy grew up during the triad of Bismarck's wars. In *Fall of Eagles,* as a boy, Willy is seen sitting at table listening to the political conversations between the Chancellor and his grandfather, the Old Kaiser. He also noticed how the Prince easily manipulated his revered grandpapa, tucking this away for future reference.

Prince Willy lit the older Chancellor's cigars, for which he received a paternalistic pat on the head and hair tousle, as seen in *Fall.* This, too, he recalled later. Prince Willy was but eleven when the Reich was forged into being. The Old Kaiser paid his financial allowance, not his parents; and reigned, not his parents.

On 15 June 1888, the new Kaiser Wilhelm II was supreme in all that he surveyed, except for one man who stood in his way, Prince Bismarck. He had to go.

The Honeymooners: Aged Prince and "The Young Master"

That His Majesty greatly admired his Chancellor was obvious to all who saw them together. The Chancellor's eldest son and heir-designate—Count Herbert von Bismarck—however, described Wilhelm II thus:

> As cold as a block of ice. Convinced from the start that people only exist to be used—either for work or for amusement—and that even then they only do their duty for a given period, after which they may be cast aside.

Otto von Bismarck had been in office for 26 years, and he fully meant to remain so until he died, at which time, his own son and familial heir would succeed him in power and name.

In fact, so confident was he of his position with the Emperor that he let slip away his initial advantage and hold over the new "Young Master," as he called Wilhelm II.

Indeed, of the first 18 months of the New Master's reign, his Imperial Chancellor spent but four at the Reich Capital Berlin, preferring instead to conduct affairs of State the rest from his country estate *Friedrichsruhe* outside the port city of Hamburg, in relaxation and at his own pace. As everything required his signature, the Reich was run via messenger boys with dispatch cases, with His Majesty left in the dark, mostly.

One of the main reasons, therefore, for Bismarck's eventual fall from power was that he failed to follow his own advice:

> The Kaiser is like a balloon. If you don't keep fast hold of the string, you never know where he'll be off to!

Herbert Bismarck's succession was secure when he himself began to fail. When one of his colleagues in the Cabinet, Bötticher, tried to warn him of his conduct and long absences, Bismarck merely replied, "In view of my record and my position, there is no risk that the Emperor will dismiss me." He was wrong.

But Bismarck was not the only one to underestimate Wilhelm II—so did his mother. The essential problem in this whole situation was a simple one: ultimately, Bismarck's entire power rested on a single pillar: the Kaiser himself. As Imperial Reich Chancellor, Bismarck was responsible to no one—not even the Reichstag!—but to the Emperor alone, whoever that person was at the time.

There was no question where the ultimate power lay: the Emperor could demand Bismarck's portfolio, whereas Bismarck couldn't demand the Emperor's crown, but would the Emperor really assert himself? He could, and did.

Wilhelm's real attitude during this time—unknown to Bismarck—was expressed to the Englishman Wheeler-Bennett by the former Kaiser in exile in Holland in August 1939 at Doorn House:

> My old Hohenzollern family pride was up in arms! Now it was a question of compelling the old hothead's obedience, or parting once and for all. Now, it was simply, "Emperor or Chancellor on top!"
>
> I began to writhe when I heard people praising Bismarck for the unification of Germany, for had not the nation sprung into being under the rule of my grandfather, Wilhelm I?
>
> Bismarck deliberately had snatched the credit to the detriment of the Sovereign. The Chancellor was no longer my servant, but my rival, and it was imperative for the dignity of the dynasty to show the world that the Hohenzollerns—and *not* the Bismarcks—ruled Germany!

The von Waldersees, General Count Alfred and Wife Mary

Count Alfred von Waldersee (1847–1904)—(Deputy) Chief of the Great German General Staff—wrote in his diary in October 1888:

The Chancellor is showing signs of age. He contradicts himself oftener than he used to do, and repeats orders given a few days before. This makes cooperation with him more difficult.

By undermining Bismarck and currying favor with first Prince, then Crown Prince, and finally Kaiser, Wilhelm for many years, Waldersee hoped to be Bismarck's immediate successor. Wilhelm II was not deceived, however, and also had taken note of how von Waldersee had plotted against his parents with the Old Kaiser, himself, and Prince Bismarck. What had happened to his father might also happen to him, he rightly reasoned. In the end, von Waldersee *never* became Imperial Reich Chancellor in anyone's place. His wife the American heiress Mary also did not fool the Young Master, although it was rumored that the two were secret lovers. As with many others, Willy told her one thing, but did another.

Old Moltke, "Silent in Seven Languages"

Field Marshal Helmuth von Moltke the Elder, 90—the old Chief of General Staff and never really a friend of Bismarck's but, rather his occasional political ally—stood aloof.

Holstein—"the Man with the Hyena Eyes"—as the Secret Anti-Bismarckian Leader

The leader of the gathering anti-Bismarck coalition that was now springing up fast was Baron Friedrich von Holstein, a minor but powerful Privy Councillor with the German Foreign Office. Through the use of bribery, fear, and extortion, von Holstein maintained his influence in foreign matters for over two decades. One of Bismarck's own creatures, Holstein nonetheless feared that the Iron Chancellor might someday discard him, and decided now to act first.

Waldersee's Best Poison Dart Hits Home

One day, von Waldersee told Wilhelm that, "Frederick the Great would never have *become* the Great if—on his accession—he'd found and retained in power a minister of Bismarck's authority and prestige."

The Kaiser Decides

Still, the Kaiser maintained an ambivalent attitude toward "his" first Chancellor, alternating between both love and hate, between retention and dismissal: "I shall let the Old Man shuffle on for six months, then I shall rule myself!" He lasted 19.

In the 1930s at Doorn, the former Kaiser told von Kürenburg that what finally brought the hidden conflict between them out into the open was Bismarck's January 1890 article in foreign newspapers attacking His Majesty's moves to placate the German anti-monarchist Social Democratic Party, the Socis.

The Foreign Bone of Contention: Russia!

The issue of Russia was a further bone of contention between the two men. The keystone of Bismarck's foreign policy had always been friendship with Russia, Prussia's old ally from the Napoleonic Wars of 1797–1815. Inherent in this was the avoidance militarily of Germany's actual bane in both World Wars: the famous "war on two fronts" that defeated her twice, with France opposite her.

Friendship with Russia, however, had never been a popular idea with the German people, who would rather *have* fought a war with their other allies the Austrians *against* the Russians, as, indeed, they did in 1914 and 1939. Bismarck was the sole friend Russia had in the Court circles of Wilhelm II.

Warmonger Waldersee the Main Anti-Russian Foe

Waldersee initially had a great influence over Wilhelm II, especially when preaching the Preventive War, and pillaried Bismarck's policy of improving relations with Russia. Instead, Waldersee plumped hard that Germany should attack and destroy Russia!

"She should also attack and destroy France before the latter grew too strong. War—not peace—was what was needed."

The Friction Intensifies

During one intense interview, Wilhelm is said to have made Bismarck so angry that the choleric Chancellor picked up his inkstand and replaced it on his desk with such force as to splash the contents all over his Young Master. Such actor's tricks had always worked with the Old Kaiser, but this one—a supreme thespian himself!—wasn't buying it.

The Climax over the Socis, 1890

Bismarck wanted to exterminate the Socis by force of arms, while the Kaiser wished instead to placate them by giving in to their more reasonable demands. The issue was brought front and center at the tumultuous Crown Council meeting of 24 January 1890, Frederick the Great's birthday, at which His Majesty proposed new and sweeping social legislation that would downgrade the Chancellor's tough anti-Socialist laws and also ameliorate the conditions of the ordinary German working man.

Sitting round a baize-green covered conference table facing their Soverign and Reich Chancellor were eight Reich Ministers, appointed by the Kaiser, but the Chancellor's men nonetheless. Seen in the current light, Wilhelm in the late nineteenth century was, therefore, on the side of progressive and enlightened reform, with the Imperial Chancellor a rank reactionary. This was the only way the dangerous Social Democrat vote could be stemmed. He read out his list: shorter working hours, no child labor, no Sunday work. When he finished, he turned to the Chancellor and asked for his opinion.

Bismarck wanted instead even harsher new anti-Socialist laws to foment anarchy for the Emperor to declare a state of emergency—exactly the policy that Wilhelm II himself later vigorously advocated—but just not *then*. Thereby, Bismarck and the Army would establish martial law, a new Constitution would be drafted by the Imperial Chancellor Prince Bismarck, and both the Reichstag and the Federal State Landtags would be dissolved. The Kaiser would become a dictator, but only via Prince Bismarck, under whose control he would be.

The Kaiser's January 1890 Retort

He wanted to be, he said, the "King of the Poor."

Bismarck answered him, "I cannot prove that Your Majesty's yielding policy will have disastrous results, but the experience of many years leads me to feel sure that it *will!* … Collisions may ensue!"

The Kaiser burst out, "Unless extreme necessity arises, I shall avert such catastrophes, instead of staining the first year of my reign with the blood of my subjects!" fully 360 degrees from his later assertions to his troops.

The two men thus had drawn the battle lines that would persist through the entire rest of the new German Empire: Liberals and Socialists (and later, Communists) on the Left versus the Reactionary Right. Indeed, the struggle that began but failed in 1848, re-ignited and partially succeeded during 1918–33.

The fact was that the Socis were *never* stamped out, usually did well at the polls, and, in the end, won. Nothing that any of the Kaiser's governments did ever halted their upward progress.

"If Your Majesty is unable to accept my advice, I do not know whether I can remain in office."

The Gauntlet Thus Thrown Down

"That puts me in a dilemma," the Kaiser said. "I beg these gentlemen for their opinion." They sat silent, afraid to cross their real boss, Bismarck. The Kaiser in a silent rage adjourned the meeting, as so ably depicted in *Fall of Eagles*. Shaking hands with Bismarck and smiling, inwardly, His Majesty smoldered. Waylaying his Minister of War in the hall, the Kaiser barked angrily, "Why did you leave me in the lurch? You—every one of you!—looked as though you'd been flogged! What had he said to you beforehand? You are no longer *my* Ministers, but the Ministers of Prince Bismarck! He has planted *his* chair in front of *my* door!"

He was right.

Bismarck in Extremis

On 31 January 1890, Bismarck gave up his post of Prussian Minister of Commerce. At the next Crown Council meeting, the Ministers *all* sided with the Kaiser against Bismarck.

Wilhelm triumphantly drafted his social ideas into a Proclamation that was then issued in the Kaiser's name alone, the very first bill to become law *not* countersigned by the Imperial

Chancellor.

Wilhelm crowed, "The Old Man is crawling! I'll leave him a few weeks to recover his breath, then *I'll* govern!"

The Kaiser Publicly Rebuffed Via the Reichstag Elections of 20 February 1890

The Reichstag elections—anticipated by both Kaiser and Chancellor—were held. The elections reached Bismarck's "Highest expectations."

The National Liberals and Bismarckian Conservatives each lost over 50% of their seats, while the Socialists, the Radicals, and the Catholic Center Parties—all opposed to Bismarck— ended with a total of nearly two-thirds of the seats.

Bismarck joyously confronted his downcast Emperor—for these were *his* losses as well, even *more* so!—and stated again his plans for a coup d'etat. The Kaiser shook Bismarck's hand, exclaiming, "No surrender!" but soon recanted.

He'd placed the Army on alert in case of demonstrations. When the results came in, the Kaiser was crushed. His liberal social reforms hadn't deleted the Social Democratic vote, but had, indeed, *increased* it by half! In the elections of 1887, the SPD had previously polled 763,000 votes, but now it had 1,427,000.

On 4 March 1890—in another stormy confrontation with Bismarck—the Kaiser rejected the Iron Chancellor's coup d'etat plan. "I won't be called the Cartridge King, like my grandfather!"

"Better sooner than later!" Bismarck shot back. "Social Democracy cannot be reformed out of existence. Someday, it will have to be *shot* out of existence!" Wilhelm exclaimed in answer, "I will *not* wade in blood!"

Bismarck revealed to the Saxon envoy in Berlin his anxiety over the future: "I think the day will soon come when even the Army will no longer be trustworthy, and then Germany's fate will be sealed," indeed, exactly as transpired on 9 November 1918.

Bismarck as a Man of the Past, and Not the Future

Bismarck failed to realize that—though he was still admired—he was seen as an *historic* figure, *not* as a leader of the modern day. A full generation of Germans had grown to maturity like the Young Master who, like him, also were impatient with the Chancellor's caution and restraint.

Like their Kaiser, Young Germany wanted great *new* achievements, not Bismarck's continued quiet life. Wilhelm II—*not* Bismarck—better represented this new Young German attitude, while the crusty Iron Chancellor seemed to be provoking civil war simply to stay in office.

The Final, Disputed Confrontation: 15 March 1890

Bismarck's next move was to attempt to cleave the alliance of Ministers and Kaiser one from another. To do this, he produced the Order of 8 September 1852—before Wilhelm II was even born!—"Forbidding Ministers to instruct or advise the crown unless the Prime Minister was present," posing himself thereby as the defender of Constitutional government combating the autocracy and irresponsibility of Wilhelm II.

On what happened next, historians differ. At 9 a.m. on 15 March 1890, a note arrived at Bismarck's home telling him that he was to report to the Kaiser in the Foreign Ministry at 9:30 a.m.

When the note arrived, Bismarck was still asleep, and got up in an angry mood at being so summoned, and crossed to the Foreign Ministry. A topic of discussion was the Order of 1852. Wilhelm II plaintively asked Bismarck, "How can I rule *without* discussing things with the Ministers, if *you* spend a large part of the year at Friedrichsruh? I have no longer *any* oral reports from *my* Ministers! I am told you have forbidden them to report to me without your consent, basing these instructions upon obsolete and forgotten ordinances."

Bismarck lost his self-control and threw his dispatch case to the ground. Would any Chief of State—monarch or President—accept such behavior? Could they?

Wilhelm II thought an ink pot might be thrown at his head—"I had my hand on my sword hilt!" The Kaiser rose and:

> Offered me his hand—in which he was holding his helmet—more coldly than usual. I accompanied him to the outer steps before the door of the house. He was just about to step into the carriage before the eyes of the servants, when he sprang up the steps again, and shook my hand vigorously.

The 1942 anti-Kaiser Nazi film *The Dismissal* shows this scene vividly, but done as a "photo op" for the cheering crowds across the street instead.

After this encounter, Bismarck's fall was only a matter of days—or even hours—off, and everyone now realized it. On 18 March 1890, the resignation finally arrived at the Berlin Palace. As seen in *Fall of Eagles,* Wilhelm and his later accused homosexual best friend and possible lover—Prince Philip "Phili" Eulenburg (1847–1921)—were playing the piano together and singing.

In the letter of resignation, Bismarck based everything on the Order of 1852, shifting the blame for his dismissal to the Kaiser, who suppressed its publication, and it was not published until after the fall of the Empire in 1918. Instead, it was announced to the public that Bismarck himself had requested to go, on grounds of ill health, a lie. On 26 March 1890, the former Chancellor took his official leave of His Majesty. The next day, he went to Charlottenburg and laid a trio of roses on the grave of Wilhelm I.

On the afternoon of 29 March 1890, Bismarck left Berlin by train for Friedrichsruh, amid a popular demonstration of several thousand Berliners and an official honor guard, but no Kaiser Wilhelm II.

As the train drew out of the station, a military band struck up a slow march. Bismarck leaned back in his carriage and sighed, "A State Funeral with full honors."

The 1942 National Socialist Film *The Dismissal* and

the Two Protagonists Reassessed

In 1942, the Nazis released their own excellent film on the fall of Prince Bismarck, entitled *Die Endlassung/The Dismissal,* directed by Wolfgang Liebeniener, whose 1940 film had been *Bismarck.*

The Nazis—especially Hitler—being both anti-monarchist *and* anti-Kaiser Wilhelm II, it comes as no surprise that this film was pro-Bismarck, based as it was on the Iron Chancellor's own memoirs, *Gedanken und Erinnerungen/Thoughts and Memories.*

Touted as "Nazi Germany's most historically accurate film biography," it actually *is,* too. It boasted a stellar cast: Emil Jannings as Bismarck, Theodor Loos as the Old Kaiser, Wilhelm I; Karl Ludwig Diel played Kaiser Frederick III, while Hildegard Grethe depicted the Empress Frederick, Vicky; Werner Hinz is Kaiser Wilhelm II, Werner Krauss plays Privy Councillor Baron Friedrich von Holstein, with Otto Gray as Count Philip Eulenburg. Published in tandem with the film's gala premiere was a *Press Book,* that states, "Frederick Wilhelm IV wrote the following words after Bismarck's name: 'Only of use when the bayonet reigns unrestrained.'"

The Young Master is quoted as asserting, "I'd rather chop off every limb, than ever part from you!" one occasion, contradicted later by a petulant, "Why does all the world only speak of Bismarck? Why does no one talk about me? It comes down to either the Hohenzollern dynasty or the Bismarck dynasty!"

Bismarck stated, "Waldersee is a confusing politician not to be counted on; what he says is worthless. He wants war because he feels he'll get too old if peace lasts much longer. It is foolish to think Waldersee could become Chancellor! He is an inadequate Chief of Staff as well." At length, His Majesty concurred.

Of Prince von Eulenberg, Bismarck wrote, "Very proper, well read, kind. Doesn't want to *be* anything—neither Secretary of State nor Chancellor. He thinks the friendship of a great man is a gift of the gods. He asks nothing more, but adoration is of no use to us."

He termed 1888—the Year of the Three Kaisers—thus: "We stand before an unnatural crack in our history."

The 1942 *Press Book* notes, the "Portrayer of Kaiser Wilhelm II" (is) "a task that requires the utmost in artistic self-discipline and acting sensitivity: Werner Hinz."

It also deftly describes what the Young Master's early ascension to the throne meant: "Not only the older generation of 70-year-olds—but also the middle generation of 50-year-olds—suddenly dropped out, and the younger generation of 30-year-olds stepped up to rule with Wilhelm II." Today, *The Dismissal* is newly available on DVD from International Historic Films, Inc.

Fall of Eagles, BBC, 1974

This outstanding, 13-part television dramatic series was created by John Elliott and produced by Stuart Burge. It portrays the period 1848–1918, "Dealing with the ruling dynasties of Europe in Austria-Hungary, Germany, and Russia: the Habsburgs, Hohenzollerns, and the Romanovs respectively. Playing the Hohenzollerns are Colin Baker as Crown Prince Wilhelm—Little Willy—son of Kaiser Wilhelm II; John Barcroft as Eulenberg, Michael Bates as General Erich Ludendorff, Isla Blair as our Willy's first love, Princess Ella; Kevin Brennan as Count Bentinck of Amerongen, Holland; Anne Castle as young Ella, Eric Carte as an aide to Kaiser Wilhelm II, and Geoffrey Chater as Prince Karl of Prussia.

Also starring is Peter Copley as Chancellor Theobald von Bethmann-Hollwegg, Gemma Jones as Empress Vicky, Curt Jurgens as Bismarck, Denis Lill as Kaiser Frederick III, Adam Cunliffe as young Willy, Maurice Denham as the Old Kaiser, Wilhelm I; Barry Foster doing an outstanding Kaiser Wilhelm II in adult life, 1887–1918; Marius Goring as Field Marshal Paul von Hindenburg, Roger Hammond as Prince Albrecht of Prussia, Laurence Hardy playing last Imperial Chancellor Prince Max von Baden, and Basil Henson as Field Marshal Helmuth von Moltke the Elder. In addition, there stars Frederick Jaeger as Baron von Holstein, Valerie Phililips as the younger Kaiserin Augusta Victoria/Dona, John Robbins depicting Navy Admiral Georg von Müller, Peter Schofield as Friedrich Ebert, John Stratton as Hesse, and Geoffrey Toone playing General Wilhelm Groener.

Fall of Eagles was released as a DVD in the US in 2006.

Edward the King, ATV, 1975

This 13-episodic dramatic series was released in 1975, and was based on the book *King Edward VII* by author Philip Magnus, starring Timothy West in the title role, with Christopher Meame playing his troublesome nephew and fellow monarch, Kaiser Wilhelm II. Felicity Kendal is Kaiserin Victoria, Willy's mother Vicky.

"He's off his head!" Bertie proclaims. *Was* he? Maybe.

The Riddle of the Sands, 1979–87

An English-language feature movie was released in 1979 starring Michael York and Simon MacCorkindale as the two adventuresome British yachters. A 1984 German version stars Burghart Klaussner and Peter Sattmann.

The 1987 German TV version stars Wigand Witting as Kaiser Wilhelm II, plotting a secret boat invasion of the UK, and is based on the 1903 spy thriller novel by Robert Erskine Childers, *The Riddle of the Sands: A Record of Secret Service* that is said to have launched that still current genre ever after.

Reportedly, Winston Churchill "Later credited the book as a major reason why the Admiralty had decided to establish" several new naval bases at Scapa Flow, Invergordon, and Rosyth in Scotland opposite Germany's North Sea coast to meet this "potential threat" from the sea.

Two similar books were *The Great War in England in 1897* (1894) and *The Invasion of 1910* (1906), both by William Le Queux. In the German version of the latter, the German Army enters the smoking ruins of London. Reportedly, Kaiser Bill read both. The former title has France and Russia combining against the UK, with the Second Reich coming to the rescue of the British Isles.

As we'll see, Scapa Flow was to figure prominently in the Kaiser's life in June 1919 as the future graveyard of his Imperial High Seas Fleet, where the ships sunk remain to this day, no less.

Great War Era Feature Films Starring the Kaiser, 1916–18

It is for England!, Leonard Shepherd as the Kaiser,1916

The Fall of the Romanovs, Georges Deneuberg, 1917

A Scrap of Paper, Gleri Cavender, 1918

Swat the Kaiser, Gustav von Seyffertitz

The Kaiser: The Beast of Berlin, Rupert Julian

My Four Years in Germany, Louis Dean

To Hell with the Kaiser! Lawrence Grant

The Geaser of Berlin, Ray Hanford

The Geezer of Berlin, Ray Hanford, US title

Me and God, Paul Weigel

The Prussian Cur, Walter Lawrence

Why America Will Win, Ernest Maupain

Kultur/Culture, William Burress

The Bond, and *Shoulder Arms*, Syd Chaplin

The Birth of a Race, Louis Dean

Kaiser's Finish, Louis Dean

Postwar Kaiser Filmography, 1919–2014

The Grand Victory: Wilson or Kaiser? The Fall of the Hohenzollerns, Henry Kolker, 1919

Yankee Doodle in Berlin/aka "The Kaiser's Last Sequel" USA, Ford Sterling, 1919

Three Faces East, Rupert Julian, 1926

Annie Get Your Gun, John Mylong, 1950

Die UnbeseigbarenThe Invincible, Hanns Groth, 1953

Die Deutschmeister/The German Master, Wolfgang Lukschy, 1955

The Adventures of Arsine Lupin, O.E. Hasse, 1957

Die Letztwn Tage der Menschheit/The Last Days of Mankind, TV, Hubert von Meyerinck, 1965

Solange leben in mir ist/As Long as Life is in Me, Harold Halgardt, 1965

The Scandal of Mr Leberecht von Kotze, TV, Gunter Wolf, 1966

Der Affaire/The Affair Eulenburg, Hans Caninberg, 1967

Those Fantastic Flying Fools aka Rocket to the Moon, Dan Cressy, 1967

Wenn Ludwig iris Manover ziehtWhen Ludwig Has a Maneuver, Dieter Borsche, 1967

Die Flucht nach Holland/The Flight to Holland, Hans Caninberg, 1967

Krupp and Krause,TV, Fred Delmaire, 1969

Oh! What a Lovely War! Kenneth More, 1969

Six Dates with Barker, Dennis Ramsden, 1971

Von Richthofen and Brown, Seamus Forde, 1971

The Fall of Prince von Arenburg, TV, Gunter Wolf, 1972

QES: Target London, TV, Frederick Jaeger, 1982

Das Luftschiff/The Airship, Reinhard Straube, 1983

Bruno H. Burger-Berliner Firmament, TV, Michael Gerber, 1983

Weltuntergang/The End of the World, TV, Wolfgang Hoper, 1984

Was zu beweisen war/What Did We Have to Prove?, TV, Martin Held, 1986

Magnat, Alfred Struwe, 1987

Emma, Queen of the South Seas, TV series, David Nettheim, 1988

Bismarck, TV series, Heikko Deutschmann, 1990

Archangel, Robert Kougheed, 1991; Stephen Snyder in stage version

The Great War and the Shaping of the 29ᵗʰ Century, TV series, Jurgen Prochnow, 1996

Houdini, TV, Jack Marston, 1998

Majestat brauchen Sonne/Majesty Needs Sun, Otto Sander, 2000

The Lost Prince, TV, David Barrass, 2003

Kronprinz/Crown Prince Rudolf, Robert Stadlober, 2006

Der Rote/The Red Baron, Ladislav Fredj, 2008

Die Deutschen/The German: Wilhelm and the World, TV, Udo Schenck, 2008

Juliana, Princess of Orange, TV, Rene van Asten, 2009

Krupp: A Family Between War and Peace, TV, Michael Schenk, 2009

Reichsgrunddung/Die nervose Grossmacht/Reich Establishment/The Nervous Great Power, TV,
    Florian Fischer, 2012

Europas letzter Sommer/Europe's Last Summer, TV, Hubertus Hartmann, 2012

Das/The Adlon: A Family Saga, TV, Michael Schenk, 2013

37 Days, TV series, Rainer Sellein, 2014

5

"Kaiser Bill" 1890–1914

The Kaiser and Annie Oakley, "The Little Sure Shot of the West"

Shortly after his accession, the new Kaiser was watching the American production *Buffalo Bill's Wild West Show*, one of whose star performers was female sharpshooter Annie Oakley/ Phoebe Ann Moses (1860–1926), who fired a .22 caliber rifle.

Reportedly, at His Majesty's personal request, Miss Oakley knocked the ashes off his cigarette. Some later ventured that—if Annie had shot Wilhelm and not his cigarette—she could have prevented the Great War.

Legend also has it that she sent the Kaiser requesting a second chance; he never responded. True or not, the anecdote makes undeniably great copy.

Wilhelm II's Wealth in Land and Castles

Kaiser Wilhelm enjoyed being around other wealthy people, especially the newly rich American "Captains of Industry" and financiers, like J. P. Morgan of New York, who was said to have more money personally than the entire United States Treasury.

In like fashion—according to van der Kiste—His Majesty was literally the richest resident of Berlin, and owned a reported 73 palaces and country estates, Reich-wide, as well.

He seemed to be indiscriminate in accepting the hospitality of rich men. At both Kiel and in Norway, Wilhelm was the guest of the "dollar kings," and had the ancient Teutonic Knights Castle of Marienburg redecorated to receive the 26-year-old son of Vanderbilt.

His Majesty's Humor

He enjoyed recalling the time when he used to visit Prince Bismarck's country estate: "I shall never forget the servants holding the wine bottles between their knees to draw the corks, or the Prince putting his plate on the floor to feed his dog. I, for one, could not get rid of the idea that it might be *I* who would eat from the same plate the next day!"

In telling such stories—according to one eyewitness—the Kaiser would laugh:

With absolute abandonment, opening his mouth to the fullest possible extent, shaking his whole body, and often stamping with one foot to show his excessive enjoyment of any joke.

His Majesty frowned far too often in his formal, oil painted portraits, and also in stern-looking studio photographic visages, but he was far from being devoid of a sense of humor, even if that was most often at the expense of others, rarely himself.

He was, indeed, notorious for practical jokes that his victims dreaded. He had met American humorist Mark Twain, but found him boring. According to the two volumes of name-dropping personal memoirs of socialite Daisy Princess of Pless in formerly Austrian Upper Silesia:

> In the evenings, we talked—or rather the Kaiser did … and then he half acts while he tells … stories. One evening, he went on from 11 till a quarter to one.

In 1908, "Emperor Bill"—as some English wags tagged him—wrote to Baron von Lyncker—the Chief of his Military Cabinet—"Not dry reports only, please, but now and then a funny story."

Even when in exile in Holland at Doorn, his humor never failed him. He told his official biographer, "One of the books by the Princess of Pless is called *Better Left Unsaid*. Too bad she didn't *do so!*" Too often, however, the Kaiser's humor backfired against him. He once irritated the Austrian heir to the throne Archduke Franz Ferdinand by telling him at the railway station, "Don't imagine that I've come to meet *your* train—I'm expecting the Crown Prince of Italy!"

Savoyard Italy was Austria's longtime foe, and yet the Kaiser also managed to insult its Crown Prince by referring to Victor Emmanuel as, "The Dwarf" due to his short stature. Moreover, Princess Daisy swore that he talked behind the backs of all his "friends,"—one to the other, never thinking or caring that they might compare notes. More ominously, he did the same thing with all his fellow monarchs, alienating them, too.

The Kaiser's Diplomacy

What almost everyone—from commoners to kings—was turned off by in the conduct of the Kaiser was that his affected excessiveness in all his varied moods and emotions came across as just plain phony, in a word, fake. He wasn't and isn't the only person guilty of that, however.

Most of his relatives and almost all of the crowned heads of Europe and their statesmen didn't like him, friends and foes alike. If King Edward VII was the best Royal diplomat, the Kaiser his nephew was the worst. That having been said, however, he did induce both Turkey and Bulgaria to join the Central Powers after the Great War commenced. For this, the Kaiser must be given credit, for—in modern political terms—it happened on his watch.

Bismarck—as first Prussian and then Imperial German Foreign Minister—constructed an elaborate system of military alliances. In 1882, he established the Triple Alliance of Germany, Austria, and Italy as signatories, followed two years later by the Alliance of the Three Kaisers/ the *Dreikaiserbund*, those of Russia, Austria, and Germany.

A three-year treaty, it was renewed in 1887, but *not* again in March 1890 after the Iron Chancellor's fall. The aim of his treaties was to keep Austria and Russia at arm's length, especially in the volatile Balkans, "The powder keg of Europe." Thereby, Imperial Germany would not be drawn into a conflict between the Great Powers there, which happened, in fact, during the Great War of 1914–18. There was also a top secret additional Russo-German Treaty that Kaiser Wilhelm failed to renew in June 1890 that as a result set Russia adrift diplomatically, while Austria—defeated by Prussia in 1866—remained Germany's only real ally in Europe under the pact of eight years earlier.

By 1894, the Russians were on their way to an understanding with the French—their foes of both 1797–1815, and again during the more recent Crimean War—mortal enemies of both Prussia and its created German Reich, of which they were the very core. Moreover, at Reval in 1908, the ancient Russian antagonism toward Imperialist England was also buried, and the Romanov Tsar Nicholas II in time became an ally of Edward VII's Great Britain.

The Unachieved Bjorko Treaty of Wilhelminian Alliance with Russia, 24 July 1905

Wilhelm II almost regained Russia as a treaty ally on his later Eastern Front by a signed pact with his first cousin, Romanov Tsar Nicholas II, a treaty that was immediately afterwards nullified by the Foreign Ministers of both Imperiums as being not consistent with Russia's alliance with Republican France.

Thus—despite having been personally signed by both Willy and Nicky—the famed phantom Bjorko Treaty died stillborn, never came into effect, and contributed at length to the overthrow of both their dynasties during the First World War.

Wilhelm II also blundered by allowing the centuries old rift between England and France to heal, which is all the more remarkable when one recalls the paternal grandfather Prince Wilhelm had ridden against Napoleon I at Waterloo, coming to the aid of Wellington, thus helping to end the 1st French Napoleonic Empire. France was eager to avenge the military and political Prussian humiliations of both 1813–15 and 1870–71, while the British felt themselves mortally menaced by the Kaiser's spanking new Imperial Battle Fleet, as well as annoyed by his clamor for German colonies abroad, particularly in Black Central Africa. Before he died in 1898, Bismarck accurately predicted, "The crash will come 20 years after my departure if things go on this."

The Unachieved Anglo-German Alliance

Twice—during 1897–98—the English had proposed a direct military alliance with Imperial Germany, but had been rebuffed by the Kaiser's government both times. The British even wanted a new, trans-Atlantic Ocean Triple Alliance of Great Britain, the German Reich, and the emerging power of the United States as partners, and so did he. Allegedly—partly because his rival Bismarck was for this idea—the Kaiser rather stupidly turned it down, much to his later regret during the Great War.

Bucking the British and French: The German Colonial Empire, 1883–1914

Bismarck was also initially against the colonial idea that Wilhelm II fully embraced in 1888. The Old Hothead felt that the colonial risk wasn't worth, "The bones of a Pomeranian grenadier," reportedly.

Aside from spiting Bismarck (who partially reversed his course on colonies in 1883), the Kaiser was unabashedly *pro*-colonies overseas, partially as a way to justify his building of the vaunted Imperial German High Seas Fleet. One aim supported the other, hand-in-glove: the fleet was needed to protect the colonies, while the latter thus needed the former.

Wilhelm also viewed the colonies as future naval coaling stations, prestige for his New Course policy of World Politics abroad, as markets for Germany's manufactured goods, as sources of raw materials that the Second Reich needed, and, finally, to stem the flow to the New World of the Americas of German emigration that had begun after 1848 and intensified before and after the American Civil War of 1861–65.

In the final analysis, the Kaiser's love-hate relationship with "Bertie" his English uncle and "Georgie" his English first cousin—British Kings both—was that England formed with France the *Entente Cordiale* at the Algeciras Conference over Morocco in 1906, followed by the Reval accord of 1908 between King and Tsar, both against Wilhelm. Thus was accomplished the iron ring around his Reich that had been Bismarck's constant nightmare, established long before the actual firing began in August 1914.

His Majesty Both Pro and Con the United States of America

By at least 1906, the German Navy had a tentative plan in place to invade North America from several points along its Eastern Seaboard, very much along the lines that Great Britain utilized during both the American Revolution and the War of 1812. In May 1910, the Kaiser amazed and set his Imperial Household Staff on edge when he asserted that he planned to go in person to the train station to personally greet a man who was an American commoner, former President of the United States Theodore Roosevelt, then out of office and touring Europe before King Edward's State Funeral in London, where he again met the Kaiser, representing the Second Reich as mourner.

Known as "Bully Teddy," Roosevelt was making a world tour on the order of his late former Republican President a generation earlier, Union General Ulysses S. Grant. The Kaiser's Foreign Office protocol advisors were shocked to their diplomatic marrow that His Majesty was greeting a private citizen without any current political post. Noted one, "It was unheard of for an Emperor to pay such a mark of respect in this way." "I can hardly believe it!" sniffed another. Surprisingly—after his own fashion—the Kaiser was not a stuffed shirt snob, and was also one of the few who also recognized formally the commoner wife of Austria's Franz Ferdinand for what she was: his consort.

Regarding Roosevelt's Berlin jaunt, then British Ambassador to Germany Sir Edward Goschen reported on 23 April 1910, "I'd heard that his entourage" (that of Wilhelm) "were so much against it that he'd given it up. If His Majesty *really* does this, it'll be going rather far. I still cannot believe it!"

As usual, though, in the end, Wilhelm did what he wanted, and met Roosevelt with a full State welcome at Berlin, later reviewing with him as well a review of 100,000 German Army troops at Doberitz, the former President doffing his hat and placing it over his heart in respect. He bacame Imperial Germany's enemy in 1914, however.

A Religious Monarch— The Racist Kaiser

By all accounts a devoutly religious Protestant Christian, His Majesty often took the pulpit himself to preach a sermon—in church, aboard ship, and, lastly, in the entrance hall of his house at Doorn, Holland, where the entire staff was daily invited to participate, and did. During his reign, Her Majesty the Kaiserin built 32 churches in Berlin alone.

Despite his religious beliefs, the Kaiser typified the latent and overt racism of his era, disliking Jews and Slavs, and disparaging Africans and Indians as "niggers," the term he used. In 1895, Wilhelm II told the then British military attaché in Berlin—Col. Leopold Swaine—that:

> England has … threatened her old friend, the German Emperor, with war—and this on account of a few square miles' territory, all niggers and palm trees!

Of the Jews, he asserted, "There are far too many of them in my country! They want stamping out. If I didn't restrain my people, there would be Jew-baiting." Nor did it help the Jews that they had been allies of his liberal parents, the Fredericks.

He liked Americans, however, but grew critical of their desire to buy everything in sight, such as one who wanted to purchase the Brandenburg Gate for the St Louis World's Fair!

He could not endure, though, the seeming mania of Americans to buy things from him, such as the Star of the Black Eagle, or the Kaiserin's ostritch feather fan. One rich woman from Baltimore offered any price to have a cuirass that had been worn by him.

The Scientific/Technocratic Emperor

As a believer in science and automotives, His Majesty the Kaiser and King established technical high schools in his Second Reich on the level of universities, and the later V1 and V2 rockets of the Third Reich of the Second World War were at least in part products of his foresight in this regard. The Kaiser Wilhelm Institute also researched the un-built Nazi atomic bomb. Like his younger brother Prince Heinrich, Wilhelm was an early fan of travel via the new internal combustion engine, and asserted that the twentieth century would be lived "Under the sign of the motor." Under his reign, the steel, iron, engine, electrical, railroad, aircraft, automotive, banking, arms, shipbuilding, and radio industries all prospered as never before. For that he must also be credited.

His Majesty's Reich/Imperial Chancellors, 1888–1918

He had eight, and wisely used each one as a separate chapter in his book of memoirs on his reign as Kaiser.

They were: Prince Otto von Bismarck (1815-1898), in office under Wilhelm II, 1888–90; General Georg Leon von Caprivi (1831–99), 1890–94; Prince Chlodwig zu Hohenlohe (1819–1901), 1894–1900; Bernhard von Bülow, created Prince by him (1849–1929), 1900–09; Theobald von Bethmann-Hollwegg (1865–1921), 1909–17; Dr Georg Michaelis (1857–1936), July-October 1917; Count Georg von Hertling (1843–1919), 1917–18; and Prince Maximilian von Baden (1867–1929), October-November 1918.

Of these eight—as we have seen—he had only one titanic battle for mastery, with Prince Bismarck. At Doorn in the 1930s, he told von Kürenburg, "I had three bitter enemies during my reign: old Bismarck, August Bebel, the Socialist; and Edward VII."

With the departure of Bismarck, what Röhl calls the Kaiser's "Personal Rule" began in earnest, and continued unabated until the First Abdication Crisis, of 1908. After the Emperor fired von Bülow the following year, it resumed in a more muted form than before, until it ended with the Second Abdication Crisis, of late 1918 that overthrew His Majesty, costing him both his crown and his throne for good.

During his reign, not only the civilian Reich Chancellor and his government ministers reported to him, but the Kaiser also had a trio of Cabinet chiefs: Military, Naval, and Civil, thus effectively placing the overall direction of matters outside the control of the country's elected Parliament, the Reichstag, where the Emperor found himself opposed by both left and far right parties.

The Pan-Germans

The Reichstag was the bastion of His Majesty's least popularity, and he never appeared in the building that was constructed during his reign and still exists in modern Germany.

He was duly opposed therein by both the far left and the far right, both of which helped overthrow him in 1918. The left opposed rampant German militarism and all wars of conquest, while the right had no use for his later fleet-building program and colonial aspirations abroad.

The Pan-Germans—formed in 1891 in direct response to his trade of Zanzibar for Heligoland—were the precursors of the Greater Germany of Hitler and his Nazis who wanted Austria and all the other German-speaking lands united into one great Germanic Empire. As such, it was finally disbanded under the Nazis in 1939.

Both Bismarck and the Kaisers were opposed to this view, however, wanting only a Little Germany that would be dominated by Prussia without any interference from their Austrian neighbors. One who did favor the Pan-Germans, however, was Crown Prince Wilhelm, in open defiance of his father the Kaiser, thus opening a gulf between himself and His Majesty that endured for the rest of their lives together.

The Political Cancer at the Core of the Second Reich, the German Social Democrats

Of all the parties in the Reichstag, however, Wilhelm II despised the newly-arrived Social Democrats—or Socis—the most: "I regard every Social Democrat as an enemy of the Empire and Fatherland!"

Once—when shown the house of a black king at a colonial exhibit—with the skulls of enemies stuck on poles outside it—Wilhelm blurted out, "If only I could see the Reichstag strung up like that!" The Kaiser went further, however. In 1889, His Majesty told new military recruits taking their oath of allegiance to him, "It'll come to this in Berlin—that the Social Democrats will proceed to plunder the citizens. I shall have loopholes cut in the Palace walls, and we'll see how much plundering will take place!"

When in 1918 the latter occurred at the Berlin Palace, it was looted, and many of his own uniforms and all his civilian clothes were stolen. Many German Army soldiers went over to the by then fully Red Independent Socis, the Spartacists, named for the leader of the anti-Roman slave revolt in Italy prior to Christ.

What the Socialists really wanted was the end of capitalist society, it being replaced with a workers' state that would also mean the end for the aristocratic-backed Hohenzollern dynastic monarchy.

Around 1900 the Kaiser came to see this clearly, but in 1890, he had not. Bismarck opposed his New Master's course of appeasement of the Socis then thus:

> I consider all hesitation in dealing with Social Democracy to be a mistake. Sooner or later, the Social Democrats will have to be shot dead!

. . . a goal achieved by Hitler and Hermann Göring in 1933 while the ex-Kaiser cooled his heels at Doorn House.

Without bloodshed—and despite all his other efforts—the fortunes of Social Democracy steadily increased in the main during the entirety of the Wilhelmine Age of 1888–1918. Indeed, during the first 25 years of his reign to 1913, Social Democracy went from 750,000 votes to 4½ million; from 9 to 35 percent of the electorate overall.

The Kaiser's Belief in the Divine Right of Kings and Relations with the Federal Princes

Wilhelm II was one of the very last of the Old Divine Right of Kings monarchs, firmly believing that his crown came to him from God himself. In 1915, the Kaiser was told that Italian King Victor Emmanuel III would be forced to ally Italy with the Allied *Entente* against the Central Powers of Germany and Austria-Hungary by his politicians, one of whom was then the young Italian Socialist and later Fascist Benito Mussolini.

The Emperor retorted that when it came to Judgment Day, the Savoyard King would not be able to evade his responsibilities. God would say:

> No, no, my little man, that won't work with me. Who made you a King—your Ministers, your Parliament? No! *I* placed you in that exalted position, and you are responsible to me alone. Go to Hell, or at least to Purgatory.

In reality, however—due to the legalities of the German Constitution of 1871—he very nearly was the Absolute Monarch he imagined. Asserted one Württemberg politician, "The Emperor is not my monarch. He is only the commanding officer of my Federation, My monarch is in Stuttgart." Accordingly, the Kaiser often ran into difficulty with his Federal Princes because he believed that he was their superior, and not only the first among equals.

The Reise/Traveling Kaiser

One way in which Wilhelm II's nervousness found release was in his constant, far-flung travels, with 199 such trips in 1894 alone. This nervousness of his was also reflected by the constant entries, processions, and receptions at municipal gates and guildhalls, all with full dress uniforms and maids-of-honor, the removing of veils from statues, the launching of vessels from slips, plus parades, reviews, cheering and banners galore, elaborate floral tributes, and the ever-present grand farewells at railway stations, both at home and abroad.

These all resulted as well in His Majesty's even now still infamous speeches: in 17 years, fully 577 such public addresses were given, for an Imperial speech every 11 days.

Eventually, his traveling schedule became a matter of a science, a routine course run annually: there was a spring voyage to the Mediterrannean Sea followed by the Kiel Week Regatta every June; in July, he yachted along the coast of Norway, cruising in the Baltic afterwards; then came August and Wilhelmshöhe Naval Base near Kassel; and in September, His Majesty was off to the Imperial Hunting Lodge at Rominten Heath on the Russian frontier; in November, he went to Max Egon II Prince zu Fürstenberg's Donaueschingen country estate to hunt stags at the latter two locations.

Again, a Most Talkative Emperor!

His Majesty was truly the first—and, therefore, the last—"speech Kaiser." Indeed, by 1900, there had been published four bulky volumes of speeches by Wilhelm II. Balfour describes the Kaiser's speeches as, "Oratorical derailments" to use a railway metaphor. There follows a typical sampling of some of Wilhelm II's better known "Kaiserisms:"

> The will of the King is the supreme law ... There is only one person who is master in this Empire, and I am not going to tolerate any other!... I am the sole master of German policy, and my country must follow me wherever I go.... What the public says is a matter of entire indifference to me.
>
> I make decisions according to my convictions, and expect my officials to reply to the mistaken ideas of my people in a suitable manner... I've never read the Constitution, and know nothing about it.

but, of course, he had read it, and knew all about it, especially as regards his powers—and the Reichstag's check upon them via the budgetary process.

What first brought him low—and precipitated the First Abdication Crisis of 1908—was the English newspaper *Daily Telegraph* interview of 28 October 1908, wherein he publicly discussed his policies of 1900, eight years earlier.

Reaction to its publication was swift and vocally violent: the Japanese felt threatened, Russia and France felt betrayed by the Kaiser's indiscretions (he'd opined that they wanted a coalition of powers against Great Britain over the Boer War then being waged), and the Germans themselves were angry at their Emperor's secret military advice to the hated British on how to defeat the popular Boers in South Africa. Most Germans in 1900 strongly sided with the Boers versus the Brits, and so, too, had their Kaiser at that time, at least publicly so. The *Daily Telegraph* affair meant that His Majesty had somewhat to curtail his public remarks, but he returned to them as soon as he felt that he could.

The faith of the German people in their ruler had been severely shaken, however, and in the long run, his inflated rhetoric helped to hasten the Red revolution that he so much feared. Conversely, however, at Düsseldorf on 7 May 1891, the Kaiser asserted that, "I wish that European peace lay in my hands alone. I should see to it that it was never disturbed," and yet, most of the world came to see in him the main disturber of the peace, whether accurate or no.

His Most Infamous Speech: The "Hun" Outburst, 1900

This was made in response to the Boxer Rebellion against all foreigners in China, and during the later Great War of 1914, was used against him by an astute Allied propaganda machine. It was given at the port city of Bremen as his German Expeditionary Force set off to help crush the Boxers:

> You must know, my men, that you're about to meet a crafty, well-armed, cruel foe! Meet him, and beat him! Give no quarter! Take no prisoners! Kill him when he falls into your hands!
>
> Even as—a thousand years ago— the Huns under their King Attila made such a name for themselves as still resounds in terror through legend and fable—so may the name of German resound through Chinese history a thousand years from now, and may you so conduct yourselves that no Chinaman will ever again so much as dare to look crooked at a German!

As commander of this force, His Majesty named the very man he had fired as his Chief of the Great German General Staff nine years before, Alfred Count von Waldersee, creating him Field Marshal especially for this occasion.

As he was to become overall commander as well of the joint, multi-Allied forces once in China, Waldersee was duly christened, "The World Marshal," but by the time he and his men arrived in-country, most of the real fighting was already over, the Boxers vanquished, and in retreat.

Returning home to the Reich, Field Marshal von Waldersee died on 5 March 1904, leaving behind a most interesting memoir that denounced his former protégé, Prince Wilhelm, later His Imperial Majesty Kaiser Wilhelm II.

Cartoonists as His Majesty's Bane

With his studied martial glare, waxed upturned moustache in the shape of the letter W, and his myriad of showy uniforms topped off by gaudy, shiny helmets, His Majesty the Kaiser was the darling of all political cartoonists everywhere of his time, most notably in the pages of the satirical British publication, *Punch.*

As noted by Coupe, the W effect was duly achieved by the wearing of a *Kaiserbinde* strap to restrain the moustache and "train" it during his sleep at night, and sold by the Imperial and Royal barber Haby, along with creams, under the name *Es ist erreicht/It has been accomplished.*

Like all other rulers both then and now, publicly Wilhelm II fumed and raged at these comic portrayals of him, but more quietly, some of the ones he admired found their way displayed on the walls of his yachting cabins, no less.

A Peaceful, Prosperous Reign of 26 Years Nonetheless!

Not everything the Kaiser did was wrong. In 1888, he personally and successfully negotiated an end to a miners' strike, and repealed Bismarck's prior anti-Soci laws in 1890.

Moreover, under this most saber rattling of monarchs, the general peace of Europe was unbroken for a full 26 years. Aside from building the German Navy—for which he has been roundly castigated by almost all historians—the German Emperor also constructed and increased a vibrant Teutonic merchant marine that plied the oceans of the globe with German wares, all highly prized.

By 1914, indeed, Germany was one of the most industrious and prosperous countries anywhere on Earth, with its renowned ruler a patron and sponsor of the arts and sciences, one who personally conducted archaeological excavations on the Greek Island of Corfu prewar, and himself funded a magnificent tomb of Saladin in Palestine as well.

The Kaiser as City Architect: The Siegesalle/Victory Avenue of Reich's Capital Berlin

On the Kaiser's 35th birthday on 27 January 1895, he commissioned to be built nearly a hundred white marble statues of previous Hohenzollern rulers over the entire course of the history of his dynasty. It was located 750 meters in length on a broad boulevard in Berlin's famous *Tiergarten* park, where he rode every morning when in his capital. It ran through the park itself from Kemper Plaza near Potsdamer Platz to Königsplatz, where stood the 1870–71 Berlin Victory Column, then in front of the new Reichstag Building, itself also commissioned and built during His Majesty's reign.

Along its length, the Kaiser's new Victory Avenue also ran through the Charlottenburger Chausee (today's 17 June Street) running east to west through the park and on to the famed Brandenburg Gate. It was first laid out under Kaiser Wilhelm I in 1873, but did not achieve its later real fame until under his grandson and successor.

The statues were sculpted by noted sculptor Reinhold Begas (1831–1911) with the aid of 27 of his students during 1896–1901. It was formally dedicated on 18 December 1901 with the first 32 primary statues in place.

Each were about four-five meters tall, including their pedestal bases, in double rows of 16 each, spaced at intervals along each side of the wide boulevard, behind which were pairs of busts of prominent advisors of their times of rule—such as Prince Bismarck—placed on a low, semicircular wall, making 96 sculptures in all.

Art critics ridiculed it, and sarcastic Berliners dubbed it the *Puppenallee/Avenue of the Dolls*, as well as Plaster Avenue and Avenue of the Puppets. Despite this, however, the Kaiser achieved his goal—the celebration of his noble forbears—and in time, even the Berliners came to enjoy their strolls there. In 1938 Hitler had it removed altogether because it interfered with his own plans with architect Albert Speer to make of Berlin the new World Capital *Germania,* with the Victory Avenue to be a part of their projected North-South Axis, itself never built due to the Second World War.

The Kaiser's former Victory Avenue was simply moved to a new location, however, to the Great Star intersection of roads in the park's center, re-titled as the New Victory Avenue, and thus it survived. The Victory Column was moved as well, to the center of the Great Star, where it remains now.

Some of the statues were damaged during the Allied bombing of the Second World War, and in 1947, the New Victory Avenue was located in the British Zone of Occupation of Berlin.

The British deconstructed it, and Berlin State Curator Hinnerk Schaper had the remaining 26 statues and 40 side busts buried for safekeeping. Exhumed in 1979 for redisplay, in 2006 the sculptures were moved to the Spandau Citadel, where they are currently being restored for yet another display as part of the permanent exhibition entitled, *Inaugurated: Berlin and Its Monuments.* Thus, the life and work of Kaiser Wilhelm II will be commemorated in this way, just as he intended it.

His Majesty's Homosexual Scandal, 1904–09

Prior to—and later in tandem with—the 1908 First Abdication Crisis, there was also the "outing" of several top figures of the Kaiser's regime as secret but practicing homosexuals that received great play in the German popular press of the period during the years 1904–09. After Bismarck's departure in March 1890, three men came to exert a powerful influence over Kaiser Wilhelm II: his bosom friend German Foreign Office diplomat Count Philip Eulenburg, Imperial Chancellor Prince Bernhard von Bülow, and Foreign Ministry First Privy Councilor Baron Friedrich von Holstein. It has been charged that all three were gay lovers— of others and possibly of each other as well—and that the Kaiser himself may have been the lover of Count Eulenburg also. Of the four, three were in favor of His Majesty's personal rule that came fully into play during 1897–1908. The fourth member of this quartet—Baron von Holstein—was opposed to personal rule, believing—along with both Bismarck and the Dowager Empress Victoria—that it would result in catastrophe for Imperial Germany.

It is believed that Baron von Holstein secretly fed information to German-Jewish journalist Maximilian Harden (1861–1927)—editor of *Die Zukunft/The Future*—that was published in a series of scandalous articles that resulted in the end in the fall of the Kaiser's three public servants. In order to shield himself from removal from his throne, the Kaiser duly accepted the resignations of all three. After a friendship lasting 20 years, His Majesty never saw Eulenburg again, and he died in 1921. Holstein had been fired in March 1906, blamed Eulenburg for his fall, and thus had contacted Harden. The Baron died in April 1909. Bülow was fired in July 1909, never returned as Reich Chancellor, and died in 1929.

Thus, the Kaiser both outlasted them all in office and outlived them all as well, having made good his needed exit from Eulenburg's famous Liebenberg Circle of fellow homosexuals. Not until the Nazi Röhm Purge of 1934 would another such gay scandal burst onto the German newspaper scene. It had, indeed, been a close call for *The Darling.* Harden had sought Wilhelm II's actual overthrow, but failed.

A German Plan for the Invasion of Holland and Belgium, 1897

As is known, the second did, in fact, occur in August 1914, thus bringing into the Great War England against the German Reich, since Britain could not afford to have a possible German invasion force present on the English Channel facing it.

According to Steinberg, the first option was also considered, but then abandoned, it being felt that having the Netherlands as a source of imports and a window to the outside world was preferable to having it as just another occupied German country.

Had it happened, however, and the war still been lost, the Kaiser might have had to consider as his place of exile either Sweden or Switzerland, both of which were contemplated in 1918 anyway.

Onset of the World War, 1914–1916

In July 1914, his ally Austria threatened Serbia, Russia's sphere of influence. The Russians began to mobilize their army, and the Germans likewise began the mobilization of their army in response. No one would back down, and at the same time, the modified Great German General Staff Schlieffen Plan of invasion went into effect in the West, frightening Republican France.

"Gaul"—as Wilhelm called her—was Russia's military ally, and England was France's ally. The German invasion of Belgium to better attack France brought into the war irrevocably the British. Germany's "ally" Savoyard Italy stalled, forsook the Triple Alliance of 1882, and joined the Allies against Austria in 1915 and then against Germany three months later, as did Rumania in 1916. Bulgaria and Turkey joined the Central Powers of Germany and Austria in 1914.

Bismarck—wags asserted—rolled in his grave, confounded. The Kaiser is important for the world of today because—not wanting it—he nevertheless stumbled blindly into the war. Modern historians believe that he neither planned it nor is totally responsible for it, although they feel that he bears a heavy burden of its guilt. So do all the other statesmen and monarchs of his time, though, making him their convenient scapegoat to escape their own collusion thereof. Many historians believe that his main guilt was in allowing his war machine and its generals and admirals to escape both his and other civilian governmental control, to precipitate 'the war on two fronts' that the Second (nor the Third!) Reich could not win to be implemented, merely because The Plan asserted that it must be so.

6

Navies, Merchant Marines, and Ocean Liners of Kings & Kaisers 1701–1914

Setting the Nautical Scenery in Place

British Foreign Office Secretary Sir Edward Grey once opined of the Kaiser that:

> He is like a battleship with steam up and screws going, but with no rudder, and will run into something one day and cause a catastrophe.

As apt an accurate description of His Majesty as, perhaps, has ever been penned.

By all accounts, Wilhelm had a fascination with the sea from his earliest years, noting in one of his memoirs that, "It sprang of no small extent from my English blood." In his childhood, Willy's most pleasant memories were of playing at Osborne on the Isle of Wight, the seaside resort of his grandmother, Queen Victoria.

At Portsmouth, Willy saw all classes of ships:

> There awoke in me the wish to build ships of my own like these some day, and when I was grown up, to possess as fine a Navy as the English.

When he did attempt to accomplish that tremendous undertaking during the main building years of 1897–1907 and beyond, the embryonic Imperial German High Seas Fleet became the prime bone of contention between Germany and Great Britain.

Not too surprisingly, the British logically reasoned thus: the Germans already have the strongest army in the world. Why do they want a fleet, if not to attack us with it? Once again, though—according to some authors—the Kaiser's real desire for a fleet like those of his British Royal cousins was his vanity—he wanted to show off, not to attack the British Lion.

Other less kind authors suggest that he did, indeed, plan to attack and destroy British naval power as a first step to conquering the British Empire for Germany. It would be finished by 1920, but was forestalled by the Great War of 1914–18. Did one lead inevitably to the other? At any event, from such childish antecedents did, in fact, the First World War spring, and, with it, the loss of 10 million lives. For this, the Kaiser shares the blame.

Prince von Bülow wrote in his postwar memoirs:

What William II most desired ... was to see himself at the head of a glorious German Fleet, starting out on a peaceful visit to England. The English sovereign—with his fleet—would meet the German Kaiser in Portsmouth. The two fleets would file past each other, the two monarchs—each wearing the naval uniform of the other's country—would then stand on the bridge of their flagships. Then—after they had embraced in the prescribed manner—a gala dinner with lovely speeches would be held in Cowes.

German Naval Hierarchy Organization, 1871–1918

Under Kaiser Wilhelm II during 1889-99, "the Admiralty" as a former single entity was divided into three distinct bodies with His Majesty overall: the Supreme Command, the Reich Marine Office, and the Naval Cabinet. During 1899-1918, this triad was yet again reorganized into ten separate commands, again, all directly under His Majesty: the RMA, Naval Cabinet, Naval Station Baltic (commanded by his brother, Prince Heinrich, during the war, 1914-18); Naval Station North Sea, the Training Inspectorate, Admiralty Staff, Cruiser Squadron, First Battle Squadron, and Independent Ship Commanders in Foreign Waters.

All ten departments had direct access to the Kaiser as their Supreme Warlord at all times. In 1903, the First Battle Squadron was renamed Fleet Command with the addition of the Second Battle Squadron.

Britain's Royal Navy the Ultimate Object of the German Navy's Reason for Being

What foreigner—especially an Englishman—could believe that the Kaiser meant no harm with his new Navy? He already had the most powerful army in Europe, and all that stood between him and it and England was the English Channel and the Royal Navy. "Would not a Navy combined with his already huge Army put the Kaiser within effective striking range of Great Britain?" was the reasoning of many, and indeed, compellingly logical.

"What other purpose could Wilhelm's fleet be for?" This naval rivalry helped start the First World War, as much as any other of the many factors that also did so.

Wilhelm II was obsessed by a single, overwhelming urge: winning fame for the House of Hohenzollern by overshadowing Bismarck's accomplishments with even greater ones of his own, an understandable goal. Since Bismarck had united the Second Reich, making it into the greatest power on the Continent, the Kaiser naturally wanted to make a giant step ahead on the path to greatness, by making it an international power, but with no real thought of war, and only wishing to be duly listened to across the global oceans. He thus threw down the Hohenzollern gauntlet into the global arena with the expansion of his colonial possessions and the construction of his Navy, and no more; again, maybe and maybe not. Britain's statesmen and admirals decided not.

When Worlds Collided: Two "Aryan" Navies Square Off

This "building a Navy" brought Wilhelm—and with him, Germany—into direct confrontation with Great Britain. On 20 August 1942, the Kaiser's successor as German Chief of State Chancellor Adolf Hitler stated, "The young fool writes to the 'Ruler of the Pacific'" (Tsar Nicholas II) "and signs himself, 'The Ruler of the Atlantic!'—The acts of an imbecile! Can you ever see *me* signing myself 'the Ruler of Europe?'"Actually, the Kaiser had used the word "Admiral" instead of "Ruler."

It was, moreover, a very unlikely confrontation in the first place. All of Wilhelm II's life had been lived in the shadow of the illustrious British-Prussian cooperative alliance against Napoleon at Waterloo in 1815, when even Lord Wellington admitted that Field Marshal Prince Blücher's timely arrival on the battlefield that evening was one of the major factors in the overall Allied victory.

Britain and Germany had never fought a war against each other. Indeed, Wilhelm's own mother was the daughter and first child of the august Queen Victoria of England, making the fabled *Faerie Queen* the Kaiser's own maternal grandmother, whom he dearly loved. A favorite story of his concerned one of the little known aspects of Victoria's life, and has a nautical flavor as well, occurring at a family luncheon at Osborne when Wilhelm was was 12, and here recounted by him:

> The British sailing frigate *Eurydice* had been sunk near Portsmouth, salvaged, and towed into harbor. The Queen had commanded Admiral Foley to luncheon at Osborne to receive his report of it.
>
> After she had exhausted this melancholy subject, my grandmother—in order to give the conversation a more cheerful turn—inquired after his sister, whom she knew well, whereon the admiral, who was hard of hearing and still nursing his train of thought about the *Eurydice,* replied in his stentorian voice: "Well, Ma'am, I am going to have her turned over and have a good look at her bottom and have it well-scraped!"
>
> The effect of this answer was stupendous. My grandmother put down her knife and fork, her face in her handkerchief, and heaved and shook with such laughter until the tears rolled down her face!

Nephew Willy versus Uncle Bertie

If the later young Kaiser got on well with his English grandmother, however, he did not enjoy such a good relationship with her son and therefore Wilhelm's uncle, Edward Prince of Wales, later King Edward VII. They were rivals almost from the time that they first met, and yet they briefly put aside their personal animosities at the old Queen's death in 1901, when the Kaiser and the new King with his younger brother the Duke of Connaught placed the Queen into her coffin.

It was, therefore, the poisonous relationship with the new King Edward VII after 1901 that determined much of the building of the Kaiser's Navy, of the combat record of his Imperial High Seas Fleet during the First World War, and its tragic aftermath in 1919. Beyond that, many of the Kaiser's young naval officers—such as the future Grand Admirals Erich Raeder and Karl Dönitz—would go on to serve the re-builder of the German Navy after 1933, Hitler.

Genesis of the Royal Prussian Navy

The original Germanic naval tradition dates back to the Viking era, and from there to the mercantile Hanseatic League port cities of the thirteenth century. Ironically, the African colonial empire of Wilhelm II also began under his seventeenth century ancestor, the Prussian Great Elector of Brandenburg Frederick Wilhelm, who—before his death in 1688—established both a small Prussian Navy and merchant marine, as well as founding a colony in West Africa.

All of this was funded by the Court, not private commercial interests, as was the case with most other European colonial powers. All three were soon sold, however, under Frederick the Great's father, King Frederick Wilhelm I. The more famous son, Frederick II, also neglected the sea in favor of building up the Royal armies instead, plus consolidating the territories he conquered from Austria.

Still, by 1806—well into the Napoleonic Wars—there were at least "300 Prussian barges and coastal vessels," according to Herwig. These were taken by the British when Prussia was compelled to fall under the sway of Napoleon's Continental System of anti-English blockade. Moreover, while subsequent Prussian victories against the French were won wholly on land, Britain dominated the world's oceans for the next 100 years after Nelson's stunning victory at Trafalgar in 1805.

The Royal Prussian Navy was reborn, however, when it was awarded six Swedish vessels and the Baltic Sea Isle of Rugen by the Allied Peace Congress of Vienna in 1815 after Waterloo. Thus—for the next 33 years—its only two officers (!) were both Swedes!

In 1841, Prussia joined the other maritime powers in abolishing the Atlantic Oceanic slaving traffic, but looked to Holland—once England's prime nautical rival—as the "German" sea power on the Continent.

The Nautical Aspect of the 1848 Revolution

The Revolution of 1848 brought with it cries for a German Navy to help unify the various Teutonic states, and these ships were taken over by Prussia in 1852. Under Prince Adalbert of Prussia (1811–1873), this force transitioned from the Royal Prussian Navy to the North German Federation Navy of 1867–1870.

In 1853, a separate Prussian Admiralty was established apart from the War Ministry, but the proposed title for the Prince of Fleet Admiral was vetoed by King Frederick Wilhelm IV because—as he stated succinctly—"We do not have a fleet!" Instead, the Prince became Admiral of the Prussian Coasts. The following year, Prussia received the future North Sea site of the naval base of Wilhelmshaven from German Oldenburg, and the opening of the decade of the 1860s saw the creation of the Ministry of Marine under the crusty Prussian General Albrecht von Roon, then also busily fine-tuning the Royal Army for the future three wars of Prince Bismarck. The first of these—with Denmark in 1864 over the Danish Provinces of

Schleswig-Holstein—was the Prussian Navy's inaugural operation in foreign waters since the time of the Great Elector.

The fighting, though, was done by the Army, but that August, the first Prussian armored vessel—the *Arminius/Hermann*—was launched in London, as the Kingdom had no yards of its own yet. The year 1865 saw Prussia acquire Kiel, her future Navy School site on the Baltic Sea coast. The steel-clad vessel *King Wilhelm* was launched in 1868 and remained her largest ship until 1891! The next year, Wilhelmshaven harbor became operational.

Both in the war with Austria in 1866 and against France during 1870–1871, the Prussian Navy took little part, although Hanoverian forts on the Elbe and Weser Rivers were seized in the former struggle by Royal monitors, while in the latter, two separate French fleets blockaded Wilhelmshaven, and took 40 German merchant ships before Napoleon III was defeated at Sedan and the great German Empire proclaimed.

Transition from Royal Prussian to Imperial German Navy

Now the Royal Prussian Navy became at last the Imperial German Navy, but from 1872–88 was again commanded by Army officers, with its principal mission being coastal defense of the new Reich forged by the Army's bayonets in conflict, and not by naval shot and shell. The first ten-year building plan, though, was announced in 1872 by Admiral Albrecht von Stosch, a former general, presaging the later ambitious programs of Kaiser Wilhelm II. Admiral Stosch resigned in 1883 because he couldn't get along with the man who was to prove the nascent Navy's greatest impediment—Prince Bismarck—but not before the Navy had a fleet of seven armored frigates and four corvettes. His successor—General Leo Graf von Caprivi—was another "coastal defense" man, in the course of whose administration was built a German torpedo boat fleet, with divisions at both Kiel and Wilhelmshaven.

In 1887 was laid the cornerstone of the Kaiser Wilhelm Canal that was to connect the North Sea to the Baltic Sea when it opened in 1895 under Wilhelm II.

During this final period of Bismarck's long rule in Germany, his main policy was to protect the Empire he had created in 1871 from a war on two fronts that might destroy it, and in his view, any overseas colonial empire might also endanger that in Europe. In this stance, he would be at odds both with his initial admirer—young Kaiser Wilhelm II—and the latter's allies, the German expansionists. The "Blood and Iron" Chancellor wanted the Reich, "To remain a sea power of the second rank," in order not to antagonize her former ally, Great Britain, that had also remained neutral in all three of his European wars while he had united Germany. In this position, moreover, he was supported by the Army, whose Field Marshal von Manteuffel asserted in 1883, "That I, too, belong to the uncultured supporters of the politics of King Frederick Wilhelm I, who sold his last warship in order to create one more Army battalion!"

Colonies Also Linked to a Future Grand Fleet

Admiral Prince Adalbert—presaging Wilhelm II—had long been the promoter also of a colonial empire abroad, to cut down on German emigration to the United States, and a strong naval arm to acquire them:

> For a growing people, there is no prosperity without expansion, no expansion without an overseas policy, and no overeas policy without a Navy!

In 1870, he nettled Prince Bismarck with the demand that Prussia seize defeated France's possessions at faraway Saigon, St Pierre, Miquelon, and Martinique, to which the Chancellor retorted sourly:

> But I do not want colonies! They're only suitable as supply bases. This colonial business for us would be similar to the silken pelts of Polish noble families who do not posses even shirts!

Eleven years later, he reiterated that, "As long as I am Chancellor, we will carry on no colonial policies," and yet a mere three years later was forced by German commercial interests to indeed set up protectorates in the Cameroons, Southwest Africa, East Africa, and the Pacific Marshall and Solomon Islands, as well as New Guinea—a virtual new German colonial empire overnight!

He was bitter about this, though, and in December 1888, told the German explorer Eugen Wolf, "Your map of Africa is very nice, indeed, but my map of Africa lies in Europe! Here lies Russia, and here lies France, and we are in the middle! That is my map of Africa!" but the Navy sent its vessels to the Dark Continent nonetheless since 1884.

Enter Fleet Kaiser Billy

The month of June 1888 marked the advent to power of the man who would radically alter Imperial Germany's naval posture almost from the very start of his reign. Kaiser Wilhelm II was the catalyst who looked with increasing favor upon the desires of both the German Colonial and Navy Leagues in direct opposition to His Imperial Chancellor Prince Bismarck.

Having spent much of his early life in maritime England, the former German Crown Prince was heavily influenced by what he had seen of the might and majesty of the British Fleet, then the greatest on earth. He attended the annual British naval reviews, as well as the Royal regattas at Cowes each year, and in 1894, read Alfred Thayer Mahan's landmark work, *The Influence of Sea Power Upon History.*

Upon firing Bismarck in March 1890, the Kaiser stated in a telegram that, "The position of Officer of the Watch of the Ship of State has come to me. Full steam ahead!" Indeed, a popular cartoon of the day entitled *Dropping the Pilot* showed Wilhelm II watching as Bismarck in sailor's kit went down the side of a ship.

As he told his Berlin Army garrison on New Year's Day 1900, the capstone of his reign was to be the twin creation of a Navy on an equal footing with his grandfather's vaunted Army, and also a strong German overseas colonial empire to rival those of Britain and France.

In a series of such bombastic speeches, the Emperor proclaimed, "The trident belongs in our fist!" and that he intended to make the Reich a *Weltmacht/World Power* by the end of the second decade of his reign. Both press and people began referring to him as "The Fleet Kaiser," a title in which he reveled.

Grand Admiral Wilhelm II and German Naval Uniforms & Accoutrements

An expression of Wilhelm's love of 'his' Navy was his fondness for titles and uniforms. In addition to all his other naval titles, His Majesty had also become an honorary Admiral of the Royal Greek Navy. Wilhelm II once received the British Ambassador in the uniform of a British Admiral of the Fleet, and had even attended Wagner's *The Flying Dutchman* in naval garb.

Once—when he came to a review of the Lifeguard Hussars in a naval uniform, a friend joked with him, "I suppose that Your Majesty comes from the Berlin Aquarium?" and yet Wilhelm II was—both in the Imperial Constitution and in the public mind—"The creator of our Fleet."

The Colonial Quest Embarked Upon in Earnest by His Majesty, 1888–1914

In the first decade of his reign until 1898, Wilhelm determined that—in order for Germany to have its "place in the sun" of world colonial empires—there would have to be a re-distribution of the globe's territories already colonized by other powers, and that this might mean war: "Old empires pass away, and new ones are in the process of being formed," he said coolly. What he needed, he asserted, was, "Fleet, fleet, fleet!" and—despite his well-known impatience generally—he was prepared to wait on this important question. "After 20 years—when it is ready—I will adopt a different tone."

Like Tsar Peter the Great—who created the Russian Navy—His Majesty took part actively in all matters relating to the technical design of coastal forts, ships, houses, and motors. The Kaiser in addition sent his own warship sketches to the Navy Office, often attempting to combine battleships and cruisers into "one fast capital ship," his nautical hobbyhorse.

Wilhelm II decorated German vessels with several smokestacks to foster an illusion of power. His official naval architects and designers, however, were forced to tell the Kaiser that his personally designed ships would sink.

German Army Opposition to the Naval Building Programs

In his article, 'The Schlieffen Plan Reconsidered', Terence Zuber reveals that the German Army lacked fully 24 phantom infantry divisions on the all-important Western Front in 1914 that it simply did not have, due to the fact that the Kaiser's Navy ate up budgeted funds that should have been spent on his ground forces instead. Indeed, when the war began in August 1914, the vaunted steamroller concept German Army was actually outnumbered by the Allies on fronts both east and west. Although his top Army leaders had always secretly opposed his designs for a grand Navy—men like Waldersee and both von Moltkes (Elder and Younger), and von Schlieffen himself—none did so openly for fear of being fired like Bismarck.

The Kaiser's Naval Cabinet

In 1889, the Kaiser had created the Naval Cabinet in his official role as German Supreme Warlord, and its chief transmitted all Imperial orders on naval affairs on domestic waters, as well as for promotions and appointments of all naval personnel, decorations for foreign naval visitors, home sea and shore duty assignments, His Majesty's naval correspondence, and many other matters as well. Admiral Gustav *Freiherr/Baron* von Sendan-Bibran was Chief of the Naval Cabinet during 1889–1906, and was succeeded by Admiral Georg Alexander von Müller until November 1918, when the regime fell.

The High Command of the Navy

Also in 1889, the Kaiser replaced the Imperial Admiralty with a new Chief of the High Command of the Navy in charge of strategy, tactics, and deployment of ships in both foreign and domestic waters. A State Secretary of the Navy Office handled daily administration under the civilian Chancellor, and—a decade later—the Kaiser substituted the Admiralty Staff of the High Command of the Navy in another reorganizational shuffle so beloved of all bureaucrats everywhere, then and now.

Imperial High Seas Fleet Organization

Between 1900 and 1907, there was created successively the First Squadron, the Active Battle Fleet, and the High Seas Fleet as the Wilhelminian Navy grew in size. His Majesty interested himself down to the minutest detail, even signing personally all promotions from the grade of lieutenant upwards.

The Nautical Emperor at Sea

"I command!" he told his naval subordinates, and as if to emphasize yet again the vital importance he placed on all matters nautical, it is estimated that the Kaiser spent fully a third of his reign of three decades—sometimes as much as 200 days each year!—aboard his beautiful white Imperial yacht, the *Hohenzollern*. Indeed, the Kaiser maintained a small fleet of ships for the use of both himself and the Imperial family, and his own lavish sea voyages to Norway during the summers and later to Corfu composed a small armada. In 1891, he bought the British *Thistle* (renamed *Meteor),* then a second *Meteor*—the former *Comet*—and even later a third *Meteor,* a former American schooner, were all state-funded. His old paddle steamer also named *Hohenzollern* was retired in 1893 as the *Kaiseradler/Imperial Eagle,* and replaced in April by the new one, with gold plating from bow to stern.

Imperial Yacht *Hohenzollern*, 1893–1914

The most famous Imperial yacht of 1893–1914 was at sea roughly 1,600 days—or four and a half years—with the Kaiser on board. The Kaiserin Dona had her own private yacht, the *Iduna*, as well. The racing vessel *Meteor* was State-funded with huge sums to beat the Krupp entry in the annual, renowned June Kiel Week Regattas sponsored by the Imperial Yacht Club at Kiel, as well as by the North German Yacht Club on the Elbe River. *Kieler-Wiche/Kiel Week* was a much celebrated international event attended by global kings, presidents, and millionaires.

Hohenzollern Junior Officer Erich Raeder's Eyewttness Account, 1960

In his 1960 autobiography, the late Grand Admiral Dr Erich Raeder tells of his early assignment aboard the *Hohenzollern* in 1910 as its navigation officer:

> As a ship, the *Hohenzollern* fell far short of what an Imperial yacht would be expected to be. In construction, she could almost be called a monstrosity. With abnormally high freeboard, she rolled in rough weather to a point uncomfortable even for old sailors. Her watertight integrity would not have met the safety requirements of even an ordinary passenger ship, much less an Imperial yacht!
>
> To my amazement, even the navigation equipment was exceedingly antiquated; at a time when the ships of the fleet all had gyrocompasses, the *Hohenzollern* had only magnetic compasses aboard, yet the captain, the navigating officer, and the watch officers were responsible for the very life of the Head of State, not to speak of the nation's prestige...
>
> Life on the *Hohenzollern* during the Scandinavian cruises, however, was much more pleasant than on the other trips when the Court was in the foreground. The Kaiser abandoned stiff ceremony and was very human, relaxing like any other tourist out for a rest. I always felt that on these cruises, he showed his real self—warmhearted, quick of comprehension, interested in everything, and eager to please others ... The food on the Imperial table was always plain, even when distinguished guests were present....

The Naval Ship Building Upgrade, 1888–1914

In 1888, five armored frigates were under construction, joined four years later by two corvettes. Within a month, he appointed his first naval officer, Vice Admiral Alexander *Graf/Count* von Monts, to head the German Admiralty. He died within six months, an evil omen for the opening of the Imperial reign, but not before securing passage from the Reichstag a bill to construct the first four *Brandenburg*-class battleships, done by 1894.

The following year, money was budgeted to build five more battleships, all named after

German emperors dating from the Middle Ages, but including the current title holder!

"The Sailor Prince," Heinrich von Hohenzollern (1862–1929)

Between 1898–1902, there was also completed the *Prince Heinrich,* named for the Kaiser's younger brother who—like Wilhelm II—became supremely interested in the emerging German maritime muscle. His career to a certain degree epitomizes the Fleet's rise and fall over the course of his older brother's reign. Born in 1862, Heinrich became an Admiral of the Fleet, and was sent by the Kaiser in this capacity in 1901 to China during the suppression of the Boxer Rebellion, as three years earlier, he had been dispatched with three ships, Marines, and naval artillerymen to the Shantung Peninsula to receive a lease for Germany of 99 years to build a Far Eastern naval base and coaling station.

As Inspector-General of the Imperial Navy in 1910, Grand Admiral Prince Heinrich, 48, became the first German naval officer to receive an air pilot's license. He was also forthright enough to tell his brother two years later that the Reich could no longer afford the cost of the expensive German *Dreadnought* program.

In May 1902, the Sailor Prince made a diplomatic visit to the United Kingdom at the head of eight new German battleships at the height of a renewed anti-British invasion scare fostered within Germany and directed at Great Britain.

Sailor Prince Henry in the Great War, 1914–18

During 1914–16, Prince Heinrich commanded nine cruisers and 11 torpedo boats in the Baltic Sea against five Russian battleships, 12 cruisers, 77 destroyers, and 20 submarines, and with this tied down a sizable Tsarist fleet.

In 1914 at the war's start, Imperial Naval Cabinet Chief Admiral von Müller opposed this posting, as he described in his postwar diary:
The Prince didn't possess the necessary qualifications. The Kaiser agreed, but replied that he was in rather a dilemma—he had made a promise to his brother—and that the Baltic theater of war wasn't essential.

The Prince could be given a competent staff. This duly happened … It cannot be denied that under the Prince, the leadership in the Baltic was satisfactory in the extreme.

In his entry for 5 August 1914, however, von Müller added:

Prince Heinrich … has laid a mine field in the Langeland Belt, in Danish territorial waters—a pointless measure since we have every reason to respect Danish neutrality. I am in favor of repudiating the Prince and sending a note of apology to the Danish government.

Later, the Admiral would criticize the Prince for remaining too long away from his headquarters at Kiel in favor of touring the various German battlefronts with the Kaiser. A staunch advocate of unrestricted U-boat warfare against neutral shipping during the war, Prince Heinrich ended the conflict by fleeing from Kiel on 5 November 1918 driving a Red flag-bedecked truck, later blaming the revolution on "British 'silver bullets,'" spent by English agents funding the German naval mutineers against the Kaiser. Grand Admiral Prince Heinrich died in 1929, 12 years before the Kaiser.

The Navy's First War Flag, 1867–1892

The Navy had received its first war flag from King Wilhelm I on 4 July 1867: white cloth with black crossbars; and black-white-red ensign with the Iron Cross of 1813 over all in its upper left-hand corner, with the Prussian black eagle intersecting the crossbars, a banner that Wilhelm II altered slightly in 1892.

Gun Salutes and Music

The last German Kaiser was a stickler on detail for gun salutes: 33 for him and his wife, 21 for Crown Prince Wilhelm, 19 for a Grand Admiral, 17 for an Admiral, and so on down the line. Initially, *Deutschland uber Alles/Germany Over All* was *not* adopted as the national anthem until 1922 under the Weimar Republic that resulted from the overthrow four years earlier of the Hohenzollern dynasty. In the Kaiser's time, His Majesty was piped aboard ship to the strains of *Heil Dir im Siegerkrantz/Hail to Thee in Victor's Wreath.* In 1901, the Emperor made the Navy's own official tune the *Hollandischer Ehrenmarsch/Dutch Honor March* that commemorated a Netherlands naval victory over the English Royal Navy in 1667.

Naming Imperial Naval Vessels

In the first year of his reign, Wilhelm II directed that:

> Large naval units be given the names of German Princes, states, or famous battles; that smaller craft receive masculine names from German mythology; and that light cruisers be christened for famous females, German Royal houses, or German mythology. After 1903, light cruisers carried the names of German cities.

Navy Yards and Schools

By 1898, there were important naval shipyards at Danzig, Kiel, and Wilhelmshaven, as well as private yards at Bremen, Kiel, Hamburg, Stettin, and Elbing, plus the Imperial Navy School at Mürwik, the Naval Academy at Kiel, and in addition, Engineer and Deck Officers Schools located at both Kiel and Wilhelmshaven.

Kaiser Wilhelm Canal and Heligoland

The 100 kilometer-long Kaiser Wilhelm Canal, "doubled" the transit effectiveness of the new Imperial Navy, that in 1890 also acquired a base in the North Sea in the form of the controversial Heligoland Island. It had been traded for the African territories of Witu, Uganda, and Zanzibar, a deal that was decried by the colonial proponents as swapping kingdoms for, "A bathtub in the North Sea!" Nevertheless, the Emperor crowed that it was a genuine foreign policy triumph that not even Bismarck had achieved.

The First Decade of His Majesty's Nautical Reign, 1888-1898

As the first decade of the Kaiser's reign drew to a close, Wilhelm II could point proudly to a squadron of eight battleships, eight armored coastal defense ships, 32 heavy and light cruisers, 110 torpedo boats, and 13 gunboats afloat. His mother the widowed Kaiserin Frederick tartly noted, "Wilhelm's one idea is to have a Navy that shall be larger and stronger than the British Navy."

He was on his Imperial way, and received a powerful, internal naval ally on 18 June 1897, when he appointed Rear Admiral Alfred von Tirpitz as State Secretary of the Navy Office. For the next 19 years, these two gifted naval men would work closely together to create the Imperial High Seas Fleet of His Majesty's fondest nautical dreams.

The Arrival of Admiral Alfred von Tirpitz (1849-1930)

Alfred von Tirpitz joined the Prussian Navy in 1865, and was a Bismarckian opponent as well as an early torpedo boat advocate, believing them superior in combat to the more expensive, ponderous, and slower—and, hence, more vulnerable—capital ships so beloved of all navies, both then and even now.

Born in Küstrin in 1849 as the son of a county court judge, Tirpitz was a full decade older than His Imperial Majesty, but was a shrewd courtier able to flatter Wilhelm II's vanity, as well as coax a succession of Navy Bills out of a reluctant Reichstag time and again. A naval bureaucrat rather than a seagoing commander in the tradition of Nelson or Halsey, Tirpitz' contribution to the Imperial German Navy was second only to that of the Kaiser himself. During his famed "New Course" speech of 6 December 1897, Admiral Tirpitz declared the young fleet to be both a foreign policy tool as well as a domestic economy "pump primer" for employment purposes, noting also that the Reich had territorial ambitions in both Africa and the Pacific Ocean.

Between 1898-1912, Tirpitz shepherded through the Reichstag budgetary process five separate Navy Bills designed to provide the fleet with 101 ships, an expensive proposition that led Winston Churchill to dub it, "The Luxury Fleet" in 1912.

By 1910, Germany was second only to her main rival—the United Kingdom— in terms of naval armaments, a feat largely achieved by Tirpitz' skillful leadership and internal political wizardry. As he stated in 1894, "The bear skin cannot be divided up before the bear is killed," meaning that he planned from the start for a decisive sea battle against England, with a mighty fleet of battleships concentrated in the North Sea that would await the Royal Navy's arrival for a cataclysmic showdown upon the outbreak of war.

A "Copenhagen" Feared

His naval reorganization of 1899—that continued until August 1918— rooted the Kaiser as the "Active head of the combined Naval Command," or as Tirpitz put it to Wilhelm II, "Your Majesty can now be your own Admiral!"—a policy that he would live to regret.

In Admiral Tirpitz' calculations, Imperial Germany would not be ready to go to war at sea with the Royal Navy until 1922. His major fear was that Great Britain would, indeed, recognize this fact, and thus launch a destructive, preemptive strike of the a-building German Navy. Horatio Nelson had done this to the Danish Fleet in 1801 at the Battle of Copenhagen. This was a dangerous period that Tirpitz reckoned would be past by 1914–15, when the Fleet would at least be strong enough to protect itself.

A "battlewagon" man in addition to his support for torpedo boats, Tirpitz denigrated both cruisers and submarines, and promulgated his famed "risk theory" to the Kaiser: "The ultimate strength of the Fleet would deter any eventual opponent from risking an all-out naval encounter with Germany because—even if he emerged victorious from battle—such an enemy might find himself at the mercy of a third strong naval power, or even coalition," such as France and Russia.

In addition, Tirpitz explained, "The Fleet would enhance Germany's value as an ally, especially in the eyes of relatively minor sea powers in search of a 'place in the sun.'"

The First English Alliance Offer Rejected, 1898

Thus, Tirpitz and Wilhelm rejected an offered English alliance in 1898 in the belief that they did not need it, while the admiral assiduously cultivated domestic allies politically. He launched a public relations blitz to popularize the concept of an ocean-ranging Navy with the German home front that was most successful.

If Wilhelm II was known as "The Fleet Kaiser," Tirpitz now began to enjoy being called "The Roon of the Navy," hearkening back to Wilhelm I's Army-expanding War Minister General Albrecht von Roon in 1861.

1922 the Magic Year for Tirpitz

Tirpitz planned for a fleet of 48 battleships to be online to face John Bull at sea by the magical year of 1922, and in February 1907, Wilhelm II proudly proclaimed the existence at last of his "life's work:" the Imperial German High Seas Fleet, by which it was known for the next 11 years.

And what was the cost of all this shipbuilding for the booming industrial German Reich? Regarding naval spending only, Tirpitz' grand plan rose from 233.4 million GM in Fiscal 1905–1906 to 478.963 million GM in 1914—a massive jump of 105 percent in but nine years; British Navy spending during that period increased only 28 percent. By 1913, it is estimated that Germany spent 90.1 percent of its income on defense, with 32.7 percent of the Imperial Army's outlay being that of the Kaiser's new naval toy. The Chief of the Imperial General Staff believed that war was inevitable due to the escalating arms race—with the German Fleet being a major factor in international tension.

1 German Kaiser Wilhelm II (1859–1941) in a formal portrait by Voight of Hamburg in 1900 in the twelfth year of his rein, with new German Army Field Marshal's baton. (*Library of Congress*)

2 Castle Hohenzollern in the Neckar River area of the Swabian Alps, a thousand feet above the surrounding countryside. Reportedly, the remains of King Frederick II the Great are buried there. During 1701–1918, there were nine Hohenzollern family rulers of first Prussia—and then the German Reich—"Kaiser Bill" being the last of the line. (*Wikipedia*)

Left: 3 Prince Wilhelm—or Willy—at age 10, as a newly commissioned Prussian Army lieutenant in 1869. (*Library of Congress*)

Below left: 4 Prince Wilhelm of Prussia, 18, having reached his age of majority, in 1877. (*Library of Congress*)

Below right: 5 Formerly Princess Elizabeth of Hesse—Ella, seen here in 1893—became Grand Duchess of Russia when she married Grand Duke Sergei, after having rejected the marriage proposal of Prince Wilhelm. She was also the sister of Tsarina Alexandra of Russia and Princess Irene of Prussia, wife of the Kaiser's younger brother, Prince Heinrich. After her husband's death, Ella became a nun, and was brutally murdered by the Bolsheviks during the Russian Revolution, her body thrown down a well. (*Publisher Archive*)

Above left: 6 "Young Germany, meet your Kaiser!" seen here standing with his wife the Kaiserin (seated at center), and six of their eventual seven children, six sons and a daughter. Princess Augusta Victoria of Schleswig-Holstein-Sonderburg-Augustenburg of Primkenau was reviled by the feminists of her era. As Dona—her nickname—however, Her Majesty won the love of most German women by extolling the three Ks: *Kinder, Küche, Kirche.* (*Publisher Archive*)

Above right: 7 Father and son—a pair of Wilhelms—seen here in 1888, when the elder was the German Crown Prince. Married at age 21 in 1881, his first son and Heir to the Throne was born the next year; engraving by A'orestier. (*Brown*)

8 The new, young Kaiser in 1888 as he liked to be seen: in cuirassier's helmet and white uniform on the annual German Army fall maneuvers, wearing also on his left arm a black band of mourning for his late father, Kaiser Frederick III, in an illustration by M. Pudhe, Berlin, 1898. (*Library of Congress*)

9 Wearing the Army uniforms of each other's country, the young Kaiser (left) and his much older Austrian counterpart—Kaiser Franz Josef (right)—render military salutes at Berlin. Old enough to be Wilhelm's grandfather, it is noteworthy that the Austrian emperor's uniform jacket fits better than the younger man's, which appears too tight. (*Library of Congress*)

10 Wearing the military uniforms of each other's country, the Kaiser (fourth from left) and Tsar Alexander III of Russia next to him at right review a German honor guard at Potsdam early in Wilhelm's reign in this previously unpublished scene. Like most of the monarchs of Europe, the Tsar despised the "Young Master," and said so. The Kaiser's younger brother—Admiral Prince Heinrich—follows behind, second from left, wearing sash. (*Doorn House Collections, Holland*)

11 During a visit to his former Reich Chancellor (left center), His Majesty the Kaiser (mounted at right) presents the retired Prince Bismarck with a gift sword. Note the coachmen's garb and top hats! Again, His Majesty wears cuirassier's helmet, uniform, and breastplate. (*Library of Congress*)

12 The Kaiser always opened the new sessions of the German nationally elected *Reichstag* with an Address from the Throne in the Berlin Palace's White Hall, as seen here in 1900. The assembly was a thorny political problem for His Majesty throughout the entirety of his long reign. Note the page at right. Engraving by H. Luders. (*Library of Congress*)

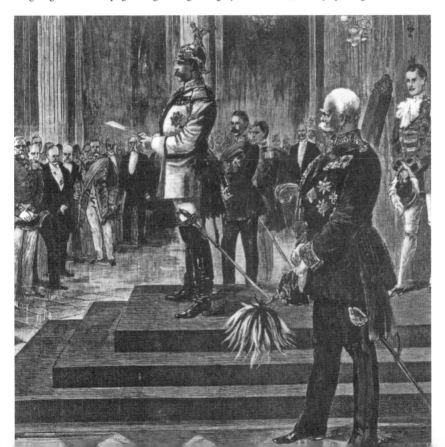

Above left: 13 A magnificent view of the Kaiser and his assembled martial entourage during the first part of his reign, a view that captures all the pomp and pageantry of these celebrated European monarchies of yesteryear, most of them being overthrown in the wake of the Great War of 1914–1918. (*Publisher Archive*)

Above right: 14 Wearing a hussar's cap and uniform, the Kaiser at center right awards the Gordon Bennett Prize motor trophy to the winner of one of the races in Imperial Germany. Note blue racing car behind them, and also the Kaiser's own family race driver, Prince Heinrich, seen here fourth from left in the crowd behind the vehicle, holding hat. US newspaper mogul James Gordon Bennett Jr.—owner and publisher of the *New York Herald*—later turned against the Kaiser. (*Library of Congress*)

15 Wearing a Royal Prussian blue Army uniform, the Kaiser receives the salute of officers of his new German Colonial Security Forces in 1897. During all of the Great War, they remained undefeated in the field in black Africa, returning home to Berlin to a rapturous welcome afterwards. (*Brown*)

Above: 16 A collage of German Colonial Security Force officers. From left to right are seen German East African paymaster, hospital attendant, surgeon, lieutenant, field grade officer in full dress, another lieutenant, corporal with native prisoner, native *Askari* infantrymen wearing red fezzes and brown uniforms, their officer, an artificer, and a senior sergeant in full dress uniform. (*Library of Congress*)

Below left: 17 A French cartoon of the German Emperor during his celebrated 1898 tour of the Middle East, during which he visited both Turkey and Palestine. This was, indeed, Wilhelm's own self-view: at the very epicenter of everything. (*Library of Congress*)

Below right: 18 Kaiser Wilhelm II in the mid-1890s, having taken his name as the second reigning Wilhelm in honor of his much revered grandfather. In Nazi times, Hitler derided such photos as this showing the German Kaiser holding a cigar. (*Library of Congress*)

Above: 19 The German Imperial Family on the terrace of *Castle Friedrichshof* at Kronberg, Germany in the Taunus Mountains on 24 May 1900, showing German Emperor Wilhelm II with his mother and siblings, from left to right: Crown Princess Sophie of Greece, Victoria of Schaumburg-Lippe, Kaiser Wilhelm II, his mother the Empress Victoria/Kaiserin Frederick (also Princess Royal of Great Britain), Charlotte, heiress to the throne of Sachsen-Meiningen; Admiral Prince Heinrich of Prussia, and Princess of Hesse-Kassel Margarethe. (*Photo by Jurgen Diener, dpa*)

Left: 20 The Kaiser in cross-legged repose in formal wear in middle age. On his left leg he wears the garter with the motto: *Honi soit qui mal y pense* (Middle French: 'shame on him who thinks evil of it'). The Most Noble Order of the Garter, founded in 1348, is the highest order of chivalry of the British Monarchy. It was awarded to him by his grandmother, Queen Victoria. (*Publisher's Archive*)

21 Their Imperial German and Royal Prussian Majesties Wilhelm II and Augusta Victoria at Windsor Castle during the mid-part of their reign. The Kaiser wears the famous black-and-silver uniform of the *Death's Head Hussars*, holding its busby cap in his right hand, with Her Majesty bearing a fan. (*Publisher Archive*)

22 Willy and Dona, his first wife: Their Majesties Wilhelm II and Augusta Victoria. The German Emperor is attired in the uniform of the Imperial German Forestry Service, complete with ceremonial dagger at the hip. (*Publisher Archive*)

23 A famed and iconic period picture postcard view entitled, *Our Kaiser with his six Sons,* from left to right, German Emperor Wilhelm II wielding Marshal's baton in clenched right fist, his left arm visibly shorter; Crown Prince Wilhelm, his son and Heir to the Throne; Princes Eitel Frederick, Adalbert (in dark blue naval uniform and bicorn hat worn fore and aft); August Wilhelm (later *Auwi* of the Nazi SA to Hitler); Oscar, and Joachim during a prewar ceremony at Reich Capital Berlin, for the Silver Jubilee of the Kaiser's reign of 25 years, June 1913. (*Library of Congress*)

24 Princess Victoria Louise of Prussia (1892–1980), His Majesty's only daughter and favorite child. She had her own regiment, outlived all the other members of her immediate family, and published one of the best and most interesting monarchist memoirs ever. (*Publisher Archive*)

25 Known as "The Hero of the Battle of Longwy" in the First World War, *Little Willy* commanded the German 5th Army—later Group—on the embattled Western Front throughout 1914–1918. German and Prussian Crown Prince during all of 1888–1918, he would have become Kaiser Wilhelm III at his father's death in 1941 had the Hohenzollern Dynasty survived, and died in 1951. (*Brown*)

26 An idyllic view of German Crown Princess Cecilie before the Great War with two of her children. Her postwar memoirs proclaimed her marriage to *Little Willy* was at first a story book romance, but he was a notorious adulterer, a reputation that doomed his ever becoming Kaiser in his own right after 1918, especially among even monarchist circles. (*Publisher Archive*)

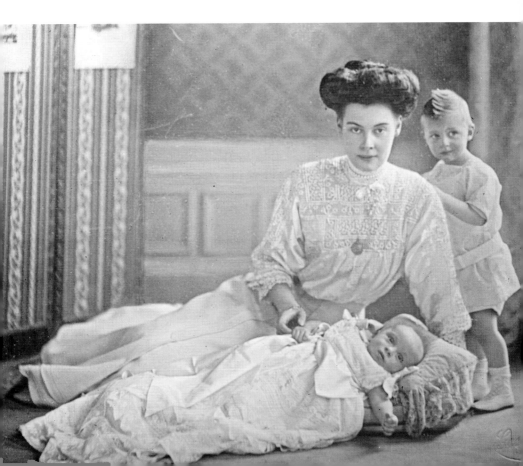

Above: 27 Again wearing Imperial Forestry Service kit and dagger, the German Kaiser poses with his grandson Prince Wilhelm of Prussia, son of the German Crown Prince of the same name. (*Beagles Postcards, Publisher Archive*)

Left: 28 A formal 1900 portrait by Voight of Hamburg of the Kaiser brandishing his new German Army Field Marshal's baton. Unlike both his father and grandfather, he had *not* won his during active combat operations in the field against the enemy, however. He was simply "awarded" it by the German Army to curry favor with him. In 1901—upon his own accession to a throne, that of Great Britain—King Edward VII made him a British Army Field Marshal as well, but the Kaiser resigned that post at the start of the First World War in 1914. (*Library of Congress*)

Above left: 29 A permanent scar was left under the Kaiser's right eye by a thrown piece of metal from a striking Bremen dockworker. The emperor took the bloody wound in stride, though, considering that he might have lost his sight in the near successful assassination attempt. If you look closely at many period photographs, you can spot them having been touched up. (*Library of Congress*)

Above right: 30 A wartime full portrait of the German Supreme Warlord Kaiser Wilhelm II in 1917, the year that the United States of America entered the war on the side of the Allies, in response to U-boat sinkings of American vessels on the high seas, and also to a secret German plan to induce Mexico to invade the western US, as a result of the Zimmermann Telegram being revealed by the British. Note the crossed marshal's batons on the two shoulder boards and the bogus equal length of both arms. (*Oil portrait by Philipp Panzer in the Michael Forman Collection, Library of Congress*)

31 Reality: His Majesty the Kaiser leads with his coveted and much prized Field Marshal's baton during an event in Berlin prewar. Note also the shorter left arm in contrast to his right, unlike the more formal oil painting portrait by artist Panzer. (*Library of Congress*)

32 The Kaiser Reviewing his Troops in a prewar view of His Majesty at center on horseback, flanked on each side by his officers. Note the martial band facing them at lower left of this frame, especially the *Jingling Johnny* chime bell tree musical instrument then common in most European armies. (*Publisher Archive*)

THE KAISER REVIEWING HIS TROOPS

33 "Cooking for the Kaiser," states this Allied period photo caption of the Great War. "His field chef is preparing luncheon near the front." Considering the prewar nature of the uniforms shown, this photo most likely was taken at one of the annual fall German military maneuvers so beloved of Wilhelm II. During the war itself, his front trips were made by rail and then car, with meals taken aboard the Imperial train mostly, or else in tents, pavilions, and open air. (*Library of Congress*)

34 A previously unpublished view of the Kaiser's famous ride through the streets of Tangier in 1905 on a strange mount, surrounded by "Spanish anarchists," as His Majesty later termed it. At left—steadying his horse—is Col. Gen. Hans von Plessen, commandant of Imperial Headquarters during most of his reign, 1892–1918. (*Doorn House Collections, Holland*)

35 A very well-known image of the be-caped German Emperor (left) with his guest at the fall 1909 German Army maneuvers, Winston Churchill. In his 1937 work *Great Contemporaries,* WSC penned one of the best word portraits of the-then former Kaiser ever published: detailed, fascinating, engaging, scathing, and fair. (*Library of Congress*)

36 Despite having made the Kaiser back down from his intended naval amphibious landing against Venezuela, His Majesty (left) truly admired American President Theodore Roosevelt. In May 1910—just prior to the State Funeral for King Edward VII that both attended at London—the Kaiser honored the-then out-of-office commoner former President (right) with a unique military review at Doberitz, Germany. For his part, TR thought that the Kaiser was mad. Note the Imperial standard at far right of this frame. (*Detail photograph, Theodore Roosevelt Collection, Harvard College Library*)

37 Opposites who did not attract! At left, King
Victor Emmanuel III of Savoyard Italy was nominally
Germany's ally under the terms of an 1882 treaty,
but the Kaiser (right) alienated him by calling the
diminutive monarch 'the Dwarf' behind his back. Italy
joined the Allies during the Great War, declaring war
on Austria-Hungary in 1915 and on Germany in 1916.
(*Library of Congress*)

38 "Foxy Ferdinand"—self-proclaimed Tsar of Bulgaria, ruled his newly formed monarchy until
late 1918, and was Imperial Germany's ally during the First World War. Here he is seen in 1914
in Germany wearing Bulgarian Army kit and cap (center), standing between the German honor
guard commander with drawn saber at left and the German Kaiser at right. Hand to face third
from left is the Tsar's son and successor—Crown Prince Boris—and his younger brother, Prince
Cyril (fifth from left.) Ferdinand abdicated in favor of Boris in 1918, and the latter reigned until a
mysterious death in 1943. Regent Cyril was executed by Communists after the Second World War.
In our own time, King Boris' son Simeon served a single term as the elected President of Bulgaria
after the fall of Communism. Note also the Kaiser's Court major domo, third from right. (*Library
of Congress*)

39 Russian Tsar Alexander III's son and successor was the last reigning Romanov Dynasty ruler, Nicholas II, seen fourth from right wearing Prussian Army blue uniform with spiked helmet. His host, the Kaiser wears Russian Army hussar's cap and uniform. The miter-helmeted men behind them are members of the elite German Army Kaiser Alexander Grenadier Guards in 1913, during the two cousins' last meeting, at Berlin, for the wedding of the Kaiser's only daughter, Princess Victoria Louise. (*Library of Congress*)

40 "The Kaiser with a former friend, King Albert of Belgium" read this 1919 picture caption of a visit that took place at Berlin early in 1914, the year in which Germany later invaded Belgium to better enter France. The Kaiser wears the dress uniform of the feared *Death's Head Hussars,* whose skull-and-crossbones emblem the Nazi SS later adopted as its own. Unlike the Belgian monarch of the 1940 German invasion, King Albert managed to lead a small army on its national territory fighting the Germans until the very end of the war in 1918. Note also the top hat Imperial outriders at rear of their State coach. (*Library of Congress*)

41 *Unser Kaiser*, a prewar picture postcard of His Majesty wearing the cap and uniform of an Admiral of the German Navy, of which he was the proud virtual creator of its vaunted High Seas Fleet that threatened the British Royal Navy during 1897–1918. It was slated to be finished in 1920, but by then the former Kaiser was an exile in Holland, and the fleet scuttled at Scapa Flow, where some of it still rests today. (*Publisher Archive*)

42 Grand Review of the Imperial German High Seas Fleet off its home base port of Kiel before the advent of the Great War. At center left is a later much-feared U-boat submarine, and at center right is the Kaiser's gleaming white yacht, *Hohenzollern*, with a backdrop of armored battleships and cruisers, with all hands on deck for the gala occasion. Painting by noted German maritime artist Willy Stower. (*Brown*)

43 Holding baton, the Kaiser—as the self-styled "Admiral of the Atlantic"—reviews a parade of the much-vaunted Imperial German High Seas Fleet before the Great War from the bridge of the battleship *Deutschland*. From left are also seen in this 1916 painting by noted German maritime artist Willy Stower, Grand Admiral of the Fleet Prince Heinrich and State Secretary of the Reich Navy Office Rear Admiral Alfred von Tirpitz. Together, this Neptunic triad built and commanded the world's second largest fleet by 1914, after that of Great Britain's Royal Navy. (*Brown*)

44 Commander-in-Chief of the Imperial German High Seas Fleet Grand Admiral Prince Heinrich was His Majesty's beloved younger brother. The two outlived a pair of younger brothers who both died early. The surviving brothers were devoted to each other throughout their lives. He died in 1929. (*Brown*)

45 A grinning Kaiser Wilhelm II (right) at prewar fall German Army maneuvers wearing a rain cape and the style of helmet that was adopted by the German Regular Police throughout Germany. The others are foreign military officers. (*Publisher Archive*)

46 During the very same event as previously, His Majesty the Kaiser shakes hands with maneuvers observer French Army General Paul Pau (1848–1932), seen here bowing as well, watched by another French officer at far right in this frame. The two Frenchmen would be foes of His Majesty during the Great War that followed. (*Publisher Archive*)

47 Imperial Germany's Supreme Warlord at ease in the service uniform of a German Army Field Marshal, complete with crossed batons atop his twin shoulder boards, and iconic spiked helmet in his lap, Potsdam. (Brown.)

3484-14 KAISER & HIS GENERALS

Aus großer Ze.

v. Mackensen v. Moltke Kronprinz Wilhelm v. François v. Falkenhayn v. Beseler v. Bethmann-Hollweg
v. Preussen Ludendorff v. Einem
v. Bülow Kronprinz Rupprecht Herzog Albrecht v. Kluck v. Emmich v. Haeseler v. Hindenburg v. Heeringen
v. Bayern v. Württemberg Kaiser Wilhelm II. v. Tirpit

48 A very well-known but still most informative wartime picture postcard of the Supreme Warlord with the Crown Prince, the Reich Chancellor, and all Kaiser Wilhelm II's major Army field marshals and generals—as well as Admiral von Tirpitz seated at far right—during the Great War of 1914–1918. (*Publisher Archive*)

49 His Majesty takes tea at one of his several wartime Imperial Headquarters, with from left an enlisted man pouring, the Kaiser, General Josiah von Heeringen (1850–1926), and Navy Grand Admiral Prince Heinrich of Prussia (1862–1929). (*Publisher Archive*)

50 A wartime chat between the Kaiser (left) and the Chief of Staff of the Austro-Hungarian Army, General Count Conrad von Hotzendorf (1852–1925), seen here wearing a black mourning armband, possibly for the late Kaiser Franz Josef, who died in 1916. Unlike Wilhelm II in 1914, the Austrians were keen to go to war with Serbia, but it took the German Army to conquer her two years later. (*Publisher Archive*)

51 Kaiser Karl succeeded the late Franz Josef as Imperial Germany's main ally upon the latter's death in 1916. He and his pro-French empress—the Kaiserin Zita—were both anti-war and pro-French almost from the very start of their brief reign, making a separate peace with the Allies that saw them forced from their thrones nonetheless. Photo by E. Forster, 1917. (*Publisher Archive*)

52 His Majesty the German Emperor traveled to the Turkish capital of Istanbul three times—1889, 1898, and 1918—thus welding Turkey into a valued member of the Central Powers. Here, in 1918, the Kaiser renders a hand salute to a Turkish imam in white (left center), while Turkish Army officers and civilian ministers watch. (*Library of Congress*)

53 *The Kaiser at Gallipoli: the Kaiser during a visit to one of the Dardanelles forts,* during his final 1918 visit to his ally the Turks. His Majesty—wearing Turkish Army helmet and uniform second from left, also carries his informal Field Marshal's stick baton in his right hand and rests his left on the hilt of a curved Turkish sword. Turkey was a far more useful and productive ally to the Second Reich than Austria-Hungary ever became. Cementing the German-Turkish alliance was almost entirely the Kaiser's own doing, for which history should credit him. (*German Picture and Film Office*)

54 The Kaiser visits part of his far-flung Eastern Front on 22 April 1915, meeting with his favorite First World War Field Marshal, August von Mackensen (second from right), and the latter's Army chief of staff, General Hans von Seeckt, smiling, with left hand holding sword hilt at center. It would be von Seeckt who would reorganize and modernize the defeated German Army after the Great War. Over top of the sentry's head at far right is a sign that reads, "Imperial German Mail Expedition of the High Command of the 11th Army," Bain News Service. If you look closely to the right of the Kaiser's belt buckle, you can see the Crown tipped informal Marshal's baton. (*Publisher Archive*)

Above: 55 A wartime Imperial Front Visit of His Majesty (far left in cape) that includes infantrymen passing by in review from the right. (*Publisher Archive*)

Below: 56 The old and the new face off, 1916, as the Kaiser wears the former *pickelhaube* with camouflage cover of the German Army since 1871, and the about to be decorated infantryman at right wears the more modern and practical helmet then adopted and worn until 1935, when it was succeeded by the version made famous during the Second World War. Note also His Majesty's sweater head warmer, and an Iron Cross medal box in his right hand at bottom left. (*Library of Congress*)

57 During the Great war, the Kaiser's Imperial Headquarters were at several locations in both western and eastern Europe, this view being in the east at *Castle Pless* at Pszcsyna, in what is today Poland, where he spent much of 1915–17. Its luxurious accommodations were a far cry, indeed, from the mud and blood of the trenches, just as were those of the Allied commanders—it should be noted—most of whom resided in swanky French châteaux.

58 Perhaps one of the most famous pictures from the Great War, its actual location is almost never identified: inside *Castle Pless* in modern Poland, today a museum open to tourists, and with its own website. From left to right, Army Field Marshal Paul von Hindenburg, His Majesty the Kaiser and King, and Army Quartermaster-General Erich Ludendorff. (*Library of Congress*)

59 *Caricature of the Kaiser as a man of evil, death, and destruction,* an example of Allied wartime propaganda that also accused the German Army of bayoneting Belgian babies. This is a most interesting graphic, so taking your time to examine every part of it is recommended. (*Publisher Archive*)

60 A magnificent Allied wartime propaganda poster by the French artist Devambez of Paris depicting the defeated Kaiser with broken sword bowed down (left) by the sheer weight of numbers of those countries fighting Germany by 1918 (right), including Japan and Savoyard Italy. (*Library of Congress*)

61 A grainy—but strangely compelling—postwar oil full portrait of the former Kaiser in his Dutch exile of 1918-1941. Reportedly, the adoption of his younger brother's Van Dyke beard as seen here had a very practical purpose: in case the Kaiser was forced to escape incognito Allied trial by fleeing elsewhere suddenly. Note also that he still has his wartime camouflage helmet, and is also wearing a holstered sidearm for protection no less. (*Publisher Archive*)

62 Doorn House, Holland, where the former Kaiser spent most of his Dutch exile during 1922-1941 until his death there. It was here that he received Nazi party spokesman Hermann Göring during 1931–1932, as an emissary from Hitler to discuss the possible restoration of His Majesty to his former thrones. The Kaiser had his personal office and study in the white Tower at the far left in this frame. (*Library of Congress*)

63 The Squire of Doorn in a new dress uniform for the occasion of his remarriage there, following the death of his first, Dona. He wears the Blue Max medal just below his high shirt collar, as well as the 1914–18 Iron Cross 1st and 2nd Classes, plus the larger Grand Cross of the Iron Cross at center, with his initial W in the middle surmounted by his Crown above. For the 1939-45 war, the W was replaced by a Nazi swastika until 1945, and later in turn replaced with an oak sprig. Note as well, the Kaiser's florid signature at bottom: *Wilhelm*. (LC.

64 Part of the exile's new family at Doorn, 1931, left to right, former Princess and Kaiserin Hermine of Reuss, His Majesty, her daughter Henriette—nicknamed *The General*—and one of several estate dogs. He also created his wife Princess Liegnitz. She was both pro and anti-Nazi by turns. Ironically, Wilhelm II appears dressed as the Edwardian Era country squire he always said he wanted to *be*. (*Publisher Archive*)

65 World famous as *The Woodcutter of Doorn*, Wilhelm II here wields his trusty hatchet. Once on neutral Dutch soil, the former Kaiser never rode horses again, nor hunted animals. (*Library of Congress*)

66 *The Kaiser on His Deathbed*, Doorn House, Holland, 4 June 1941. In funereal repose, Wilhelm's right hand rests over top his *left*. (*The Michael Forman Collection, Library of Congress*)

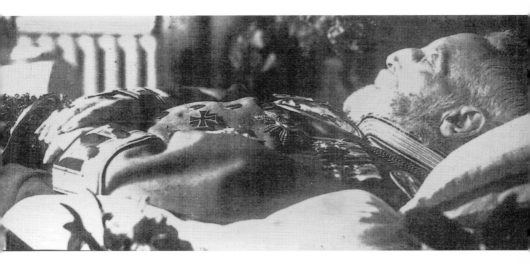

67 The Nazi Führer's giant wreath for the Kaiser's funeral at Doorn, then in German-occupied Holland, June 1941. Note the German soldiers at right for perspective. (*Doorn House Collections, Holland*)

The Emergence of the Kaiser as the World's Newest Naval Neptune: China, 1900

And now—at last—the German Emperor began to keep his promise of long ago that the world would hear differently from him once his Fleet was built. Three German gunboats had been built specifically for service off China, and in 1900—when the Kaiser sent Prince Heinrich there to punish the Boxers—he exhorted his brother to "Drive in with the mailed fist!" The German East Asia naval detachment at Tsingtau was quickly sent, and an heroic battle occurred at the Pei Ho River mouth when the supply artery to Tientsin was nearly sealed off by the Boxers.

The colonial navies—standing offshore— realized the impending danger, and organized a small force of gunboats to capture the four enemy forts guarding the sides of the narrow river.

Over the night of 16–17 June 1900, nine small vessels sailed over shallow water mud flats and attacked the Taku Forts, one being the gunboat SMS *Iltis* of the Kaiser's Navy, skippered by Korvette Captain Wilhelm Lans. She was 200 feet long, with a displacement of but 900 tons, unarmored and with a crew of 121 men. Having a top speed of 13 knots, the *Iltis* had small bore guns, with four-inch quick fire weapons both fore and aft. She and seven other Allied ships attacked the forts in the six-hour battle of 17 June 1900, when, at dawn, a shell blew up one of the forts' magazines. Troops landed and took them by bayonet attack. Two enemy destroyers were boarded early, thus ending all enemy naval resistance.

Gunboat *Iltis* suffered 20 enemy shell strikes, her boiler blew up, killing seven men and wounding ten, including the skipper. She remained afloat and engaged, though, fighting to the end, firing more than 4,000 shells against the fort.

Captain Wilhelm Lans was decorated with the coveted Blue Max medal by his grateful Kaiser. In 1903, His Majesty—in a unique award—presented the *Pour le Merite* as well to the ship itself for the brave conduct of the entire crew, but the latter could not itself receive the decoration, as by tradition it could only be awarded to officers. Instead, the ship received a large Order badge mounted on the bow.

In another unique award, the Kaiser bestowed the famed Blue Max on both the winning and losing navies of the Russo-Japanese War of 1904–05—just to cover all bases politically.

German Navy League/Fleet Association Formed 30 April 1898

This was a special interest group formed by von Tirpitz to promote the expansion of the Imperial Navy by persuading the Reichstag to pass his naval funding Fleet Acts of 1898 and 1900, and succeeded. Admiral Tirpitz had an internal deadline of 17 years for the eventual construction of a German fleet of two flagships, 36 battleships; 11 large, and 34 small, cruisers to challenge the British Royal Navy when completed. There ensued a mass enthusiasm for the German Navy as depicted in many magazines and adventure books and also collectible cards and childrens' sailor suits that included both the Kaiser's sons and grandsons. By 1898, the Navy League boasted more than 300,000 dues-paying members, and 770,000 affiliated via other groups.

During 1890–1913, Germany's population grew by 40%, and she also became the premier steel producer in all of Europe—much of it going to build His Majesty's floating "castles of steel," as noted by author Robert Massie. Both the Navy League and Pan-German League tried to curb the political influence of the growing Social Democratic Party, but failed. Was this all for nought? According to the admiral's own postwar memoirs, the Navy played no decisive part in the First World War until the Wilhelmshaven mutiny of 1918 that helped spark the overall German Revolution of 1918–19. At Scapa Flow on 21 June 1919, fully 70 ships of the fleet were scuttled by its own officers and men, an ignominious end, to say the least. Today, some of these sunken hulks are still visited by deepsea divers filming TV documentaries.

1898: Face Off with Admiral Dewey, USN

Tirpitz opposed the Boxer Rebellion relief expedition, but, nonetheless, desired naval coaling and re-supply stations in the Far East. Three years before, in 1897, the Kaiser had bombastically declared:

> I am determined—when the opportunity arises—to purchase or simply take the Philippine Islands from Imperial Spain—when her liquidation approaches.

This design, however, was frustrated the following year by American Admiral George Dewey's stunning victory at Manila Bay over the Spanish Fleet. There was even a brief confrontation between the normally calm Admiral Dewey and the commander of a German Naval squadron led by Vice Admiral Otto von Diederichs, who sent his flag lieutenant—Paul von Hintze—to meet with the American admiral.

Dewey exploded, "Why, I shall stop each vessel"—there was a blockade established—"whatever may be her colors! And if she doesn't stop, I shall fire at her! And that means war, do you know, sir? And I tell you—if Germany wants war, all right—we're ready!"

The Germans relented, and so hostilities between the Reich and the US were postponed for another 19 years thereby.

Seizing Kiaochow

On 10 November 1897, von Diederich on the Kaiser's orders seized China's Kiaochow region with a squadron including the cruisers *Kaiser, Cormoran, Prinzess Wilhelm, Irene,* and *Arcona,* plus a landing force of Imperial German Marines, whose 717 troops routed the garrison of 2,000 Chinese soldiers.

Prince Heinrich rushed there with reinforcements that included the ships *Gefion, Deutschland,* and *Kaiserin Augusta,* as well as another detachment of 1,155 Marines and 303 Naval artillerymen to add naval muscle, resulting in Imperial Germany on 6 March 1898 receiving a formal 99-year lease of the Chinese Shantung Peninsula.

Germany's 1899 Pacific Ocean Acquisitions

In 1899, the Reich received most of the Samoan Islands, and also bought from a defeated Spain the Caroline, Palau, and Mariana Islands, with the exception of Guam. These 2,000 square miles of new territory led the Kaiser to declare in 1900 that the formerly "German" Empire was now a "world" Imperial structure at last, and thus was another of His Majesty's ambitions realized.

Kiaochow became a Navy colony with a force ultimately of 1,850 men, a free port designed to upstage the British Hong Kong, and by 1913—as China's sixth most important port—the Reich had spent 200 million GM on its colony. Meanwhile, the German colonies in Central Africa, too, proved to be more of a financial drain on the Mother Country than an economic asset.

Showing the German Naval Ensign Globally

The Kaiser was determined that his new fleet would show the German flag everywhere, and the cruisers SMS *Bussard, Falke, Gazelle, Geier,* and *Vineta* were seen off Haiti, Venezuela, the West Indies, Mexico, Brazil, Chile, Peru, California, and British Columbia. During 1902–03, the *Vineta* bombarded Venezuelan Forts Puerto Cabello and Maracaibo, and in 1905, the light cruiser *Habicht* landed German Marines ashore at Swakopmund in black Africa to suppress the native Herero Revolt. During 1905–06, *Bussard, Seeadler,* and *Thetis* battled the native Maji-Maji Rebellion in German East Africa as well. When the small Island of Ponape saw native troubles in 1911, the German warships *Emden, Nürnberg,* and *Kondor* were duly dispatched. The cost of maintaining such naval flotillas in peacetime at Germany's overseas colonies in 1909 alone was 1.4 million GM.

German Navy Gunboat Diplomacy, 1911–12

Indeed, both the Kaiser and Admiral Tirpitz seemed to glory in German gunboat diplomacy on 1 July 1911 when *Panther* appeared off Agadir during the Moroccan crisis, and later was joined by the cruiser *Berlin*. This naval brinksmanship by the German Foreign Office backed by the Kaiser pushed the French and British closer in an alliance that three years later led to the First World War. In 1912, the Germans created their own Mediterranean Squadron with the new battle cruiser *Goeben* and the light cruiser *Breslau*, as well as sold older German warships to a future German ally, Ottoman Turkey.

Despite the pre–1914 crash naval building program and the German drive worldwide for overseas colonies, it was galling to the German Emperor that—between 1871–1901—German emigration abroad was not to the new territories, but to the United States. Tirpitz, too, was mortified in that he never really achieved his dream of securing a workable chain of German naval bases, and yet the German home ports—Bremen, Danzig, Kiel, Hamburg, and Wilhelmshaven—were all online and in full operation, where a generation before there had been virtually none.

U-Boat Submarines, Zeppelin Airships, and Seaplanes

In 1906, both the first *Unterseeboot*—or U-Boat—submarine as well as the initial Zeppelin dirigible airships for the infant German naval air arm had been constructed. Admiral Tirpitz had been opposed to both new developments in favor of spending more money on battleships. The forward thinking Kaiser, however, encouraged this type of futuristic research, and in 1911, Tirpitz finally authorized the formation of an experimental air station at Putzig outside Danzig on the Baltic Sea coast.

In Britain simultaneously, Tirpitz' opposite number—Admiral John Jellicoe—was fully aware of the reconnaissance danger to his own fleet that the Imperial Navy's Zeppelins represented.

Initially, Tirpitz opposed seaplane development as well for the Imperial Fleet—while the British embraced this new concept fervently—but later proposed a long-range plan for the Reich to have six naval air stations by 1918, each with eight aircraft.

Considering his later extensive urging of usage of the U-boat arm, Tirpitz dragged his feet also with its buildup at first, again favoring the battleship fleet for government funding, so that Germany came late to the submarine scene. On the outbreak of the war in August 1914, she actually had fewer units than her rivals at sea. The Reich had 28 operational vessels, while France possessed 77, Britain had 55, and even the US had 38. In Germany, the diesel engine for U-boats was introduced in 1910—six years after France made the switch—and the reason was simple: petrol engines many times gave away the boat's position via the emission of heavy, white smoke. The transition to diesel engines made the submarine a decisive strategic naval combat unit to decimate the Royal Navy battleship muscle.

Complex Tirpitz Described

The man who dominated this force under Wilhelm II's aegis was a complex personality like his Imperial master. In 1900, Rear Admiral Alfred von Tirpitz seemed to be the very epitome of the irascible seadog, with his famous twin-pronged beard, colorful admiral's Navy blue uniform with gold epaulettes and arm stripes, saber on his left hip that all made it easy to envision this salty sailor on the wind-swept deck of a swaying warship at sea, yelling orders above the din of a fierce North Sea storm. Having won his spurs as a torpedo boat skipper in the 1880s in the Bismarckian Navy, Tirpitz then served during 1892-96 as Chief of Staff of the Naval High Command at Berlin, and had seen his last active sea service the next year when Chief of the Cruiser Squadron for East Asia. Thus, Tirpitz never skippered a modern battleship, far less a capital ship squadron or fleet. His 19 years as State Secretary of the Reich Navy Office occurred behind his massive wooden desk on Berlin's Leipziger Plaza, or from his summerhouse at St Blasien.

Imperial stag hunts at the Kaiser's Rominten Heath lodge and fox hunts at Max Egon II Prince zu Fürstenberg's Donaueschingen estate over time replaced both the North Sea and the Atlantic Ocean as his action locales.

His Majesty's Grand Admirals, 1888–1930

These included the Kaiser himself as Supreme Warlord; Hans von Koester (1844–1928), who was presented his ceremonial baton of office on 5 June 1905; Prince Heinrich (1862–1929), 4 September 1909; von Tirpitz (1849–1930), also ennobled by His Majesty on 27 January 1911; and Henning von Holtzendorf (1853–1919), 31 July 1916.

His Majesty's Naval Son Prince Adalbert of Prussia (1884–1948)

Named for the original naval Admiral Prince Adalbert of Prussia, the Kaiser's son was the only one of his six sons to join the Imperial Navy as an Ensign, being promoted lieutenant junior grade through 1908. In 1914, he served as a staff lieutenant aboard SMS *Luitpold,* and two years later was promoted Korvette Captain of SMS *Danzig.* In 1918, Prince Adalbert served as Frigate Captain in command of a Torpedo Boat Flotilla off Flanders, and also had a commission in the German Army. Born at Potsdam on 14 July 1884, the Prince died at Vaud, Switzerland on 22 September 1948, aged 64.

Officers and Seamen, Uniforms and Accoutrements

And what of the officers and men of the Imperial High Seas Fleet created by this Germanic Neptune and his vainglorious "Admiral of the Atlantic," Wilhelm II von Hohenzollern?

When Tirpitz took over in 1897, there were about 26,000 officers and ratings of all ranks, and by 1914, there were 80,000. The Tirpitz Navy derived its initial officer corps from those of the already-existent Imperial Army, with the Naval Infantry—or Marines—dating back to 1886. By 1901, there were even Naval cavalry, and also a machine gun company. In 1895, the Naval Infantry were removed from aboard ship duty to serve as Colonial Troops. In the rarified atmosphere of the Wilhelminian Navy, ships' captains were on a lonely, Olympian height on the larger warships. They lived in private cabin suites at the ships' sterns, and dined alone. The Kaiser's birthday each 27 January was a rare occasion for a captain to mess with other executive officers.

In 1890 and 1892, the Kaiser himself specified officer corps uniform insignia, with an Imperial Crown and Wilhelm's monogram on its epaulettes, and by 1899, the latter had been altered with both anchor and eagle, with the Crown added close to the collar button. Reflecting the Kaiser's own lifelong fetish for uniforms, there were 36 Navy shirts, while in 1873 side arms had been replaced by swords, that—in turn—gave way to daggers in 1901, in time for the visit of the Emperor's cousin, Tsar Nicholas II, to the High Seas Fleet. The stratified Imperial Officer Corps admitted no Jews nor the hated Social Democrats who would help overthrow the regime in 1918, but did welcome young men of independent means, particularly nobles. Raeder, Dönitz, and the later Pastor Martin Niemöller, however, were all commoners who served in high posts in the Imperial Navy, two as Grand Admirals under the Nazis, one of whom became President of the Reich in 1945.

Daily Life in the Imperial Navy

A ship was seen as a barracks of iron at sea, with rigid discipline, and even flogging when Dönitz entered the Navy in 1910. Officers took a personal loyalty oath to the Kaiser, and were then elected to the corps by their peer members on each ship, achieved by secret ballot without any appeal—in case a final blackballing might be desired for exclusivity's sake. Drinking, gambling, and dueling among officers were all frowned upon—but went on nonetheless, and the rigid class structure was maintained all through the Great War with a major schism between executive and engineer officers. No non-commissioned officers received direct or battle promotions to the officer corps, either, as in other navies.

Enlisted sailors were trained by the naval petty officers. Sail gave way to steam, wood was replaced by steel for ship construction, and gun turrets replaced mobile cannon on side decks. This created a demand for highly technical specialists with requirements of their own elite within the elite.

Duty took place during both day and night shifts. In port, it began at 5 a.m. with washing, laundry, and ship cleaning; breakfast was eaten at 6:45 a.m., then more duty and instruction continued until 11:30 a.m., when "clear deck" was piped. Noon lunch was served, then general rest to 2 p.m.

Afternoon duty and training training took place during 2–6 p.m., next came supper. At 8 p.m., everyone except those on watch received hammocks. Shore leave was granted during 7–11 p.m., and on Sundays, free time was during noon–5 p.m. No scheduled recreation occurred aboard ship. Food was hard bread, canned potatoes, and dried salt meat. This, then, was the Imperial German High Seas Fleet on the eve of the outbreak of the First World War in August 1914. Even at that point, it was crystal clear for both a frustrated Kaiser Wilhelm II and an agitated Admiral von Tirpitz that the latter's detailed, extensive 1897 master plan for the Navy had not met its goals in the main, despite the great progress that had, indeed, been made.

The Navy as German Domestic Political Weapon as well as Foreign Policy Tool

State Secretary Tirpitz insisted that a mammoth fleet would unite all German political parties against the Social Democrats, rally German workers behind the Empire via steady work and higher wages, solidify the Federal states by having one great German armed force, enhance the image of the Crown both domestically and abroad, and, finally, curb the power of the Reichstag over the Kaiser's policies. He asserted that this would make the Reich far more attractive as an ally among the minor European naval powers, plus extract colonial concessions from London via threatening Britain's European security by a massive German battle fleet concentrated in the North Sea.

Too, the very best material, personnel, and tactics would provide the High Seas Fleet a "genuine chance" of beating the British Royal Navy with only a 2.3 numerical ratio. None of this occurred, however. Indeed, by 1912 Social Democracy became the Reich's dominant political party, the Fleet was not a unifying force—the imagined "darling of the nation" as formerly boasted of by Tirpitz—and the Crown's glitter was deeply tarnished via the Boer War, the successive Moroccan crises in which Germany came up short diplomatically, and the Anglo-French-Russian Entente versus the Fatherland was an accomplished fact. Moreover, the Reichstag controlled the Navy's budget more than ever, and no single European naval power had sought an alliance with Germany. Great Britain surrendered no colonies; and, after Algeciras in 1906, Wilhelminian Germany had been completely isolated in Europe, with but the sole and fateful exception of her one ally, Austria-Hungary.

The Army Pushes back against the Kaiser's Navy

At home, the Imperial Army, too, was making its road back to re-achieve its former fiscal ascendancy over the Navy within the parliamentary budget process that was achieved in 1912. There was also bitterness against the admirals in Navy blue from within the Great General Staff of the Army, as noted in 1898 by General Count Alfred von Waldersee:

> The Navy more and more cultivates the notion that future wars will be decided at sea, but what will the Navy do if the Army should be defeated, be it in the East or the West? Those good gentlemen do not like to think that far ahead!

It was to be a telling prophecy for 1918.

And meanwhile, what had been the response of Great Britain and its own Royal Navy to the most unprecedented naval buildup in modern history? How would the Imperial German High Seas Fleet actually fight in time of war? How did it react, in fact, in 1914 to a global conflict that—for the sailors—seemed to be a war too soon?

How did Admiral von Tirpitz' theories play out in daily practice, and how did His Imperial Majesty Kaiser Wilhelm II by Grace of God Emperor of Germany, King of Prussia, and German Supreme Warlord, conduct Reich naval operations during the First World War? And—in perhaps the greatest irony of all—what role did the Kaiser's vaunted "barracks of iron at sea" really play in the demise of one of Europe's great ruling Houses, the loss of the war, and the fall of the German Reich in 1918? We shall learn the answers to all these and other questions as well as the Great War unfolds.

The Imperial German Merchant Marine

The German Merchant Marine fleet—second largest on the sealanes of the globe before 1914—had an unintended but decisive role in the Second Reich's defeat in the Great War. This happened when its vessels in the US—interned when America joined the war against Imperial Germany in April 1917—sailed under the US Navy transporting the million-man American Expeditionary Force over the Atlantic Ocean to France, a feat that neither the Kaiser nor his admirals and generals ever thought they would live to witness. It is worth noting here that not one single Allied troopship was sunk by U-boats during all of both World Wars *en route* to Western Europe, a remarkable achievement on the part of all the

Allied navies, and a stupendous loss for those of the Central Powers and, later, the Axis Pact.

By 1914, the HAPAG/Hamburg-Amerika Line shipping of owner/manager Albert Ballin (1857–1918) and that of his great rival—Heinrich Wiegand's North German Lloyd—plied the world's oceans, and today remain known as among the greatest seagoing ships in all maritime history. His Majesty's stellar Merchant Marine was on par with the *Imperial Navy's* quality in every way. In June 1914, the Germans boasted 5,135,000 tons of merchant shipping afloat, second only to Great Britain. When the war ended in 1918, however, the Reich's shrunken tonnage was but 419,000, and all but one ship—the *Victoria Luise,* named for the Kaiser's only daughter—seized as war reparations by the victorious Allies.

During the Great War, five large Merchant Marine vessels and many smaller ones became armed raiders attacking Allied ships, while some passenger liners were converted to armed auxiliary cruisers also. Submarines, though, were always preferred to surface raiders by the German Navy, simply because they were more effective in sinking Allied ships.

Ballin opposed the Great War from the start, and would have made an excellent Foreign Office State Secretary to conclude a just peace. AEG electrical magnate Walther Rathenau could have done the same—and both might have made superb Imperial Chancellors—but as they were Jewish and commoners, neither was ever appointed to those posts. During the Kaiser's reign, he named only Christian noblemen and/or military or naval officers as Imperial Chancellors and/or Foreign Secretaries.

"Seizing the Trident:" The Kaiser's Ocean Superliner Fleet, 1889–1914

In addition to building his grandiose navy to challenge that of Great Britain, the Kaiser in 1889, according to Burgess, decided to "Seize the Trident" from the UK in the arena of ocean-going passenger liners. Just as Tirpitz was His Majesty's naval architect, so, too, was Ballin that of first his merchant fleet, and then also of his passenger liners. The liner *Wilhelm the Great* won the world speed record for liners in 1898, and after 1900, the Germans maintained this edge both into the Great War and afterward. Germany built a liner assembly line for vessels with typically both larger and more luxurious interiors than any others afloat to 1914.

In 1902, the Kaiser himself brokered a financial deal wherein both HAPAG and NDL were bought by American tycoon J. P. Morgan, who thus placed Germany's entire peacetime civilian fleet under foreign ownership—his. The liner *Imperator* was larger than the famed but doomed *Titanic,* and was launched by Wilhelm II on 23 May 1912, five weeks after the latter sank. Burgess notes that the Kaiser was almost hit by a falling plank, and also that the entire reviewing stand was almost struck by the ship's hull when its anchor chain broke and sank to the bottom!

The Kaiser met Ballin in 1891 at the ceremonies for the *Kaiserin Augusta,* and their productive partnership lasted until the onset of the Great War in 1914. Ballin saw himself as leading a liner race with Britain as a peaceful endeavor, as opposed to Tirpitz's bent for war. The *Imperator* had as a figurehead a nine-foot-long golden eagle wearing a crown, bearing the legend, *My Scope is the World,* but was too heavy, and rolled worse than any other ship of its type, until concrete was poured into its hull for ballast.

By 1907—when the *Dreadnought* battleship race began—the concurrent liner race was also well underway. When the US entered the war in 1917, it called Ballin's interned liners, "The fleet the Kaiser built for us." Those remaining under German control were converted into an Auxiliary Fleet of merchant surface raiders.

Ballin—mocked by his foes as, "The Napoleon of the Sea"—nevertheless built, "The world's greatest shipping line," and for his personal help the Kaiser also deserves partial credit for its success. Indeed, Ballin's trio of jumbo ocean liners—the *Vaterland, Imperator,* and *Bismarck*—were bigger vessels than the British ever constructed, and continued thus for the next two decades. Ironically, it was the sinking of the passenger liner *Lusitania* by a U-boat on 7 May 1915 that almost brought the US into the war two years earlier than its actuality. The Great War was the undoing of Ballin's lifelong work for peace, as he lamented before his death from a drug overdose on 10 November 1918:

> My ships didn't need the protection of a German Fleet, and I should have said so to the Kaiser, but I could never summon the courage to do so. We were all too weak toward the Kaiser. No one wished to disturb his childlike, happy optimism that could shift at once into an almost helpless depression if anyone criticized any of his pet projects.
>
> And among these, the fleet was the greatest. Now we have the result of our lack of courage!

After the war, the first German ocean liner launched in 10 years was named the *Albert Ballin* in August 1924.

The British and German superliners—though in symbolic opposition to each other— ironically witnessed that their greatest effect would in time be achieved in tandem. Jointly, they transported a new generation to the United States, and also carried over the waves the American Expeditionary Force that altered the course of the First World War. Jointly, they radicalized the business of sea transportation ever after. The merging of these two maritime fleets after the Great War is their crowning irony, however, only as seen from the perspective of the Anglo-German rivalry. The greatest irony was that—despite their seeming antipathy, they had been a sister fleet throughout it all.

7

The German Overseas Colonial Empire 1888–1914

The Kaiser's long reign saw the continuous expansion of the Reich's overseas possessions, By 1914, the German Colonial Empire encompassed German Southwest Africa, German East Africa, Togo, Cameroon, Kaiser Wilhelm Land, the Bismarck Archipelago, the Caroline and Marianas Island Groups, Samoa, and also the Tsingtao naval base on China's Shantung Peninsula.

The "British" Kaiser's Positive Accomplishments, 1888–1914

Kaiser Wilhelm II was seen by many as earnest, forthright, and curious. A soldier by training from age 10, Wilhelm II's speeches cited valor and military glory, but he was at heart both a warrior and a man of peace. His reign was marked by the increase in Germanic might and commercial prosperity unparalleled in any previous era of German history. In 1888, electric lighting had just debuted in Berlin, and by his Throne Jubilee of 25 years in 1913, the Second Reich ranked among the five wealthiest nations on Earth.

Although Germany began industrialization relatively late, the German Empire witnessed an instant boom in railway construction, coal mining, and shipbuilding, thus providing a strong impetus to its overall economic development. By 1910, Germany's steel production had doubled that of Great Britain, and German manufactured goods were sought after in all global markets. Germany's scientists dominated chemistry, microbiology, and physics, and Teutonic architects, engineers, and industrialists built railroads, factories, harbors, and housing over the entire planet. Germany' middle class grew steadily, and German workers were protected by the most comprehensive social legislation system in existence.

During the period from 1870 to 1914, the German Empire saw a population incease from 41 million to 67.8 million people, while the Imperial Capital Berlin also advanced steadily from a once medium-sized city to a vast metropolis that rivaled Paris in size by 1910.

The German Army was a model for military science students and practitioners, but in spite of its well-deserved reputation for excellence, in 1914 it had a peacetime strength of but 760,905 NCOs and men that—while proportional to the national population—was actually far smaller than that of its neighbor, Republican France.

As his mother was called "the English Princess," it was also partially correct to call Wilhelm II, "the British Kaiser," as he had a distant blood lineage that put him in line to succeed as well to the United Kingdom's throne. Indeed, during the vaunted Wilhelminian Age, the German Reich stood at a pinnacle of achievement and an apogee of power never before and never again accomplished, measured by and in prestige, prosperity, and security.

Germany was where the automobile industry was invented in 1885, and she was also world-famous for her X-rays in the field of medicine. Germany led the world in educational reform, while the German optical industry was the globe's finest, even in 1919, after the lost war. Indeed, during the war, the British were forced to buy 32,000 pairs of German-made field binoculars via the neutral Swiss for their British Expeditionary Force officers on the Western Front.

The Curtain Falls on the Emperor's Overseas Colonial Empire, 1914

The First World War saw the end of Germany's dreams of empire, and the Tsingtao Chinese holdings fell first, to Japan in the autumn of 1914. What happened in Africa follows later herein.

PART 3

Supreme Warlord in the Great War
1914–1918

THE COMING OF THE COSSACKS.

Wilhelm II. "WHAT IS THIS DISTANT RUMBLING THAT I HEAR? DOUBTLESS THE PLAUDITS OF MY PEOPLE!"

"The Coming of the Cossacks." Cartoon by L. Ravenhill, published in *Punch* 26 August 1914.
(Publisher Archive)

8

In the West

Wilhelm found happiness as an adult only in the Prussian Army: 'I really found my family, my friends, my interests—everything in which I had up to that time had to do without.' It was the Army therefore, that moulded the hardness of Wilhelm's character.

The Uniformed Warlord Fishing for Applause

The Kaiser seemed perpetually to be in uniform, all a-glitter with medals, orders, and decorations, and truly was fascinated by them, but once scoffed at Tsar Ferdinand of Bulgaria for being "Festooned with decorations like a Christmas tree"—oblivious of the quantity he himself wore. In his first 16 years on the throne, the Kaiser altered uniforms 37 times, donned that of a General of Engineers for dinner at the Berlin Motor Club, and was in love with showing off. A Hamburg lady asserted: "The trouble with the Kaiser is that he wants to be the bride at every wedding and the corpse at every funeral."

At least part of this craving for attention was due to his constant need of applause, as Imperial Chancellor Theobald von Bethmann-Hollwegg once frankly told him straight up: "Your Majesty finds life impossible unless Prussia applauds you daily, Germany weekly, and Europe once a fortnight!" Prince Philip von Eulenburg asserted that the Kaiser's successful Army maneuver victories were prearranged. Wilhelm II insisted that this insulted his generals, who merely treated him as one of themselves; the Prince rejoined that, 'I should be very glad to learn someday that Your Majesty had been defeated!'"

Enraged at the Fall 1891 maneuvers when Chief of the General Staff von Waldersee criticized His Majesty's military prowess in front of the assembled generals, the Kaiser fired him, demoting him to Altona to command an Army Corps instead.

In 1906, von Moltke the Younger made his acceptance of the post as Chief of the General Staff based on His Majesty's ceasing to take part in the annual war games so that his side would stop winning. He also demanded that the Kaiser lead no more massive, but militarily useless, cavalry charges therein, because they would be decimated in the next war by the future "King of the Battlefield," automatic machine guns.

Meekly, Wilhelm II complied, going on record as stating that it was better to tell a monarch the truth than to flatter him to the detriment of the nation. Still, once the World War broke out, his wife the Kaiserin made his aides promise not to tell His Majesty bad news for fear of fraying his already poor nervous system; they complied.

How War Came in 1914

In July 1914—following the assassination at Sarajevo by Serbian terrorists on 28 June of the Austrian Heir to the Throne, Archduke Franz Ferdinand, and his wife—Austria threatened Serbia, which was in Russia's sphere of influence, and the Russians mobilized their army. Germany then began to mobilize its army, and neither side would back down. Meanwhile, the modified German Army Schlieffen Plan went into effect in the West, frightening Republican France, Russia's ally, and also England, again, France's ally.

The German invasion of Belgium—to better attack France—brought the British into the war on the side of the two European Allies. Savoyard Italy failed to honor its 1882 Triple Alliance with Germany and Austria, and later joined the Allies outright during 1915, first against Austria alone, and then also versus the Reich.

In 1916, Rumania also joined the Allies. Bulgaria and Turkey both joined what became known as the Central Powers of Germany and Austria in 1914, and with the entry of the United States in 1917 with the Allies, the conflict became a truly global World War. The legacy of the Kaiser is important for the twenty-first century because—although not wanting it—he nevertheless stumbled blindly into the war by backing Austria in whatever it decided to do to punish Serbia, his famed "blank check" diplomatic blunder.

Modern historians mostly now agree that the Kaiser neither planned it nor was totally responsible for the outbreak of the Great War, but—as Allied propagandists charged later—also concur that he bears a heavy burden of the guilt. So do most of the other monarchs and statesmen of his time for creating the climate in which it seemed natural to occur. Populations on both sides applauded the arrival of the war, and marched off to it with bands playing and flags waving. That all stopped by the end of 1914.

Wilhelm's main guilt in 1914 seems to be in allowing his generals and war machine to run away from him at its start, to elude civilian control in so doing, and so also precipitate the dreaded "war on two fronts" to be implemented, merely because their railroad troop movement timetable scheduling said that it must be so, despite his protests.

The Warlord's Enduring Image

Wilhelm's carefully cultivated image of 26 years before 1914 as a saber-rattler and maker of overblown, warlike speeches came back to haunt him when quoted out of context by these same Allied propagandists. It is interesting to note that—had he not been overthrown in 1918, after 30 years on the throne—and ruled instead until his death in mid–1941, his reign then of 53 years would have been the longest in all of German history.

His Army Chiefs of General Staff, 1888–1918

A military monarch by upbringing, this soldier king had six Chiefs of General Staff for his Imperial Army: Field Marshal Count Helmuth von Moltke the Elder (1888), General Count Alfred von Waldersee (1888–1891); General Count Alfred von Schlieffen (1891–1906); General Count Helmuth J.L von Moltke the Younger (1906–1914); General Erich von Falkenhayn (1914–1916), and Field Marshal Paul von Hindenburg (1916–1918.)

He also had two Chief Quartermasters-General under the last Chief of the General Staff chief, Erich Ludendorff (1916–1918) and Wilhelm Groener (1918). Normally, these men worked under the direction of the Kaiser himself—who, as the vaunted Supreme Warlord—had the ultimate power and responsibility in time of war for all matters military.

Previous biographers have almost universally suggested that when the war actually did break out, just the opposite quickly became true in reality. In their scenario, it was as if all Wilhelm's previous life had been but a preparation for the test of the First World War, and he failed it, by seemingly allowing the military to run the war in his place. The Kaiser was, instead, a shrewd domestic politician, and he realized that if the war was lost, it was far better for him as Emperor not to be blamed for having lost it, as he was anyway in 1918. His prewar military critics—such as the late World Marshal von Waldersee—panned His Majesty for wanting to be his own Chief of Staff and fighting the war on his own, as a modern day Frederick the Great. When he let the generals run it while reporting their every action to him at daily military conferences, he merely approved or not what they had done, or suggested.

Ever since 1918, his critics have wanted to have it both ways: being critical of him for exercising too much "personal rule" before the war, and then an alleged non-control after it began.

His Majesty's Wartime KHQs: Kaiser/Imperial Headquarters

Typically, military historians and biographers of the period refer to OHL/General Headquarters of the Armed Forces High Command generally, and almost never to what they really were: His Majesty the Kaiser's Headquarters, especially so since he was almost always present in person at all of them from the first day of the war to the last.

Initially, they were at Koblenz on the Rhine on German soil, then were moved forward to invaded Luxembourg to be nearer to the Western Front, to Mézières and Charleville, on to Kreuznach and Bad Hamburg in 1917, and finally, in 1918, to Avesnes, and later to Spa in occupied Belgium, all also in the West. When the war focused more on action on the Eastern Front, His Majesty's Imperial Train sped eastward to both Posen Castle in Poland and that in Upper Silesia of the Prince of Pless during 1915–16; then back and forth between the east and Krueznach in the west as the situation demanded. In between, the Kaiser looked to domestic and civilian affairs at both his Berlin Castle and also Potsdam's New Palace.

Col. General Hans von Plessen—attached to the Kaiser's staff since 1892—was in charge of all his wartime KHQs during the Great War.

KHQ Castle Pless, Pszczyna, Upper Silesia, now Poland, 1914–17

According to its official Internet website:

> Between 1914–17, the … castle played an important role housing an Emperor's Headquarters and the General Staff of the German Army. It was here … where the Emperor, the Chief of General Staff, Marshal Paul von Hindenburg, and the Chief of Eastern Staff—General Erich von Ludendorff—were making military decisions changing the history of Europe.

Among these was the famous Pless Conference held there on 8 January 1917 that saw the Kaiser decide that unconditional U-boat warfare would commence on 31 January 1917, "attacking all ships within the British coastal zone and Atlantic Ocean."

His Majesty resided at Castle Pless in the Royal Apartments that were later restored:

> With a lot of the original furnishings intact … Princess Mary Theresa Olivia Cornwallis-West—nicknamed Daisy—lived there during 1891–1943 as the wife of Prince Hans Heinrich XV, and left her native England…The highlight of the palace is its Chamber of Mirrors.

The site is a tourist attraction today.

KHQ Spa, *Hotel Britannique*, Belgium, 1918

Spa is a city in Belgium's Walloon Region and Liège Province, located in a valley in the Ardennes. In 1918, both KHQ and German Army General Staff Headquarters were sited there in the famous Hotel Britannique. It was there that His Majesty decided to flee to Holland on 9 November 1918, and also where the German Armistice Delegation was sent to see French Marshal Ferdinand Foch at Compiègne, France. In July 1920, the Allied Supreme Council's Spa Conference took place after the war, with German delegates invited to discuss war reparations, that were duly paid until 1933.

> The Hotel Britannique is a grand piece of architecture at the very center of the city. It was always a good looking building, but is particularly famous because of its role in the First World War, used as a headquarters by the German Kaiser, and still retains some of the changes and marks that were left by the military leader.

KHQ Imperial Train, 1914–10 November 1918

Whenever he traveled, KHQ duly shifted with him, aboard His Majesty's mobile field headquarters, the Imperial Train, which he later lived on into his Dutch exile as well.

His Majesty's Facetious Remark to Prince Max von Baden Concerning His Role

Historians have seized upon the following statement by the Kaiser as self-admitted proof that Wilhelm II was somehow unattached to what went on at and in Imperial General Headquarters during the long war:

> If people in Germany think I am the Supreme Commander, they're grossly mistaken! The General Staff tells me nothing, and never asks my advice. I drink tea, go for walks, and saw wood, which pleases my suite. The only one who is a bit kind to me is the Chief of the Railway Department [*then General Groener*], who tells me all he does and intends to do. I am nothing more than Hindenburg's adjutant, and he asks me nothing.

This was the Emperor being his sulking and facetious best, probably for not getting his way entirely at that day's military situation conference. It is also both likely and possible that His Majesty the German domestic politician was preparing his defense brief before his constituency his subjects when his marshals and generals duly lost their war, not his. He had every intention of returning to Berlin as German Emperor and King of Prussia—lost war or no!—to rebuild his country, just as had his forbears Frederick the Great afer the Seven Years' War and also King Frederick Wilhelm III during 1806–1840 after being soundly beaten by Napoleon. In these instances, Prussian history, indeed, was on his side, too.

From Short to Long War in 1914

Initially, the Kaiser thought that it would be a short war—certainly no longer than that of 1870—and he envisioned a triumphant ride on horseback through Paris, as both his father and grandfather had done before him. Indeed, at the war's outset that August, the German Army won the famous Battle of the Frontiers with the routed French Army, then invaded France itself, and drove on Paris right up to the Marne River. At that point there occurred the "Miracle of the Marne," when the defeated French and British forces wheeled and turned to fight again, exploiting a growing gap between two of the German armies on the right wing of their drive in the first 10 days of September, 1914. When Moltke told him forthrightly, "Majesty, the war is lost" because the war of movement had been halted in its tracks, the Kaiser fired him in a bold move that certainly was not the action of a somehow detached and disinterested German Warlord. Into the breech His Majesty thrust as Chief of the General Staff his then Minister of War, General Erich von Falkenhayn (1861–1922), who immediately proceeded to launch a fresh offensive in the West against all three Allied armies—those of France and still fighting Belgium—and also the plucky British Expeditionary Force. The Germans had collided with this in the earlier Battles of Mons and Le Cateau, their first combat ever with British troops.

Falkenhayn's First Battle of Ypres in Belgium ground to a halt as well during October–November 1914, and by the end of the year, both sides faced off in a war of position and stalemate in opposite trench works that stretched all the way from the North Sea Coast to

Switzerland. There the two sides remained basically until March 1918, with futile battles of attrition being waged at Verdun, on the Somme River, and again at Ypres that the Germans lost.

In 1916, the Kaiser once more fired a Chief of the General Staff, replacing von Falkenhayn with von Hindenburg from the far more successful German front in the Eastern Theater of War. Thus came "The Duo" to the Western Front.

His Majesty's Roster of Field Marshals, 1888–1934

According to *Prussian-German Field Marshals and Grand Admirals,* published by Safari-Verlag, Berlin, 1938, the former include: Helmuth Bernhard Graf von Moltke (1800–1891), awarded his baton on 8 April 1871; Albrecht Crown Prince of Saxony (1828–1902), 11 July 1871; Leonhard Count von Blumenthal (1810–1900), 15 March 1888; Georg Prince of Saxony (1832–1904), 15 June 1888;

Albrecht of Prussia (1837–1907), 19 June 1888; Alfred Count von Waldersee (1852–1904), 6 May 1900; Frederick Christian Freiherr von Loe (1828–1908), 1 January 1905; Gustav Karl Wilhelm von Hahnke (1883–1912), 1 January 1905; Gottlieb Ferdinand von Haeseler (1836–1919), 1 January 1905; Mar von Bock und Pollach (1842–1915), 1 January 1911; Colmar Baron von der Goltz-Pasha (1843–1916), 1 January 1911; Albrecht Count von Schlieffen (1833–1913), 1 January 1911; Paul von Hindenburg und Beneckendorf (1847–1934), November 1914; Karl von Bülow (1846–1921), 27 January 1915; August von Mackensen (1849–1945), 22 June 1915; Rupprecht Crown Prince of Bavaria (1869–1955), 1 August 1916; Albrecht von Württemberg, 1 August 1916; Leopold of Bavaria (1846–1930), 1 August 1916; Remus von Woyrsch (1847–1920), 31 July 1917; and Hermann von Eichhorn (1848–1918), who was assassinated on the Eastern Front.

The German Emperor's Wartime Rail Travel, 1914–1918

Wihelm II as German Supreme Warloard relished roaring through the countryside by rail during the war aboard his famous Imperial train. Attended by his suite—with standard bearer and staff trumpeter, two guardsmen of the Royal Rifles bearing the Imperial map case and field glasses—His Majesty the Emperor watched far-off battles via a periscope, tossing back the cape of his cloak while pushing his camouflaged spiked helmet off his forehead. From under its rim was seen a tuft of gray hair. Fully aware that he was being watched by everyone examining his every facial expression---searching for any clue as to the general military situation, whether things were doing well or ill on the various battlefronts—His Majesty the Kaiser and King naturally sought to inspire confidence, and many times did.

He shook hands vigorously with both officers and men with a steady look into the eyes of all: he did what he could.

In the East and Middle East

First Marne—there would be a second, in spring 1918—had, indeed, been the first turning point against Germany in the World War, and Wilhelm II had helped to lose it by requiring that two full Army Corps be detached from the Western Front and sent to the embattled Eastern Front that was then being successfully invaded by two rampaging Russian armies, both then but a mere 150 miles away from the Imperial Capital of Berlin. The twin army corps thus left France before the fighting began at First Marne, and were still in transit by rail when an unexpected smashing victory was won against the Russians at the Battle of Tannenberg. The two corps took part in neither battle, therefore.

As First Marne was, strategically by far the more important of the two battles, this decisive stroke cost Germany the outcome of the war at its very outset, mainly because the Allied armies in the West were not defeated, and Paris was not taken, as it had been in 1871. The Marne defeat was hidden from the German people by the more glorious news of the victory at Tannenberg that made its commander the national hero of the hour, and also of the next two decades—Hindenburg—but not His Majesty the Kaiser, alas.

"The Cossacks are Coming!"

"There has never been and no doubt will never be again such a war as this—fought with such bestial fury! The Russians are burning everything down!" lamented Lt. Col. Max Hoffmann (1866–1927), operations officer of the undermanned German 8th Army in lightly defended East Prussia on 23 August 1914.

Cried the simpler East Prussian villagers who fled the sweeping fire and sword of the two Russian armies of invasion, "*Kossaken kommen!*" a lament that would be re-echoed again a generation later, in 1945. A hundred years earlier—during the German War of Liberation from the hated Napoleonic yoke—the Germans and Russians had been allies, but now they were at deathly odds.

As the First World War opened, the German plan of attack focused entirely on its Western Front, in a massive assault to defeat France and the British Expeditionary Force, while the plan for the East depended on a tardy Russian mobilization to buy time for the engaged German armies to win in the West, and then strike eastward.

Throughout the Great War, the German General Staff routinely overestimated its own strengths, while always underestimating those of the Allies. When the backward Russians were thus able to assemble faster than forecast, a specter arose that haunted the Kaiser and his generals: not only would their beloved East Prussia be lost, Berlin would be taken—as during the Seven Years' War and again by Napoleon—and its Austrian ally's Vienna might fall as well! Indeed, this might occur even if and while the war in the west was being won. What to do? They ruminated. At last, the "Hero of Liège," General Erich Ludendorff—who had banged his sword pommel on the gates of that Belgian fortress city, demanding and getting its surrender—would be the new 8th Army chief of staff to reverse the Russian tide in the embattled east. But who would be his commander? Out of retirement was summoned the 67-year-old General Paul von Hindenburg, who had failed to become Chief of the General Staff because he had the temerity once to defeat the Emperor on maneuvers. A veteran of all three of the Bismarckian wars earlier, von Hindenburg had retired as an Army corps commander, and was said to have steady nerves of steel. Thus, he was seen as the perfect counterpart to offset the nervous, excitable, high-strung, but brilliant Ludendorff.

"The Duo"

Later called "The Duo," they—together with Hoffmann and others—would plan and execute what the latter would call, "One of the greatest battles in history," named for an obscure East Prussian village—Tannenberg. It was, indeed, a watershed engagement in military history, a combat that the Russians had expected to win and the Germans to lose, but the reverse occurred. It is a strange but true tale.

Each of the two Russian armies faced by the Germans was equal to their own 8th Army, and but 30 miles apart. If they linked up, Ludendorff later admitted, "We would have been beaten." Thus, the war might have ended in 1914 in signal Allied victories on both fronts, West and East, but with, possibly, the Hohenzollern monarchy thus still retained.

Russian High Command Dissension

The Russian High Command bungled, and there was no link-up of the two mighty forces. The 1st Army's commander—General Pavel Rennenkampf—hated the man he was supposed to rescue, the 2nd Army's leader, General Alexander Samsonov.

The latter had once punched the former in the mouth on a railway platform at Mukden in 1905. He was in no hurry to help, and besides, he had orders to take the Prussian fortress city of Königsberg, in another direction. The final blow was that the Germans were reading all of their enemy's wireless messages that the Russians sent in the clear! Ludendorff's subordinate commander—General Hermann von François—disobeyed orders twice: once attacking two days late after his needed artillery had arrived, and later continuing his line of advance over orders to go elsewhere. Victory rescued von François from a court martial when two entire Russian Army corps were destroyed. Samsonov shot himself, and Rennenkampf was disgraced.

The Role of Siegfriedian Mythology

Two myths emerged: the Russians had drowned in swamp quicksand—there were no swamps in the local forests, Ludendorff always maintained—and Hindenburg, promoted by his grateful Kaiser to Field Marshal, had won the battle alone. Col. Hoffmann later noted sourly if Hindenburg had won the Battle of Tannenberg, one could cease believing in Hannibal and Caesar. Taking tours of visitors through the battlefield later, he commented waspishly:

> This is where the Field Marshal slept before the battle; here is where he slept after the battle; and here is where he slept during the battle!

The war in the east continued apace, however, and the Russians neither surrendered nor retreated back into Russia, but instead won victories against the Austrian Army in Polish Galicia, with more German victories at the 1915 Battle of the Masurian Lakes and also with the fall of Warsaw. A new hero also emerged in the east in the person of the Kaiser's favorite Army Field Marshal—August von Mackensen—who, after Rumania entered the war in 1916, took its capital of Bucharest, ending the fighting. The famed Death's Head Hussar leader also was the German conqueror of Serbia, whose army had badly defeated the Austrians in 1914.

In early 1917, the Tsar was overthrown and abdicated, but the Russians stayed in the war, until it appeared likely that their capital of Petrograd might fall to the German Army. Then the new Red Communist Russian State signed the Peace of Brest-Litovsk with Germany, and thus exited the lost war; the Reich had won in the east, hands down.

By September 1918, the former border state Russian provinces of Finland, Latvia, Estonia, Kurland, Livonia, Ukraine, Georgia, Armenia, and Azerbaijan all had declared their independence from the former Great, and now Rump, Russia, and virtually joined the German Reich in waging the war in the east.

Indeed, as the war turned against the Second Reich in the west in August 1918, the German Army and its political influence was paramount on the Don up to Tsarityn (the later Stalingrad), in the Kuban, on the Krim (Crimea), and also in the oil-rich Caucasus. Thus, there had been achieved Chancellor von Bethmann-Hollwegg's September Program of 1914, including a projection of future control of all the rest of Russia as well.

The Saga of "Johnny Turk" in the Middle East, 1914–1918

For many Western readers, the view of the Turkish Army in the First World War comes mainly from two popular movies, both post-Second World War: *Lawrence of Arabia* and *Gallipoli*. As author Edward J. Erickson points out in his groundbreaking 2002 study—*Ordered to Die: A History of the Ottoman Army in the First World War*—they hardly present the full picture of this magnificent Central Powers fighting machine. Long overdue and splendidly done, this first work in English in the last 85 years notes that Turkey outlasted Russia, Bulgaria, and Rumania in the Great War, and also matched Austria-Hungary in its overall war effort to boot. Moreover, theTurkish armies never mutinied—as did those of France, Germany, and Russia—while the hardy Turks inflicted huge casualties on the Allies, fighting on a total of five fronts, of which Arabia (in which the vaunted Lawrence allegedly played so vital a role) was the least important.

Containing ethnic Turks, Kurds, and Arabs—who were more of a liability than an asset—the army that was feared by its enemies simply by its overall name of "the Turks," was weakened by a trio of Balkan Wars before mistakenly entering the war of 1914 on the Kaiser's behalf. Ironically—considering the stress placed on their importance in *Lawrence of Arabia* in the Hejaz Railway scenes—the Turkish railroad system was also a major liability throughout the entire war, one never solved either by the influx after 1915 of Railway Troops of the German Asia Corps. One of the myriad myths about the Turkish Army in this period is that its victories were won primarily due to this and other Imperial German Army aid throughout the war. True, the liaison between the two partners Germany and Turkey was far more effective than Nazi Germany and Fascist Italy a generation later, and several such famous officers as Hans von Seeckt, von der Goltz, Liman von Sanders (of Gallipoli renown), and von Falkenhayn served on the Turkish fronts.

It was, however, the Turkish commanders and their hardy warriors who both planned and fought the major campaigns and battles in the final analysis. It was in the areas of chiefs of staff and material aid to flex out major Turkish formations in the field (still with 25 divisions and a million men under arms as late as November 1918) that helped Turkey stay in the war almost until the very end as a reliable ally to the Germans, and also as an equal partner.

Indeed, Mustafa Kemal Ataturk (1881–1938)—reportedly the finest commander produced by the Ottoman Empire in the First World War—protested vigorously against his Empire becoming a colonial dependent state of the Reich. Enver Pasha performed ably as the Turkish War Minister. On mobilization in August 1914, the Turkish Army had but eight airplanes in operational units, plus four more posted to its flying school. At war's end, the Turks had about 200 aircraft in differing operational states. No Ottoman pilots became aces, true—but both pilots and observers shot down many enemy aircraft during the war, and—to its credit— Turkish air units are portrayed strafing Arab Prince Feisal's mounted warriors successfully during the first half of *Lawrence of Arabia.*

Turkey suffered tremendously in the First World War, was completely beaten, and her troops always fought at a disadvantage, but their armies' infantry marching capacity was considered amazing by all, friend and foe alike. In the Middle East, therefore, the Central Powers appeared to be winning the war at first, with Turkish armies holding the Russians to a standstill on their common frontier, and badly defeating a British amphibious landing at Gallipoli in 1915 in the Dardenelles Straits that was designed by Churchill to both aid Russia and take Constantinople.

Turkey waged an aggressive war against the French and British in all seven of its major wartime provinces. Lawrence's irregular forces took Damascus that the Kaiser had visited in 1898, and former British Expeditionary Force cavalry General Sir Edmund Allenby took the Jewish-Arab city of Jerusalem. Everything considered, Turkey had been a far more useful and results-producing ally of Imperial Germany than had the Austrians. For concluding the alliance with her, no one deserves the credit more than successful diplomat Kaiser Wilhelm II.

Health in History Revisited: An Ill German Supreme Warlord?

To forestall recurrent colds and chills, the Kaiser—in prewar days—took some unusual measures, such as changing residences whenever measles or mumps was discovered in the Palace, moving on a half hour's notice. Once, the Court had moved into the Bellevue Palace for the winter instead of the Old Palace in Berlin, and his son Prince Oscar—returned from Italy—came down with chickenpox. No sooner had they arrived elsewhere, than Prince August Wilhelm got sick with it as well. The Kaiser then blithely announced that he had had chickenpox years before, and did what his doctors ordered.

During the four-year passage of the war, the Kaiser suffered from a host of both minor and some major physical problems. At least some of these derived from his boyhood, such as his propensity for catching the common cold. During the war, Admiral von Müller notes in his diary that His Majesty suffered from colds on 4 February 1917 ("severe") for which he took "a Turkish bath cure," and on 15 January 1918, "The naval report was cancelled this afternoon because His Majesty has retired to bed…"

He further notes when Wilhelm caught "chills," as on 5 December 1914, 3 February 1916, again on 13 February ("very bad") coupled with tonsillitis, on 7 November 1916 (when the Kaiser felt he was close to having pneumonia), and yet again on 15 November 1917.

On 20 April 1917, von Müller notes in his diary the Kaiser's "grossly overheated bedroom," and that His Majesty, "Sat up in bed and confessed that he'd not slept a wink for six nights." The Kaiser would often use his inability to sleep or the discomfort of military headquarters as excuses to retreat personally further from the war zones and enjoy a life of ease in the rear areas, according to the Chief of his Naval Cabinet. The overall impression that this left on even his closest associates was one of Imperial indolence: "The Kaiser declared that he could not see the Chancellor tomorrow before six o'clock. He wanted to spend the morning in the gardens of *Sans Souci,* and he must sleep after lunch," and this in the face of mounting crises on the combat fronts both east and west.

Perhaps this was his method of dealing with them, and in the final analysis, all the necessary political, diplomatic, and military decisions were made. Still, by 16 August 1917— with the end of the war more than a year away—von Müller writes of the Kaiser's relations with his top military commanders: "He is now completely left out in the cold … because he has failed in his duty." While this was the opinion of one of his sailors, a recent reading of Fischer's 1961 wartime chronicle of His Majesty's activities gives an entirely different view, that of an engaged monarch intimately connected with all manner of treaties, negotiations, and conferences in the political sphere, activities to which the Naval Cabinet Chief was not privy all the time.

A Medical Plot to Remove the Kaiser?

As early as 18 April 1915, the admiral notes a bizarre medical plot against the Kaiser's alleged lack of wartime leadership:

[*Civil Cabinet Chief Rudolf*] Valentini … confided to me that the Kaiser's physician—Dr von

Neidner—is worried about an intrigue at headquarters to declare the Kaiser temporarily incapable of ruling, and to make the Crown Prince Regent—a wild pipe dream!

But maybe not, when one considers that his own grandfather had in exactly that fashion replaced his older brother King Frederick Wilhelm IV until the older man died and his younger brother succeeded him as King.

After the war's loss—when editing his diaries for eventual publication following the deaths of both himself and the Kaiser—von Müller added to this passage:

> I heard no more of the matter at the time. It never became dangerous, and never presumably got further than private talk.

A medical plot to overthrow His Majesty the Kaiser is not as farfetched as it might at first seem.

The Physical Supreme Warlord

Oddly enough, His Majesty was neither indolent nor disinterested in the war's outcome, his very survival as a reigning monarch dependent upon it. He was, physically, an extraordinarily active man. Before the war, the Kaiser daily walked with the Kaiserin, as well as shot, rode, drove, hunted, boated, skated, and even tobogganed energetically. As early as January 1915 during the war, Wilhelm II was sawing wood with his one good arm for exercise, and, indeed, in his postwar exile in Holland at age 60 on up, felled 17,000 trees.

Personally, he was physically courageous, too. On 25 April 1916, French planes staged a bombing attack on KHQ Charleville, in which the engineer of the Imperial Train was killed, but Wilhelm II remained there nonetheless; he didn't have to. He did, however—like most monarchs of his time—fear assassination. In November 1900, a mentally disturbed older woman tossed an ax at him, but missed, while in 1903, a mentally ill youth threw a piece of iron at his face, wounding him under the right eye. His fear of illnesses can also be found to have a rational basis, as—in 1866—his younger brother Sigismund died of meningitis, and his brother Waldemar 12 years later, during a typhoid epidemic. As we have seen, both his parents died early of cancer, a disease he had also contracted as well.

His seeming—to some—disinterest in the war sprang from his belief that Germany could not defeat the world. Despite this, however—and naturally—he wanted to believe that his country would win. Therefore, he veered from making irrational statements—about the German Army conquering all in its path, when, in fact, the news from the battlefields was bad—to ensuring that wounded English soldiers received the same medical treatment as injured German troops.

An Insane German Emperor?

This erratic behavior led some—even in his own, inner circle—to conclude that he was mad. Von Müller writes on 16 May 1916, "His Majesty does not appear to be in his right mind." In 1927—nine years after the end of the war—the admiral adds that the Kaiser's bold speeches in the face of military defeat, "Can only be explained by the presumption that the Kaiser's mental balance had been disturbed by the long, nerve-wracking war." In truth, the Kaiser's nerves were bad—and always had been, too, even before the war---that merely served as the catalyst to bring them to the attention of his officer corps. Prior to 1914, most of them had never observed Wilhelm II at close quarters except at the annual Imperial military maneuvers.

The medical profession has asserted that men can and often do suffer the emotional stresses experienced by females during their menopause. If this was the case with the Kaiser, it would explain his increased nervousness and tension in early middle age. 29 January 1899 was his 40th birthday. He wrote to Queen Victoria that the strain of his office was often too heavy to bear, and described himself as, "Her queer and impetuous colleague." She notes in her journal, "I wish he were more prudent and less impulsive at such an age!"

In 1908, we saw how the Kaiser almost left his throne during the First Abdication Crisis. Eight years later, he reportedly wept when he was forced to replace General von Falkenhayn with von Hindenburg. As the war went on, his nerves worsened. He became hard to live with, with no telling either how well or ill he would be daily; or why his mood barometer went up and down so quickly, nor how long he would be in euphoria or depression. It is entirely possible that Kaiser Wilhelm II in today's medical experience would be diagnosed as bipolar manic depressive.

Wilhelm suffered near-complete nervous breakdowns in April 1917 and October 1918 (along with the Empress), when he realized for sure that the war was lost (and was walking with a cane due to sciatica.) In addition to bouts of nervous depression, the Kaiser suffered "a slight heart attack" on 9 July 1916, and another on 18 April 1917; a sore throat on 17 July 1916, a hernia operation in February 1917, and an arthritic attack coupled with "rheumatic pains" in October 1918. Yet, he bounced back from them all to live into his early eighties nevertheless, far outliving both his parents and all his younger brothers, too. The effect of all of these things—considering his past history also—was, perhaps, somewhat predictable. He existed in his own fantasy world, rushing about inspecting troops, handing out Iron Crosses in person, reviewing parades, and continuing to address martial throngs with speeches that were too long.

Still, His Majesty's vigor and stamina were considered by his staff to be truly remarkable, he was moving so fast that generals could hardly keep pace with him. One—on a hot day— fainted from fatigue. To his credit, moreover, the Kaiser traveled to the front as closely as Ludendorff allowed, driving through burned villages in his motorcar with the yellow Imperial standard flapping in the breeze.

Again—as before—it was believed that he had aged visibly. His hair had grayed, his face becoming lined, but then, so, too, had those of Clemenceau, Wilson, Pershing, and Haig. The Great War took its toll on everyone.

Enter "The Duo" in the West, 1916–1918

In the summer of 1916, the "twin brethren Duo" of Hindenburg and Ludendorff took over the German High Command under the Kaiser's orders in the west, commanding all the far-flung battlefronts.

In Africa

In Africa, the Germans did surprisingly well during the entirety of the war there, under the inspired leadership of colonial forces General Paul von Lettow-Vorbeck (1870–1964), who waged major battles at Tanga in 1914, Jassin in 1915, and Mahiwa in 1917 with native *Askari* infantry officered by whites, outnumbered by superior Allied forces. Having previously served in both China and German Southwest Africa, Lettow-Vorbeck in April 1914 was posted to command the German *Schuttruppen* in German East Africa.

The British landed troops at Tanga in November 1914, and Lettow-Vorbeck beat them despite being himself heavily outnumbered, capturing much weaponry. At the Battle of Jassin in January 1915, Lettow recognized that such pitched fighting was exhausting both his finite supplies of men and ammunition, just as, indeed, on the Western Front as well. He switched over to guerilla warfare tactics. Evading far larger British forces, Lettow-Vorbeck led his 3,000 whites and 11,000 Africans in a raiding campaign of ambushes, living off the land, and faulting all attempts to engage him in further pitched battles he could not win. Despite greater hardships, discipline and loyalty stayed high. Lettow-Vorbeck's exploits in East Africa made for several excellent German propaganda posters.

A Hero's Return to Berlin, 1919

In October 1917, Lettow-Vorbeck fought the Battle of Mahiwa—losing 500 men—while inflicting five times the casualties on his foes, then escaped into Portuguese Mozambique, being entirely unbeaten at war's end. Thus—as on the Eastern Front with defeated Russia— Imperial Germany could and did claim an undefeated standoff. Returning as a hero to Berlin in 1919 with a parade through the Brandenburg Gate, Lettow-Vorbeck was dismissed from the Army after having taken part in the failed March 1920 Kapp *Putsch* that aimed to overthrow the Republic and restore Germany to monarchical rule. He made his Kaiser and people proud.

Born on 20 March 1870, von Lettow-Vorbeck took no part in the Second World War, but lived to see the founding of West Germany, dying on 9 March 1964.

After the fall of Tsingtao in China, both Togo and the German Cameroons fell to the French, while German Southwest Africa surrendered to Botha's mixed forces, but German East Africa remained unconconquered until November 1918, and the loss of the war in Europe, not Africa. The Versailles Treaty took them away from the Reich forever.

In the Air and on the Sea

The Imperial Air Service

German military air power and civilian air passenger travel was created during the Wilhelmine Age, and in 1909—as part of the annual fall Kaiser maneuvers—military aircraft took part for the first time, and the Kaiser rightly deserves credit for having the Imperial Air Service created during his reign. In 1910, civil and military pilots were licensed by the German Aviation Association; in 1907, German Aeroclubs had already been established under the Kaiser's aegis. Although His Majesty never flew, Ludendorff did, and also Wilhelm II's son and Heir to the Throne Crown Prince Wilhelm—with American flight pioneer Orvile Wright, no less. As noted earlier, Grand Admiral Prince Heinrich learned to fly a plane as well, being awarded a pilot's license. Before the war, German aerial emphasis had been on dirigibles, not fixed wing aircraft. Indeed, the very first German Army balloon detachment had been created in 1884, and in May 1907, there was formally established the Imperial Army Air Service as well. The first German airfields were built in 1909, and on 4 July 1910, the first combat flight pilots began training; later, the first seven airplanes were bought.

On 1 April 1911—the same year that the first aerial combat operations began in the Italo-Turk War in Libya—the Germans founded their initial military aerial high command structure. German military aircraft took part as observers at the fall 1911 annual maneuevers, attended by the Kaiser, and at the year's end, there were 37 military aircraft.

Expansion of airship service and new flying schools soon followed, with formal observer training added. More bases were built in 1913. Training was speeded up in 1914, and the first experimental bombing sights were introduced. The cost of German martial aviation during 1906–1914 was 118 million Reich marks, but when the war broke, German airpower was still inferior to that of France. Belgian Liège was bombed from the air during 6–7 August 1914, but there were also 50 percent aerial losses in that month alone.

Hindenburg asserted that—without aerial observation of his enemy—the Battle of Tannenberg would have been lost, not won, and in October 1914, there was founded the formal Flying Corps of the Eastern Army as a result.

Regarding the now famous fighter planes of the Second Reich, 3,668 frontline German military airplanes were deployed on the Western Front on 21 March 1918 for the final *Michael* offensive, while 307 more were posted in Macedonia, Italy, and the Middle East theaters of war. In early 1918, there were 4,500 air officers and men, with the Kaiser awarding 75 Blue Maxes to the German Army Air Service officers, 27 of whom were later killed. GAAS personnel war losses were 6,840 killed; 7,350 wounded, and 1,372 missing. Aircraft losses were 3,128 airplanes, 546 balloons, and 26 airships.

Although German police forces used aircraft in a restricted way postwar, the Treaty of Versailles from 28 June 1919 destroyed even these last remnants of the GAAS, and it officially ceased to exist on 8 May 1920. The air war also gave the annals of martial aviation the names of many famous German aces who still today outshine those of the Second World War in the public imagination: Manfred and Lothar von Richthofen, Max Immelmann, Oswald Boelcke, Ernst Udet, Hermann Göring, and many others as well.

The Imperial German Navy at War

At war's outbreak, the Imperial Navy had ready 22 pre-*Dreadnought* battleships, 19 *Dreadnought*-class battleships, and seven battlecruisers. The main German Navy forces were the High Seas Fleet, and the U-boat fleet. Smaller fleets were deployed at the German overseas protectorates, the most prominent being that of the East Asian Station at Tsingtao, China, captured by the Japanese early in the war, as were, also, all of Germany's other Pacific Ocean holdings as well, kept by Japan until lost during the Second World War.

The Navy fought many sizable and noteworthy battles, among them being Heligoland Bight, Coronel, the Falkland Islands, Dogger Bank, the Gulf of Riga, Jutland on 31 May 1916—a German victory in terms of losses of men and ships—but a British win relative to overall grand naval strategy of containing the Germans at sea. There was also *Operation Albion* that included Moon Sound, and the First Battle of the Atlantic submarine war. There were as well several minor naval battles, including Gotland, First and Second Dover Straits, Cocos; the raid on Scarborough, Hartlespool, and Whitby; the pursuit of SMS *Goeben* and SMS *Breslau,* the bombardment of Yarmouth and Lowestoft, and Trindale.

The major battle, of course, was that of 31 May 1916 off the Danish coast in the North Sea called Jutland by the Royal Navy's Grand Fleet and the Skaggerak by the German Navy's Imperial High Seas Fleet. Who won? Fully 6,094 British sailors were killed in action, versus 2,551 Germans. The British commander—Admiral Jellicoe—admitted to losing the following:

> The battle cruisers *Queen Mary, Indefatigable,* and *Invincible;* and the cruisers *Defense* and *Black Prince* were sunk.

According to one of the British Admiralty's official press statements:

> The *Warrior* was disabled … and had to be abandoned by her crew. It is also known that the destroyers *Tipperary, Turbulent, Fortune, Sparrowhawk,* and *Ardent* were lost, and six others are not yet accounted for.
> Three of these also lost were HMS *Nestor, Nomad,* and *Shark.*
> The British won the Battle of Jutland, according to the British. In his own after action

reports, Admiral Reinhard Scheer admitted to losing the battle cruiser *Lutzow*, the pre-*Dreadnought Pommern*; the light cruisers *Elbing, Frauenlob, Rostock,* and *Wiesbaden*; as well as five destroyers sunk: *S35, VV4, V27, V29,* and *V48*. Not surprisingly, the Germans also claimed victory.

The Royal Navy Blockade of Germany, 1914–1920

The later vaunted Royal Navy blockade cutting off the "encircled" Reich from all outside supplies was very loose indeed, up to early 1917, for fear of angering the one neutral that counted the most: the United States of America. Once it entered the war on the side of the Allies in 1917, the Royal Navy at last was enabled to mine the North Sea. The real blockade lasted into 1920, months after the Versailles Peace Treaty ended the war officially on 28 June 1919. The remaining 74 ships of the German fleet surrendered to the Royal Navy on 28 November 1918, and scuttled themselves at Scapa Flow on 21 June 1919, by order of the last commander of the German Navy Imperial High Seas Fleet, Rear Admiral Ludwig von Reuter.

By then, the fleet's creator the Kaiser was already living in exile in Holland.

Unrestricted Submarine Warfare Brings America into the War, 1917

Against his better—and correct, no less—political judgment, His Majesty allowed unrestricted German submarine warfare against neutrals in early 1917. By April, this brought the United States into the war on the side of the Allies, just as he both feared and predicted. During the massive battles of 1918, it was the influx of fresh American troops that helped decide the war on the Western Front against Germany.

Total British Empire shipping sunk during the Great War encompassed 7,133,000 tons by submarine, versus 442,000 by surface ships. Great Britain also lost 82 ships—182,000 tons—that were interned in Central Powers ports.

German Naval Aviation at War

Reportedly, the German Navy deployed 14 Zeppelin reconnaissance dirigibles over the North Sea and the Baltic Sea, whereby several Allied vessels were spotted; 1,200 wartime scouting missions were duly flown by 1918, and these also aided in halting Royal Navy raids against the German coastline. There was also a Naval Aviation First Aerial Battle of Britain, whereby on 9 January 1915 the Kaiser approved Zeppelin attacks on cities, excluding London, but it, too, was later assaulted.

Defeat in the East and the West

By the Treaty of Brest-Litovsk, signed on 3 March 1918 Russia was taken out of the war and Imperial Germany came out the winner on the Eastern Front. The last major turning point—the final great *Michael* campaign of March 1918 in the west—was the monarch's final hope to avoid a final German defeat, and he—like both Hindenurg and Ludendorff—staked everything on it.

However, the Second Marne, like the first, was also a German defeat, and again Paris failed to be taken. The Allied counterattack shattered the German Army in August, and by mid-October 1918, the Allies were massing their armies for the destruction of the Hindenburg Line completely. This was to be followed by an invasion of the Reich in 1919. *Der Tag*—The Day of Judgment—seemed, indeed, to be at hand for the Second Reich of Wilhelm II von Hohenzollern.

The Fall of the Kaiser Approaches

In 1901, Wilhelm II proclaimed:

> My Alexander Regiment is called upon to act as a bodyguard both by day and night, to be ready to fight to the death for the King and his Household ... to drive those insolent and unruly subjects before you with your bayonets!

In 1911, he told his men:

> It may come about that I order you to shoot down your own relatives, brothers, or parents, but even then you must follow my orders without a murmur.

In 1888, Bismarck told the young ruler that a true Hohenzollern, "Would rather die fighting—sword in hand on the steps of his throne—than give in!" The Kaiser was informed by the Duo of Hindenburg and Ludendorff that the Allies had driven back the latest German offensive in the West and even managed to crash through their own lines in August 1918.

The Black Day of the German Army, 8 August 1918

Indeed, Ludendorff termed 8 August 1918 as, "The black day of the German Army!" for it was then that he realized that his last throw of the dice *Michael* Offensive of March—also called, "The Kaiser's Battle"—had failed to crush the Allies on the Western Front. The vaunted Hindenburg Line would be cracked wide open, with victorious Allied armies surging ahead. The German Supreme Warlord on 2 September 1918 thundered, "I trust that we shall not give up a single foot of the soil we have won!" Later—at *Schloss Wilhelmshöhe*—The Kaiser slammed his fist on the table and ranted: "Now we have lost the war!" and rushed into the dining room to tell his guests that he had serious, shattering news:

> The 17th Army has suffered a heavy defeat and is being harassed on both flanks. The political effect of such a defeat is disastrous! We have suffered defeat after defeat. Our army is at the end of its tether. The senior officers have all gone. It means nothing more or less than that we have lost the war!

His listeners were stunned, a deathly silence reigning overall. Some tried to console the truly stricken German Emperor. Admiral von Müller—believing little of what he heard—mentioned that they'd been in far worse positions. After a nervous breakdown of 24 hours, His Majesty rebounded, and later in September 1918 at the mammoth Krupp Works at Essen addressed 1,500 steelworkers, many of them Socis, who felt almost nothing for their militaristic, rightwing, archconservative Emperor.

The Kaiser's adjutant Capt. Sigurd von Ilsemann presented His Majesty with a speech text, but Wilhelm II instead spoke off the cuff. The leftist workers hated his very field gray uniform, and when he called them, "My dear friends," their faces asked, "Since when?" For half an hour, a too-excited monarch spoke so fast that his face perspired, and as His Majesty commented on the suffering and starvation of the people, it was obvious to them all that he knew nothing of such things. When Wilhelm asked them to call out, "Yes!" if they were committed to fighting the war to the end, there were only a few who so stated, then furtive laughter, and an overall, awkward stillness from his massed audience. Indeed—after three decades on his once-solid throne, Kaiser Wilhelm II was in deep political trouble at home because of the never-ending war abroad and the now successful Allied naval blockade domestically that kept food out of the war-torn, embattled Second Reich.

He was still Supreme Commander of all the armed forces, but had kept more out of public view far more than he had in peacetime, thus losing contact with his own people. His main wartime appearances had been with and to his soldiers in the field, not civilians. They looked to Hindenburg—if anyone—for salvation, not the absent Kaiser. His day and era was clearly a shade of the past, not the present, much less the future. He had only visited Reich Capital Berlin sporadically during the four wartime years, preferring instead to run his civilian governmental affairs via both telephone and telegraph, much as had Bismarck earlier from both *Varzin* and *Friedrichsruhe*. Out of sight became out of mind.

His Majesty Fires Ludendorff and Resists Abdication

In a fit of extreme anger, on 26 October 1918, the Kaiser fired the despised Ludendorff—a scene well depicted in *Fall of Eagles*—telling von Hindenburg abruptly, "You stay!" As his troops asked forlornly, "Where is the Kaiser?" His Majesty fought off both civilian governmental and military leaders' assertions that he must abdicate his twin thrones as both German Emperor and King of Prussia, if he was to save his ruling dynasty, the House of Hohenzollern, at all. The same was true of his womanizing son, Crown Prince Wilhelm, still commanding his 5th Army Group on the besieged Western Front. Perhaps, it was stated, that one of the Kaiser's grandsons might save the throne in a Regency, until he came of age to rule. This would be within the framework of a new constitutional monarchy along the lines of the House of Windsor in England—shades revived of his long dead parents, the Fredericks. It was not to be, however, for as the Kaiser stubbornly dug in his political heels over the course of late October into early November 1918, events outpaced him in the capital city of Berlin while he remained at KHQ Spa.

The Navy Mutinies, and Revolution Follows

On 29 October 1918, the German Navy—the Kaiser's very own, personal creation— mutinied *en masse* at Kiel, and from there the Revolution spread to every major urban center in the Second Reich. By 5 November 1918, Hamburg, Lübeck, and Bremen had fallen to the councils of soldiers, sailors, and workmen, and two days later, all German cities were in their hands. On 8 November 1918, Bavaria in southern Germany split away from the Reich to form a separatist state under its own monarchy, and Bismarck's work was thus undone after only 47 years.

The majority of the revolutionaries were not Reds, however—nor even Socialists—but those who just wanted an end to the interminable war. The Social Democratic Party—long hated foes—took over the government. Announced prematurely by Prince Max and the Socis was both the end of the House of Hohenzollern in its entirety, and also of all the lesser German ruling houses that had created the German Empire. The Allies—particularly US President Woodrow Wilson—had made it known publicly that only the person of the hated Kaiser Wilhelm II himself stood between the German people and an honorable peace. This, however, turned out to be one of modern history's great deceptions. The Kaiser had to go, his people murmured. In historical retrospect, it has been argued that Wilson's pressing for the Kaiser's removal was a grave mistake, as it left an abnormal power vacuum in defeated Germany that was filled first in 1925 by von Hindenburg, and in 1933–34 by Corporal Hitler. It is difficult to imagine Hitler coming to office as Imperial Chancellor under Wilhelm II, as he did under Reich President von Hindenburg, alas.

When the terms of the 28 June 1919 Versailles Peace Treaty were published, the Kaiser accurately predicted in astute political terms—forseeing another war of 1939—"The war to end wars has resulted in a peace to end peace." As a final swipe at the Kaiser, on 19 November 1918, German Admiral Reuter led a 50 kilometer-long procession of German warships in column to surrender to the Royal Navy at Scapa Flow in Scotland. Germany was permitted to retain six small battleships, six light cruisers, 12 destroyers, and 12 torpedo boats, but all of the deadly U-boats had to be surrendered. As a concluding irony of the sea war, the pre-*Dreadnought* Royal Navy battleship HMS *Britannia* was torpedoed and sunk off Cap Trafalgar by a U-boat on 9 November 1918, as His Majesty was leaving for his exile in the Netherlands.

12

At Berlin & Spa
Autumn 1918

On the evening of 9 November 1918, the Kaiser sat down in shock—after having celebrated the 30th year of his reign but six months before, on 15 June—to write the following letter to the eldest of his six sons, Crown Prince Wilhelm, the 36-year-old Army commander, his dynastic Heir:

Dear Boy,

Since the Field Marshal [*Hindenburg*] can no longer guarantee my security here [*at Imperial General Headquarters at Spa*] and since he also will no longer assume responsibility for the loyalty of the troops—I have decided, after severe inward struggle, to leave the collapsed army.

    Berlin is totally lost in the hands of the Socialists, and two governments have already been formed there, one by [*Friedrich*] Ebert as Reich Chancellor, and another at the same time by Independents … Your deeply grieved father, Wilhelm.

The Suddenness of the Long Expected Imperial and Royal Collapse

As recently as March 1918, it had appeared that the German offensive on the Western Front had at last broken the back of the Allied lines and ended the trench warfare and stalemate that had existed since the fall of 1914. Then—in the fourth grim year of the war—it looked like the Central Powers might yet prevail after all, as an elated Kaiser had learned that, "90,000 British soldiers and 1,300 guns" had allegedly been taken. Indeed, on returning that night on the Imperial train to Charleville, the Kaiser was so excited that he shouted to the guard on the platform, "The battle is won! The English have been utterly defeated!'" but it was an illusion that soon faded in the light of stiff Allied resistance and renewed counterattacks.

    Thus the euphoria of 18 March 1918 passed, but still the German Army was fighting everywhere on foreign and not German soil, and might yet regroup for fresh campaigns in 1918. There were still the years 1919, 1920, and 1921 to think of militarily, but that would also mean more and more trained American Army troops crossing the Atlantic Ocean safely every day. No matter what they did, Germany's political and military leaders were convinced that they could not win the war in the long run, and that their beloved western Reich would be invaded by foreign armies for the first time since Napoleon in 1813.

The Spectre of Murder by the Reds Ala' Nicholas II in Russia

This was no idle fear, as just the previous July 1918 the Romanov Tsar Nicholas II and his entire immediate family had been brutally murdered by the Reds in Russia. Willy's own first love—Princess Ella, sister to the later murdered Tsarina Alexandra—had also been murdered by the Bosheviks, and her mutilated body thrown down a well. Rightfully so, both the Kaiser and his circle dreaded such a possibility happening to him and his at the hands of murderous German Reds. The problem was: where to go? Aside from Sweden, there were two other neutral destinations to which Wilhelm II might flee to safety and seek political asylum: Switzerland and Holland, with the latter being much closer. He opted, therefore, for The Netherlands. A further problem was that Red soldiers might have already seized the railway lines, and so seize His Majesty *en route*, just as, indeed, had the Russians in early 1917 when the Tsar was returning from the front to his capital, St Petersburg. Time, therefore, was critically of the essence.

The Kaiser as a Reluctant Holland-Bound Traveler

On the early morning of 10 November 1918, the famous cream-gold-and-blue Imperial train was steaming toward neighboring neutral Holland, as the now Royal fugitive prepared to give up two thrones and cross the Dutch border as an exile in a foreign land. How had such an event come to pass?

At first, the Kaiser adamantly refused to abdicate, vowing that he would die fighting with his troops, living up to the credo of his dead enemy, Bismarck. His lucid and compelling argument against abdication was:

> Very well, supposing I did. What do you suppose would happen? My sons have assured me that none of them will take my place, so the whole House of Hohenzollern would go along with me!
>
> And who would then take on the Regency for a 12-year-old child, my grandson—the Imperial Chancellor perhaps? I gather from Munich that they haven't the least intention of recognizing him down there! [*in Bavaria*] So what would happen?

"Chaos!" he was rightly told.

> All right then, let me tell you the form the chaos would take. I abdicate. All the dynasties fall along with me, the Army is left leaderless, the frontline troops disband, and stream over the Rhine, the disaffected gang up together, hang, murder, plunder, assisted by the enemy!
>
> That is why I have no intention of abdicating!

He was then informed by almost all his chief military advisors—from von Hindenburg on down—that, indeed, there were no more loyal troops left with which to carry on the fight either domestically or at the fronts. He was told, moreover, that his presence on German soil would provoke civil war, with German slaying German in bitter and bloody fighting. He would become, "The Cartridge Kaiser."

General Groener secretly expressed another idea:

He should go to the front—not to review troops or confer decorations—but to look on death. If he were killed, it would be the finest death possible. If he were killed or wounded, the feelings of the German people toward him would completely change. He should go to some trench that was under the full blast of war.

Informed curtly by General Groener that his troops would neither fight for him nor follow his lead homeward, Wilhelm II reflected that no such words had ever before been uttered to a reigning King of Prussia or sitting German Emperor!

His famed blue eyes blazing in anger, Wilhelm shot back:

Excellency! I shall require a statement from you in black and white—signed by all my generals—that the Army no longer stands behind its Commander-in-Chief! Have they not taken the military oath to me?

General Groener sadly answered with words that would haunt him for the rest of his life until his death at age 71 in 1939: "In circumstances like these, Sire, oaths are but words."

The Lightning Strike from Berlin

While "the Field Marshal" was agreeing with General Groener at Spa, there was more humiliation in store from the Reich's capital, Berlin. His Majesty's abdication was duly announced there from both his thrones at once.

Prince Max had resigned the Chancellorship and—on his own authority—had asked Socialist Friederich Ebert to take over, then said they should set up a Regency. However, the other Socis present—seeing their chance for real power at last—began chanting in unison, "Too late! Too late!"

Meanwhile, Soci Reichstag Deputy Philipp Scheidemann was eating a bowl of soup in the legislators' restaurant. The main fear of the Majority Socis was that—once the Hohenzollerns and other dynasties were overthrown—the German Communist Party, the Spartacists (named after the slave revolt versus ancient Rome)—would forestall them, declare a Red state, thus inciting civil war. Some workers and soldiers rushed in, demanding that Scheidemann address the large crowd outside. Karl Liebknecht—leader of the Radical Socialists—was even then speaking from the balcony of the Royal Palace, planning to announce a Soviet Republic. Leaving his soup, Schiedemann rushed to the balcony of the Reichstag's reading room, climbing to its ballustrade, having an associate hold his ankles as he spoke:

Fellow citizens! Workers! Fellow Party men! The monarchical system has collapsed. Many of the garrisons have joined us. The Hohenzollerns have left! Long live the great German Republic!

To stormy applause from below, having just announced the first German republic on his own authority alone, Scheidemann returned and finished his soup. He died in 1939.

The world press picked up the story, and its publication helped create the eventual, actual reality. Wilhelm's rage was boundless, and he never forgave Prince Max:

> Treason, gentlemen! Barefaced, outrageous treason! I am King of Prussia, and I will remain King! As such, I will stay with the troops!

At 5 p.m. that night of 9 November 1918, Hindenburg instead decided to accept the Berlin proclamation with the Friedrich Ebert government as the new political reality, and also advised the Kaiser to go to the nearest neutral country—Holland—by the Imperial train. Casting a withering glance at General Groener, the stricken monarch blurted out, "You no longer have a Warlord," refusing to ever speak to him again. To the downcast von Hindenburg, the Kaiser asked angrily, "Do you think I am afraid to remain with my troops? Signal one of the entourage to make preparations for the journey." Admiral Scheer mumbled that the Fleet's loyalty was likewise very much in doubt, to which an infuriated Wilhelm II retorted, "I no longer have a Navy!"

The Decision for the Final Dutch Journey

On this basis, His Majesty decided to abdicate at last in neutral Holland, a decision bitterly criticized later by both contemporary politicans and historians as, "running away." As the Crown Prince also later fled to Holland and abdicated, it meant the total collapse of the Hohenzollern Dynasty at one fell swoop, after more than three centuries of rule, first in Brandenburg-Prussia, and then in Germany as a whole.

In 1935, Wilhelm's handpicked Doorn biographer—von Kürenberg—told the former last German Emperor to his face upon being asked to do so that his flight to the Netherlands, "Was wrong!" Von Kürenberg and all others were and are entitled to their opinions, but they were not the ones on the spot at the time whose unenviable task it was to have to make such a weighty decision under such great duress. Nor was it their families who might be massacred in barbaric fashion, and and humiliated in captivity—the fate of French Queen Marie Antoinette comes to mind. One may at least grant Wilhelm II some sympathetic consideration on this score.

Bismarck opined that his Young Master had, "No sense of proportion," and possibly a good deal of his reported nervousness was due to a reportedly dull home life with his first wife, the Kaiserin Augusta Victoria, nicknamed Dona. Again—according to Bismarck—she satisfied him sexually, but John C. G. Röhl in his books and others now note both his pre-marital and extramarital affairs with other women, and possibly also with men. Once as he sat up late reading, she stayed at his side sewing. Suddenly, he asked, "Do you mean to spend the night here?" "No, Wilhelm, but I didn't want to disturb you as you've been so busy reading the whole evening."
"What else could I do? It's so incredibly dull here."
Certainly the Kaiser is neither the first nor the last man to treat his wife this way, but he

always knew that she loved him and had only his best interests at heart, and this feeling for her only deepened during the grim war years, when most of the news he got was bad—and getting worse. Still, the Kaiser always repaired to Dona in an hour of need, and she overlooked these slights, realizing his true feelings for her. When alone with him, he would pour out his heart to his devoted wife for hours. When they were separated, the Kaiser wrote her long daily letters.

In addition, she was one of but three humans—the other two being his longtime valet, Schulz, and his second wife, Empress Hermine—who most likely saw his naked left arm after he married the first time, an intimacy not to be discounted.

Dona—anti-liberal, anti-English, anti-drinking, gambling, and adultery; anti-Reichstag and Soci, anti-Prince Max, pro-Duo, and the champion of the Kaiser retaining all of his rights, privileges, and powers no matter what—backed him up, always. She remained faithful to him in 40 years of marriage to the day she died. Her successor the second wife had nothing bad to say about either her or her second husband in her published 1928 memoirs, either.

Dona emerged in her own right as one of his most trusted top advisors by 1908, when she successfully—alone—prevented him from abandoning his crown during the First Abdication Crisis. She might have done the same again during the second a decade later, had she been at Spa instead of at Potsdam, where she bravely stood up to the Revolutionaries when they plundered their New Palace. She followed Wilhelm to Holland only on 28 November 1918—the very day he signed his abdication papers—and it is felt she was only released on condition that he do so, she being sent into her Dutch exile aboard a train flying the Red flag. Her leaving for Holland set the final seal on the fall of the monarchy. Some have felt that—had she stayed in Germany, she might have served as the focus for a monarchist restoration movement; conversely, she would also most likely have been savagely murdered by the Reds.

Still, her advisers considered her leaving a grave political mistake, but entirely characteristically, Dona went to the side of the man she loved at her earliest possible instant, entirely putting aside all of the weighty political implications. Like her husband when leaving, she did the right thing. Their last two years were probably the best of their long marriage, a final marital happiness that both found after they had lost their throne and even their country forever. Oddly, theirs is a love story that has yet to be fully told. Then as now, Dona has been disdained by the more "modern" women of both her and our own times as not "their kind" of woman, i.e., an engaged political feminist. It is very much to her credit, however, that she was admired by the German people both before and after her death, and no less by her major daughter-in-law, Crown Princess Cecilie, and her husband's own second wife. How many women of any era can claim that? A study of their life together is long overdue, and, I hope, will be forthcoming soon.

Suffering from a heart condition, Dona had a stroke on 18 August 1918, in the wake of the news of the war being lost. The Kaiser spent three weeks away from headquarters to personally care for her, much to the fury of his angered inner circle.

Imperium Germanicum: What if the Kaiser had Won the Great War?

Here is what Fischer concluded in his groundbreaking work of 1961 would have been the outcome of a German rather than an Allied victory. In the west, Belgium, Luxembourg, and Longwy-Briey in northern France would all have been annexed to Germany to create an economic dependency of both France herself and Holland, too, plus to isolate beaten Britain, thus forcing her to recognize Germanys' position. In the east, Kurland, Livonia, Estonia, and Lithuania from Reval to Riga and Vilno, adding the Polish Frontier Strip plus Rump Poland, would all also be closely bound to Germany, economically, politically, and in foreign relations.

In the southeast, Austria-Hungary would be throughly "clamped into Germany as a cornerstone," then Rumania and Bulgaria, as well as the Ottoman Empire as part of Germany's Asiatic fiat.

The naval sway over the eastern Mediterranean Sea would force Greece to submit to the German yoke as well, and in addition seize the Suez Canal from Britain, with Reich domination of the Black Sea securing the economic mastery of Ukraine, the Crimea, and Georgia. The nautical command of the Baltic Sea would force Sweden and Finland—with their riches—to become yet other satellite states within the iron clasp of the Teutonic orbit.

Rump Russia would be at the mercy of the victorious Central Powers. With Middle Europe surrounded by German dominated vassal states, the fully realized Central African Colonial Empire would be safeguarded by German naval bases linked to the Near East via the Sudan and the German Suez Canal.

German Africa—reinforced with control of all strategic and technical key points *en route* to South America for even more expansion—wouls see the Reich consolidate her gains, thus making herself at last the colonial and economic power of truly world status that Kaiser Wilhelm II lusted for all his life.

Focusing on the black German African Imperium, however, meant no withdrawal from the Eastern Hemisphere of the vast Pacific Ocean. Imperial Germany would also expand her interests in Samoa, New Guinea, and China.

By ceding Kiachow to Japan, the Second Reich would renew her old connections with that country against both Russia and the Anglo-Saxon states, still in existence, regarding future wars.

Germany's political and economic *imperium* would have a critical mass of raw, naked might far surpassing Bismarck's relatively puny 1871 empire—another of the Kaiser's main life goals—both in natural and human material.

The old industrial regions of the Ruhr and Luxembourg, the Saar, German Lorraine, Saxony, and Upper Silesia would be buttressed by French Lorraine, Belgium, Poland, and Bohemia.

For iron ore—besides her own production and the assured imports of coopted Sweden— the German Reich would draw on those of Austria, Poland, Longwy-Briey, Ukraine, the Caucasus, Turkey, and Katanga in black Africa.

To Galician oil would be added Rumanian, Caucasian, and Mesopotamian rich oil preserves. To the Fatherland's own agricultural production, that of the Balkans and the northeast would be taken; to the previous colonial imports from Africa would be commandeered the tremendous produce of Central Africa. Markets before contested would be replaced by a monopoly in Georgia, Turkey, Russia, Ukraine, the Balkans, the northest, north, and west. The new, all-powerful German Reich would be in an impregnable and uncontested position of global economic power, with all economic agreements safeguarded by ironclad and rigid military pacts.

Martial conventions with Finland, the Baltic States, Lithuania, Poland, Ukraine, Georgia, Turkey, Bulgaria, Rumania, and Austria-Hungary—and in the negative sense with subjugated Belgium—would become fact, had been planned, and even initialed in summer 1918 by the Kaiser, no disinterested observer he.

Via the above economic, political, and military chains, Imperial Germany would lead a European power bloc putting her for the first time on par with the triad of world powers of America, Britain, and—if it could still be counted—Russia—providing the Greater Germanic Reich a rank far, far above that of any European power of any previous imperium, bar none.

The Actual Reality...

As it was, the Kaiser reigned for more than 30 years, but if he had continued to rule until his death in 1941, his overall rule of 53 years would have been comparable to that of his grandmother, Queen Victoria. The succeeding 10-year reign of his son and Heir Kaiser Wilhelm III would have lasted until his death in 1951.

Who can tell what 33 more years of Hohenzollern rule under those conditions might have done? It was not to be, however, as the achievement of this global aim depended entirely on victory in the west, where the new, unused power of America came to the aid of the British, French, and Belgian Armies, and together they stopped Kaiser Wilhelm II dead in his tracks. The Allies won the war, and the Kaiser lost it, ending all of any *Imperium Germanicum* until the great Iron Dice of war were rolled again, in 1939.

Far less known—but equally dead on—is this follow-up cartoon entitled, *The Haunted Ship*, also from *Punch*, 31 March 1915. (*LC*)

PART 4

Kaiser-in-Waiting and Exiled Memoir Author 1918–1941

The Undisclosed Decision:-
News Note: England and Holland have come to a decision regarding the Ex-Kaiser, 1 May 1919.
A contemporary cartoon by Clifford K. Berryman. (*Publisher Archive*)

13

The Kaiser in Holland
1918

Arriving by car on 10 November 1918 at the Belgian-Dutch border—according to a *Time* cover story of 28 June 1926—A Dutch soldier—guarding the frontier at Eysden—was struck dumb when a man in a long military cloak approached him, hesitated, and said, "I am the Emperor of Germany. Here is my sword."

The startled sentry telephoned The Hague. Queen Wilhelmina took the news by summoning her Cabinet, as the Kaiser for the first time ever cooled his heels at the border. Six hours later, the defeated Supreme Warlord was informed that he might enter neutral Holland, the very same country that years before his generals had secretly planned to invade. He had never waited before.

His own Imperial train came to the frontier to provide a temporary residence for His Majesty and entourage until a more definite site could be found for them all.

Dutch Count Godard Bentinck—like His Majesty, a fellow Knight of the Order of St John—agreed to the Kaiser's written request for shelter for himself and his aides. They met for the first time on 11 November 1918, Armistice Day on the Western Front, where the guns fell silent at last.

His stay at the Count's Castle at Amerongen—initially set for three days—lasted 18 months, ending in May 1920. As Amerongen was then in some danger of flooding, the Kaiser's enemies hoped that he might drown there.

The American Attempt to Kidnap the Kaiser, 5 January 1919

US Army Col. Lukas "Luke" Lea—a serving US Senator from Tennessee—and seven other officers hatched a plot to kidnap His Majesty and present him as a present to their President Wilson in Paris. With passports and two cars, they bluffed their way into Count Bentinck's house late on the evening of 5 January 1919.

They were halted by the searching questions of the Count at the door, even as the awakened Kaiser was dressing upstairs! Secretly, the town's mayor was called in, followed by 10 policemen and Dutch Army soldiers.

Confessing the real purpose of their visit, the men were taken by the Dutch to the frontier and sent on their way, but the news created a worldwide sensation anyway. There was fear of a second kidnap plot, a possible Red assassination attempt on the life of the Kaiser, and even a report that a Belgian plane might bomb Amerongen. A far more serious and actual threat to Wilhelm II's future emerged, however.

"The Kaiser Crisis:" His Majesty as Alleged War Criminal

In Article 27 of the Treaty of Versailles, the German Kaiser was indicted, "For a supreme offense against international morality and the sanctity of treaties."

On 4 June 1919, the Allied Supreme Council at Paris agreed he should be brought to trial at Dover or London—or possibly on one of the English Channel Islands—while another trial site venue proposed was at the Vatican, but rejected by the Pope. In both World Wars, the Papacy proved itself sympathetic to defeated German war criminals. In the end, only Britain held out for extradition and trial, while all the other Allies wanted no part of it. Officially, however, Holland was threatened with economic sanctions and possibly war by the Allies if she refused. The Dutch rejected the Allied demands of 16 January 1920 and thereafter. The "Kaiser Crisis" reached its greatest intensity by 19 February 1920, and ended when Lloyd George gave up his quest on 24 March 1920.

Knowing the fate of the Gallic leader Vercingetorix—who surrendered honorably to Julius Caesar, only to be strangled in a Roman jail cell—the Kaiser refused to surrender himself, the example of Napoleon I also being recalled.

His entourage was determined that His Majesty should not fall into enemy hands at all costs. When he refused to consider suicide, there were dark mutterings that he might be shot by an aide if about to fall prisoner to the Allies or others.

Several impractical escape plans were made, but never undertaken, and the former Emperor thus allowed his famous upturned moustache ends to droop, even growing a beard for disguise that remained to his end, thus giving his facial features a softer cast.

In December 1919, the Dutch government asked him to leave Holland, but he remained, steadfastly secure behind the walls of his self-imposed prison, his letters and those of his family read by the local authortities, the house telephone tapped. He was fenced in, and guarded by Dutch Army sentries, day and night.

Other Exile Sites Considered

Many other exile site locations were suggested by his foes: St Helena (for the UK's hated "new Napoleon"), the Falkland Islands, Java, or Curaçao—in The Netherlands' West Indies. Corfu, Algiers, Chile, Peru, and Argentina—even the notorious French prison of Devil's Island made the list, but he never resided at any of them.

14

At Doorn, Holland
1920–1941

On 16 August 1919, the Kaiser purchased Doorn House and its surrounding park, paying $200,000 that His Majesty did not yet have in hand, his word being accepted that the debt would be paid when his accounts in Germany were settled, as they duly were. On 15 May 1920, Wilhelm and Dona gave Count Bentinck their thanks and moved to Doorn five miles away. Indoor plumbing had had to be installed, as well as an elevator for the ill Dona, and a marble staircase from the New Palace at Potsdam was also transferred, to make the exiled Hohenzollerns feel more "at home."

The Kaiser appointed German Navy Admiral Magnus von Levetzow as his Imperial agent in Berlin, as by the terms of the signed Abdication, he himself was never allowed on German soil again. He settled in, importing furniture, books, and artwork of his ancestors from Germany—according to one source, a full 50 train cars' worth. Here he spent the remaining 21 years of his life as the retired country gentleman he had always swore he wanted to be. He got his wish at last. His Majesty had visited Dutch Queen Wilhelmina before the war, but she never called upon him at Doorn, the Royal exile being a hot potato in Dutch domestic politics. The Dutch people forgot their initial hostility to both the Kaiser and former Crown Prince Wilhelm in their midst, though, and they were accepted as friendly neighbors in time.

The Crown Prince settled in Holland the day after his father, on 12 November 1918, being sent to a small cottage called *The Parsonage* on the Isle of Wieringen in the Zuyder Zee. He signed his own Abdication on 1 December 1918, again a few days after his father. There were never any Allied calls for his extradition and trial as a war criminal.

No longer was His Majesty booed by hostile crowds as he had been along his 1918 ride into Holland, nor was there much further fear of possible Red assassins.

The Imperial Prisoner at Doorn and Dona's Demise, 11 April 1921

At first, the Kaiser was personally restricted to his grounds at Doorn, but in time, this was relaxed, and he was permitted to travel in his brand new, gray Mercedes-Benz touring car in the home Province of Utrecht, and later on throughout Holland if he wished. His former "traveling Kaiser" days were gone; nor did he ever hunt or ride horseback again.

When Dona died, the shattered Kaiser and his five still living sons in full uniform watched her coffin placed on the Imperial train for burial in now Weimar Republican Germany, but the Dutch government refused permission for the Imperial Exile to accompany the train to the frontier, and he was near collapse as it pulled away. Dona was buried in Berlin at the Antike Temple, seen by the largest monarchist demonstration since before the lost war.

"Hang the Kaiser!"—Lloyd George During England's "Khaki Election"

Continued *Time* magazine's 28 June 1926 cover story entitled, *Wilhelm der Zweite: Ballots for Bullets* under *Foreign News*, "Mr Lloyd George—having actually won an election with the slogan, 'Hang the Kaiser!'...' Wilhelm of Doorn, Herr Hohenzollern having already received from the Reich a sum equivalent to $1,000 for every day since his abdication...."

Finances of an Ex-Emperor, 1918–1926

In her 1928 memoirs, the later Kaiserin Hermine disputed this figure, asserting that at Doorn the residents were forced by near poverty and the German inflation of 1923 to lead frugal lives, an assertion disputed in turn by the Kaiser's biographers: he both lived and died a wealthy man all his life. On the other hand, the Kaiser arrived in Holland with no money— his aides asserted—and only uniforms, as all his civilian clothes were stolen by looters of his castles back at home. Nor had he transferred any of his fortune abroad, never feeling it was necessary, according to writer Sally Marks in 2001.

The former Kaiser did not make the same mistake at the onset of the Second World War: between October 1939–January 1940, Wilhelm II transferred two-thirds of his personal money to Swiss banks. She also quotes Karnebeck as stating that his 18 months' of Amerongen expenses were met by $80,000 that he had brought with him, and then from the sale of jewels and paintings.

In January 1919, the Prussian government periodically sent unspecified large amounts from Wilhelm's private fortune. This "shrank alarmingly" due to German inflation, as attested to in her 1928 memoir by Princess Hermine. Reportedly, the Prussian Ministry of Finance paid the former Kaiser over 45 million marks ($5.5 million) in January 1919; another $538,000 in August 1919, and a further $373,000, mainly to fund the Doorn estate, in October 1919, with about $4 million more being realized by the sale of two of his Berlin properties, plus "other figures, many disputed." This could be a separate book, and fascinating to boot!

How an Englishwoman Viewed the Ex-Kaiser in his Dutch Exile, 1920

The English-born authoress Lady Norah Bentinck attended the wedding at Amerongen on 7 October 1920 of His Majesty's ADC Capt. Sigurd von Ilsemann to Dutch Countess Elizabeth Bentinck, and thus got her first close-up full sighting of the ex-Kaiser:

> Suddenly—without any warning—two tall attendants, in long blue coats and tricorn hats, and with silver-topped staves, flung open the big double doors and announced, "The Kaiser!" ... A slight, stiffly erect figure in the uniform of a German field marshal took two short, quick steps into the room, halted near the door with a smart click of the heels, gave

a rapid succession of slight, jerky bows to right and left, and then … looked restlessly and uncertainly around the room.

He held a helmet tucked against his right side by his right arm, and his left hand pushed forward slightly the hilt of a sword that had clattered as he entered …. It was a gray man we gazed upon—gray of dress … face … hair, and steely of eye … The moustache, long and drooping at the ends, was a shade whiter; the eyebrows … were gray; the hair thick and wavy … with an unruly tuft standing up near the front …

He had small ears and, was rather short [*actually, he was 5′ 10″ tall*] …. This was the first occasion on which he'd appeared in uniform since his abdication … His friends received a short handshake accompanied by a click of the heels … His glance was always darting here and there …

Majestat … but the impressions was that of a quiet, elderly man, friendly and genial in manner, and without any pose, for by now the ice was broken, and he was quite at ease.

Wilhelm II as 'The Woodcutter of Doorn"

The first Hohenzollern family reunion was held at Doorn in May 1920 to celebrate the Kaiser's new residence, that had 15 rooms in a park of 100 acres, with nearby Doorn Village being home to about 2,000 neighbors, about five miles northwest of Amerongen, and about 30 miles from the German-Dutch frontier.

The now landed gentleman chopped wood for exercise daily, drank "good English— actually Scottish— tea," and refought the battles of the past both during his armchair evenings, and from his published memoirs, but as a widower, he truly missed his late wife.

Wrote an aide:

It was heart-rending to see the man who was once the most powerful ruler in Christendom slowly ascend—a gray and lonely figure—the steep stairs to his room. His little court was unable to make him forget his unutterable grief for the loss of his helpmate.

As his late mother had done in cases of family bereavement, so, too, did her son order the dead Empress' room locked, and kept exactly as she had left it, with all her much treasured, intimate photographs and books in their proper places. Every day for the rest of his life, the aging former monarch visited her sacred room, bowed his head, and prayed—for forgiveness?

Comes the Second Empress!

The Kaiser remarried on 5 November 1922, to Princess Hermine of Reuss, the widow of of the Prince Schönaich-Carolath, who had died during the war after a long illness. The Princess attests in her most interesting memoirs that she had worshipped His Majesty since she first met him as a child during his heyday.

Six months before, her second young son had written the Kaiser a letter, and he invited the boy and his mother to Doorn. She came by herself, and within a week, the two were engaged to be married. As with the late Empress at first, this second marriage was not a love match, but one of convenience for both: she was 34 and he 63, but they had many things in common, so it worked, despite the normal bickerings in all such unions, then and now.

Reportedly, Wilhelm's children and the Doorn staff took a different view: "She was argumentative, lively, tactless, and aggressive. No one in the Kaiser's household liked her," asserted one.

"She was hard, ambitious, and trouble-making; she had prompted her child to write the Kaiser in order to trap him; she had proposed to the Emperor herself, and married him because she believed that the Hohenzollerns would one day be restored to the throne," as did he. No surprises there! In her own 1928 account, "Hermo" as she was known, denied all. It was ghost written by the American German journalist George Sylvester Vierieck, to whom Wilhelm allegedly confided that the Empress Hermine, "Saved my reason, if not my life."

The Kaiser's first hopes for the Restoration to his thrones died with the failure of the rightwing Kapp *Putsch* in Berlin of 12 March 1920, but he still began many sentences with, "When I return to Germany."

In spite of the entourage's efforts to bring him to reality, the Kaiser envisaged a Russian invasion of Germany via Poland, followed by a mass monarchist revolt, and thence his chance to return home, and to his ancient throne. This was not as far-fetched as it seems, either, as both the Nazis feared such, and the anti-Hitler plotters desired a Hohenzollern restoration. After all, his grandfather the Cartridge Prince had returned, and so had Napoleon I. It was possible, but never likely. Hope sprang eternal, as it always does…

Kaiserin Hermine and the Nazis

His Majesty was skeptical of the new nationalist party in Germany, the Nazis, writing to von Mackensen, "The new Reich will not come from a beer joint!" referring to Hitler's failed 1923 Beer Hall *Putsch*, but it did, a decade later. The new Kaiserin Hermine was, however, pro-Hitler, mainly because she believed that—once in office—the Nazis would restore the Hohenzollern Dynasty to the Imperial throne, which the *Führer* shrewdly allowed her to think until the Third Reich was firmly established. Hitler's paladin—former First World War air ace Hermann Göring—said as much to them on his pair of secret pre-1933 visits to Doorn to meet privately with his Supreme Warlord: on 18–19 September 1931, and again the following May 1932, to induce His Majesty to support his former corporal, A. Hitler.

The last German Emperor was doubtful, though, considering Göring, "A vain creature, a mere Army captain who would be consigned to obscurity once he remounted his throne." The Crown Prince agreed, asserting, "I know my Göring: he's a windbag!" and was proven right. Hitler himself never came, however, to visit the living Kaiser, but did send a funeral wreath in 1941.

When it became clear in 1937 that there would never be a Hohenzollern Restoration under the National Socialists, Kaiserin Hermine cooled to them. Göring did, however, enact a final financial settlement with the Hohenzollerns that paid them not to criticize Nazi Germany, and to this they adhered until 1945, at least publicly.

Sunset for the Hohenzollerns, 1929–51

The Kaiser's brother Prince Heinrich died in 1929 at the age of 67. When the Germans took Paris in 1940, Wilhelm II's final political act was to send Hitler a congratulatory telegram. Holland had by then also been occupied by the German Army. Churchill had previously offered His Majesty asylum in Britain, but Wilhelm II remained instead with the people who had granted him a safe home when it was most needed, the Dutch. In May 1940, German Army sentries replaced those of the Dutch at the gates to Doorn House, and once again—for the first time since 1918—the Kaiser found himself guarded by soldiers of his native land wearing the old field gray uniforms. Respectful delegations of officers came to pay their respects to the last German Emperor. Hitler was miffed.

Taps for His Majesty, 1941

The Kaiser died at the age of 82 on 5 June 1941, and was buried on the grounds at Doorn as he willed in 1933. A military funeral was held on the Doorn House grounds and both the Crown Prince and Field Marshal von Mackensen attended, with the Third Reich being represented by its Nazi Governor General of Occupied Holland, the Austrian lawyer Dr Artur von Seyss-Inquart, hanged by the Allies five years later as a convicted war criminal at Nürnberg.

According to the *Huis Doorn* website, Crown Prince Wilhelm had German architect Martin Kieszling design a mausoleum:

> Amidst his beloved rhododendrons in the park … On the roof is a brass ball with a cross on top of it, made secretly by a Doorn blacksmith from old copper cooking pots from the kitchen. During the Second World War, copper had to be turned in to the German occupier, who used it to make guns.

Noted writer Tony Paterson in *The Independent* on 18 November 2012:

> His mummified corpse is draped with a flag displaying the Black Eagle of Prussia. On the manicured lawn outside the white mausoleum containing his remains, a stone plaque marks the grave of his dog *Senta,* that accompanied him throughout the catastrophe of the First World War….

"We do everything we can to keep the house exactly as it was when the Kaiser lived here," explained Doorn's Director Eymert-Jan Goosens.

Finale for the Kaiser's Second Empress, 1947

Sally Marks provides this intriguing statement with no further details: "Hermine, banished from Doorn by the Crown Prince…" returned to her Silesian estate in East Germany that was seized by the invading Russian Red Army in 1945.

She was kept as its political prisoner, "At the Paulinenhof Internment Camp near

Brandenburg," reportedly. She died instead, though, at age 59, in a small flat at Frankfurt while under Red Army guard on 7 August 1947.

Like the Kaiser's first Empress, Kaiserin Hermine, too, was buried at Potsdam's *Antike Tempel*—*"interred beside Dona,"* asserts Marks—as a German Empress *in* Germany at last, her dream thus realized. A few hours after her funeral—as reported on 16 August 1947 in the *New York Times*—her son Prince Ferdinand was arrested as a secret Nazi Party member when he tried to get a job as a chauffeur with the occupying British Army. Nazi Party membership files showed that he had joined the NSDAP on 1 August 1932.

Empress Hermine and the Kaiser had no children of their own, but in 1940, Hermine's youngest daughter Princess Henriette—nicknamed "The General"— married one of his grandsons, and that Hohenzollern couple did.

House Doorn in 1945, and Curtains for the Kaiser's Children

The German armed forces were routed from occupied Holland by the Allies in 1945, and the restored Dutch government seized Doorn as enemy property. Today it remains as a memorial to the Kaiser and his life. Its seizure prevented the ex-Crown Prince from selling the property to raise money, as he had other such domains.

In 1951, the ex-Crown Prince Wilhelm followed his father to the grave at the age of 69, also having survived both the Nazis and French internment at the war's end. His brothers all died as well. His youngest brother Joachim died as a suicide by pistol shot on 18 July 1920, preceding his mother, Dona; Prince Eitel-Fritz at the age of 59 in 1942 at Potsdam; Adalbert, aged 64, in 1948 at his Swiss home; Prince August Wilhelm—the "Nazi Prince" at the age of 62 in 1949, and—the last of the six sons—Prince Oskar, at the age of 70, in Munich on 27 January 1958, on his late father's 99th birthday. His Majesty's only daughter—Princess of Prussia and Grand Duchess of Brunswick Victoria Luise---passed away in 1980 at age 88.

The Kaiser and His Prior Biographers, Old, Newer, and Current

The first major biography of His Majesty was published by the famed German-Jewish author, Emil Ludwig Cohn, whose work appeared in 1927. He tried to cast the Kaiser's life in a pre-ordained, tragic mold, a sort of prolonged birth defect. He sees everything through one pair of glasses: to every question, there is the ultimate answer, The Arm. He shows extreme bias—but does not admit it—for Bismarck (whom he admired), and against the Kaiser's parents … and his son Wilhelm, the Crown Prince. He does, however, make a concrete attempt at objectivity … in one respect:

> For fairness' sake … we here design *to let no adversary of the Emperor bear witness,* but to construct our portrait wholly from his own deeds and words, together with the reports of those who stood in close relation to him … his relatives and friends, his Chancellors, Ministers, and Generals, his courtiers and officials.

A more modern and reasoned approach appeared in 1963 with Virginia Cowles, and this continued up through Giles MacDonough in 2001, and beyond, to now. Still, his Wilhelm II emerges as, "An actor, striving for effect," but what politician is not?

Among the more current biographers of the Kaiser, there stands John C. G. Röhl, the final volume of his magisterial trilogy having just appeared in 2014.

Afterword: The Kaiser Today—and Tomorrow? 1941–2014

It is unfortunate that his grandfather vetoed Prince Wilhelm's desire to visit the United States, India, and Australia, but would it have made any difference? Maybe, maybe not, but who knows? After all, he was the most traveled ruler in history during his age, and that still did not prevent the Great War. Neither did his brother's trip to Theodore Roosevelt's United States, nor his eldest son's visit to British India. Instead, Wilhelm II sailed off in his five Imperial yachts to the same places year after year, and crisscrossed the Europe he knew so well in his famed Imperial Train that is still partially preserved in the new Germany of today.

In a single day's hunt, the last German Emperor shot 550 pheasants, by 1897 had already killed 33,967 animals of all kinds, and was also well on his way to embroiling his country and its allies in a disastrous war by the turn of the twentieth century in but the 12th year of his reign of 30. He was a grandson of Queen Victoria: "What a woman!" he once said. "One could do business with her," but when the First World War broke out, he reportedly returned his British field marshal's insignia and baton, and later spoke bitterly of his English foes of the Great War. As late as August 1939, however, the Kaiser's uncle and the late Queen's third son— Arthur, Duke of Connaught—still proudly kept his Prussian Army baton in a desk drawer at his home in England, according to Wheeler-Bennett. He carried it next to King George V and the Kaiser at the May 1910 State Funeral of his late brother, King Edward VII, at London.

Huis Doorn Today

In an e-mail to me from noted author and collector Ray Cowdery on 7 August 2005, he asked, "Isn't it amazing that a little country" (Holland) is so museum-rich that the idea of closing a museum containing over 300 of the Kaiser's uniforms is a likehihood?"

As of this year 2014, *Huis Doorn* is still open to the public as a museum.

Kaiser Wilhelm II: The Adventure of His Orders & Medals by Michael Forman, 1992

This stunning little booklet contains photos of The Forman Collection of His Majesty's decorations that were used in the 1974 BBC TV production *Fall of Eagles,* the real ones being actually worn by actor Barry Foster portraying the Kaiser.

The booklet tells how the decorations came to be both found and then acquired, including this anecdote from 1950:

In Berlin, he was taken to an office in the Russian Zone [*of Occupation*], where on a large table were Kaiser Wilhelm's Orders, except for a few at Doorn in Holland, and those in the *Zeughaus of German History* on the *Unter den Linden* Street. The collection was priced at 4,000 Marks...

Later, I was fortunate to discover an original photograph of the Kaiser on his deathbed at Doorn, wearing the Group of Orders and Medals, and Black Eagle Breast Star. After the Kaiser's death, most of the Orders and Medals together with uniforms were taken to Berlin, *Exhibition Catalogue Kaiser Wilhelm II in Exile*. We continued to add to the collection when in Germany, principally West Berlin and Wiesbaden...

During one visit to Berlin ... we completely filled the car, so that two highly visible Garde du Corps helmets had to be placed in the back window, for all to see.

We were stopped by an East German Border Guard at Marienborn, who asked, "What is this?" I replied in English, "Garde du Corps helmet of the Kaiser." Very quickly, I took out one of the helmets, gesturing to him to put it on his head, which he did. His colleague made a comment in German.

I then took the second helmet and placed it on the second guard's head. They were very amused. As this point, I said, "For a museum." They ... smiled, handed back the helmets with a little bow, and waved us on. Much relieved, we crossed into West Germany with all speed...

In 1988—on the 100th anniversary of Kaiser Wilhelm II's accession to the throne—we decided to display all his Orders and Medals, with photographs and commemorative items in a single case, as part of the exhibition in the Dungeon.

The Kaiser's American Dentist's Accurate Predictions, September 1918

American Arthur N. Davis, DDS, was the Imperial family's dentist during 1903–17. He last saw the Kaiser on 27 November 1917, asserting that his patient never flinched in his chair from pain.

Dr Davis took over from American Dr Alonzo H. Sylvester, DDS as assistant. Sylvester shot himself due to debts on 10 January 1905. Dr Davis left Germany on 22 January 1918, predicting in his September 1918 memoirs that the Kaiser would fall via a mass uprising and the desertion of his own Army officer corps, exactly as occurred.

EPILOGUE: *How a German Soldier Still Loves His Dead Kaiser,* 17 February 2014

In *The Heritage of the Great War* there appeared an excellent article by Rob Ruggenberg entitled *Clanging of Swords, Sounds of Trumpets and Kettledrums: Germans Pay Honor at the Grave of Their Beloved Kaiser*:

No, to them he is no war criminal, no war inciter. To them he is their beloved Kaiser, the personification of a brave Germany, the victim of biased historians and a mean, Leftish press.

That's why they are here today, sounding their trumpets and beating their kettledrums and clanging their swords. They traveled with busloads from Germany to the Netherlands, because here the German Kaiser and *Oberste Kreigsherr* Wilhelm II lies buried...

Kaiser Wilhelm lived in exile for 22 years. The Germans never wanted him back. He died on 4 June 1941, and he was buried in a small mausoleum on the lawn of *Huis Doorn*, a small castle he had bought in 1919.

He was buried there on purpose, because the Kaiser considered his Dutch castle and its precincts "German soil." His body must stay there—he ordered in his Will—until in Germany the monarchy is restored.

Now every year in ... June, hundreds of German monarchists—yes, they still exist—come to Doorn to pay respect to the grave. Usually, the mausoleum is firmly locked, but for this special occasion, the keeper of the Hohenzollern family gives permission to open it up.

And so they arrive, with white flowers and military music: civilians and people marching in Prussian blue toy-soldier uniforms. They wear boots with spurs and bear skins and [carry] banners *Pro Patria et Gloria: Die Deutschen Kaiserfreunde.*

Among them this year is a subaltern officer of the *Bundeswehr*, the official German Army. He is in uniform. He carries the flowers and he stands firm at the grave of his Kaiser.

The *Bundeswehr* subaltern knows that the German government does not want her soldiers to take part in political happenings in uniform, "But I consider this not a political occasion," he says.

And besides that, his direct superior—an officer who has the picture of the Kaiser hanging in his office—has allowed him to attend this commemoration in his uniform, he says.

Yes—he is a strong monarchist, he loves the Hohenzollerns—but he refrains from answering further questions on this subject, "Because statements on this matter in the press will surely cause problems for me and for the *Bundeswehr*."

The commemoration begins. Knut Wissenbach—President of *Tradition and Life* from Cologne—addresses the gathered audience, all Germans. He tells them that for 80 years one-sided historians have given the world a wrong impression of the Kaiser...

"Now it is time for all Germans and other people of good will to stand up and protest against these biased versions of history.... Wilhelm II, [he says], had a *good judgment*, whatever others may say about that. The Kaiser may not have been completely free of some racial prejudices. On the other hand, he foresaw the problems with the Bolsheviks ... He was also a good Christian."

And because of that, all monarchists present join him in saying, *The Lord's Prayer.*

The Hohenzollern family is still going strong. Crown Pretender is Prince Georg Friedrich of Prussia, born in Bremen on 10 June 1976...(and who) "studied business at the Technical University Mountain Academy Freiburg, in Germany.

"The Crown Pretender visits *Huis Doorn* and the grave of the Kaiser occasionally. He even met with some members of the Dutch Cabinet there. When we took pictures of the commemoration, Prince Georg Friedrich was absent. His uncle Prince Michael von

Preussen came a few days later, and laid flowers on behalf of the family.

During his exile in Doorn, the Kaiser daily *sawed down trees*—more than 40,000 in total. He did so to get physical training. When he died in 1941, the country seat around the Castle looked almost as barren as a First World War battlefield.

Huis Doorn is a museum now. The Dutch government seized the Castle and the household effects in 1945 as being hostile German property. Many new trees were planted.

The Hohenzollern family was allowed to take personal belongings from the household, but what remained still forms a gigantic collection. The Castle has been renovated, and can be visited daily. The furniture is just like it was when the Kaiser lived.

During the 22 years Wilhelm II lived in The Netherlands, he embarrassed the Dutch government many times. He'd gotten political asylum because of his family relations with the *Dutch Royal family.* He had to promise that he would refrain from political activities.

Instead, the ex-Kaiser continuously worked for his return as an Emperor to Germany. When Hitler took Paris in 1940, he sent him a telegram of congratulation. He invited and received German politicians, including Nazis like Hermann Göring, but the Nazis did not want him back.

Nevertheless, two of his sons—including Crown Prince Wilhelm [*and also Prince August Wilhelm and his daughter Victoria Luise*] joined Nazi organizations (*sic*). Hermine von Reuss—the Princess he married in 1922 … was also a devoted follower of Nazi doctrines …

There were a few attempts to murder Wilhelm in Holland, but they were all ill-prepared, and were easily stopped by his staff.

Thus Wilhelm II remains, still discussed in death as if he were still alive.

A Final Glimpse of the Last German Emperor, 1911

In his postwar memoirs, German-Jewish electrical magnate Walther Rathenau (1867–1922) recalls first meeting his Imperial master thus:

> How different from what I'd expected! I knew the energetic, youthful pictures with broad cheeks, bristled moustache, threatening eyes; the dangerous telegrams, the speeches and mottos that exuded energy.
>
> There sat a youthful man in a colorful uniform, with odd medals, the white hands full of colored rings, bracelets on his wrists; tender skin, soft hair; small, white teeth.
>
> A true Prince, intent on the impression he made, continuously fighting with himself, overcoming his nature in order to wrest from it bearing, energy, mastery. Hardly an un-self-conscious moment; unconscious only—and here begins the part that is humanly touching—of the struggle with himself. A nature directed against itself, unsuspecting. Many have seen this besides me: neediness, softness, a longing for people, a childlike nature ravished, these were palpable behind athletic feats, high tension, and resounding activity, these people grasped and sympathized with.
>
> This man must be protected, guarded with a strong arm, against that which he feels, but

does not know, that which pulls him into the abyss.

The latest *Lesen & Schenken* German language book and artifacts catalog on my desk now shows many books and pictures of all manner of former German rulers and soldiers of all wars, but the very least is devoted to the still scorned last German Emperor, with even the Nazis taking pride of place over him. Will I live to see this altered? In the final analysis, the Kaiser—although unique in many ways, and for a long time as all-powerful as few mortals have been—was as complicated as many of the rest of us. To His Imperial Majesty Kaiser Wilhelm II, RIP.

Bibliography

Books

The Rise of Brandenburg-Prussia

The Teutonic Knights: A Military History by William Urban, London: Greenhill Books, 2003.

The Vanished Kingdom: Travels Through the History of Prussia by James Charles Roy, Oxford: Westview Press, 1999.

Forgotten Land: Journeys Among the Ghosts of East Prussia by Max Egremont, New York: Farrar, Straus, and Giroux, 2011.

Iron Kingdom: The Rise and Downfall of Prussia, 1600–1947 by Christopher Clark, Cambridge: The Bellknap Press of Harvard University Press, 2006.

The Great Elector by Derek McKay, London: Longman, 2001.

Frederick the Great: A Biography by Ludwig Reiners, New York: G. P. Putnam's Sons, 1960.

Frederick the Great: The Magnificent Enigma by Robert B. Asprey, New York: History Book Club, 1986.

Frederick the Great: A Military History by Dennis Showalter, London: Frontline Books, 2012.

The Hussar General: The Life of Blücher, Man of Waterloo by Roger Parkinson, London: Wordsworth Editions, 1975.

Kaiser Wilhelm's Family

The Prussian Princesses: The Sisters of Kaiser Wilhelm II, United Kingdom, Fonthill Media, 2014.

The Soldier Kings: The House of Hohenzollern by Walter Henry Nelson, New York: G. P. Putnam's Sons, 1970.

The Kaisers by Theo Aronson, Indianapolis: The Bobbs-Merrill Co., 1971.

An Uncommon Woman: The Empress Frederick/Daughter of Queen Victoria, Wife of the Crown Prince of Prussia, Mother of Kaiser Wilhelm by Hannah Pakula, New York: Simon & Schuster, 1995.

Royal Web: The Story of Princess Victoria & Frederick of Prussia by Ladislas Farago & Andrew Sinclair, New York, 1982.

Dearest Vicky, Darling Fritz: Queen Victoria's Daughter and the German Emperor by John Van der Kiste, Stroud, England: Sutton Publishing, 2001.

Frederick III: German Emperor 1888 by John Van der Kiste, Gloucester: Alan Sutton, 1981.

Frederick III: Germany's Liberal Emperor by Patricia Kollander, Westport, CT: Greenwood Press, 1995.

Diaries of the Emperor Frederick During the Campaigns of 1866 and 1870–71 as well as His Journeys to the East and to Spain edited by Margarethe von Poschinger, London: Chapman & Hall, Ltd., 1902.

The Year of the Three Kaisers; Bismarck and the German Succession, 1887–88 by J. Alden Nichols, Urbana and Chicago: University of Chicago Press, 1987.

Death of a Kaiser: A Medical Narrative by Jain I. Lin, MD, Dayton, OH: Landfall Press, Inc., 1985.

The Life of Crown Prince William by Klaus Jonas, London: Routledge & Kegan Paul, 1961.

The Bismarckian Era

1848: Year of Revolution by Mike Rapport, New York: Basic Books, 2008.
Bismarck: Von der Wiege bis zum Grab/From the Cradle to the Grave by Bruno Garlepp, New York: The Werner Co., 1898.
Bismarck: The Story of a Fighter by Emil Ludwig Cohn, Boston: Little, Brown, and Company, 1929.
Bismarck: The Man and the Statesman by A. J. P. Taylor, New York: Alfred A. Knopf, 1955.
Bismarck by Werner Richter, London: Macdonald, 1962.
Bismarck: A Life by Jonathan Steinberg, Oxford: Oxford University Press, 2011.
Bismarck and Germany, 1862–90 by D. G. Williamson, London: Longman, 1999.
Gold and Iron: Bismarck, Bleichroder, and the Building of the German Empire by Fritz Stern, New York: Vintage Books, 1979.
The Army of the German Empire, 1870–88 by Albert Seaton and Michael Youens, New York: Osprey Publishing, Ltd., 1973.

The Wilhelmine Age

Imperial Germany, 1890–1918 by Ian Porter and Ian D. Armour, London: Longman, 1999.
The Arms of Krupp, 1587–1968 by William Manchester, New York: Bantam Books, 1970.
The German Genius: Europe's Third Renaissance, the Second Scientific Revolution, and the 20th *Century* by Peter Watson, New York: Harper Perennial, 2010.
Germany's Road to Ruin: The Middle Years of the Reign of the Emperor William II by Karl Friedrich Nowak, New York: The Macmillan Company, 1931.
The Proud Tower: A Portrait of the World Before the War: 1890–1914 by Barbara W. Tuchman, New York: The Macmillan Co., 1966.
Imperial Berlin by Gerhard Masur, New York: Dorset Press, 1970.
Berlin by Dieter and Anke Adler, New York: Chartwell Books, Inc., 2008.
The Boxer Rebellion: The Dramatic Story of China's War on Foreigners that Shook the World in the Summer of 1900 by Diana Preston, New York: Berkley Books, 1999.
A Field Marshal's Memoirs from the Diary, Correspondence, and Reminiscences of Alfred, Count von Waldersee, Westport, CT: Greenwood Press, Publishers, 1978.
The Berlin-Baghdad Express: The Ottoman Empire and Germany's Bid for World Power by Sean McMeekin, Cambridge: The Belknap Press of Harvard University Press, 2010.
The Entourage of Kaiser Wilhelm II, 1888–1918 by Isabell V. Hull, Cambridge: Cambridge University Press, 1982.
1913: In Search of the World Before the Great War by Charles Emerson, New York: Public Affairs, 2013.
July 1914: Countdown to War by Sean McMeekin, New York: Basic Books, 2013.
The War That Ended Peace: The Road to 1914 by Margaret Macmillan, New York: Random House, 2013.
The Origins of the War of 1914: European Relations from the Congress of Berlin to the Eve of the Sarajevo Murder Volume 1; The Crisis of July 1914 from the Sarajevo Outrage to the Austro-Hungarian General Mobilization, Vol. 2; and The Epilogue of the Crisis of July 1914, the Declarations of War, and of Neutrality, Vol. 3 by Luigi Albertini, New York: Enigma Books, 2005.
The Kaiser as I Know Him by Arthur N. Davis, DDS, New York: Harper & Brothers Publishers, 1918.

The First World War 1914–18

History of the German General Staff, 1657–1945 by Walter Gorlitz, New York: Prager Paperbacks, 1953.
War Book of the German General Staff by J. H. Morgan, Mechanicsburg, PA: Stackpole Books.
Tannenberg: Clash of Empires by Dennis E. Showalter, Hamden, CT: Archon Books, 1991.
Helmuth von Moltke and the Origins of the First World War by Annika Mombauer, Cambridge: Cambridge University Press, 2001.
The Real German War Plan, 1904–14 by Terence Zuber, Stroud, UK: The History Press, 2011.
The Military Attache by Alfred Vagts, Princeton: Princeton University Press, 1967.
Germany's Aims in the First World War by Fritz Fischer, New York: W.W. Norton & Co., Inc., 1967.
The Great War by Cyril Falls, New York: G. P. Putnam's Sons, 1961.

The First World War by Hew Strachan, New York: Viking, 2003.

The Great War: A Combat History of the First World War by Peter Hart, Oxford: Oxford University Press, 2013.

The Swordbearers: Supreme Command in the First World War by Corelli Barnett, New York: Signet Books, 1963.

The Guns of August by Barbara W. Tuchman, New York: The Macmillan Co., 1962.

Opening Moves: August 1914 by John Keegan, New York: Ballantine Books, 1971.

The Marne by Georges Blond, New York: Pyramid Books, 1967.

The Marne, 1914: The Opening of World War I and the Battle That Changed the World by Holger W. Herwig, New York: Random House Trade Paperback, 2011.

Catastrophe 1914: Europe Goes to War by Max Hastings, New York: Alfred A. Knopf, 2013.

The Kaiser's Army in Color: Uniforms of the Imperial German Army as Illustrated by Karl Becker, 1890–1910 by Charles Woolley, Atglen, PA: Schiffer Military History Books, 2000.

Uniforms & Equipment of the Imperial German Army 1900–18: A Study in Period Photographs by Charles Woolley, Atglen, PA: Schiffer Military History, 1999.

Headdress of Imperial Germany, 1880–1916 by Paul Sanders, Atglen, PA: Schiffer Military History, 2001.

The Prussian Orden/Order Pour le Merite/For Your Merit: History of the Blue Max by David Edkins, Falls Church: Ajay Enterprises, 1981.

The Price of Glory: Verdun 1916 by Alistair Horne, New York: MacFadden-Bartell Books, 1964.

Verdun: The Lost History of the Most Important Battle of World War I, 1914–18 by John Mosier, New York: NAL Caliber, 2013.

The German High Command at War: Hindenburg and Ludendorff Conduct World War I by Robert B. Asprey, New York: William Morrow & Co., 1991.

Brushes & Bayonets: Cartoons, Sketches and Paintings of World War I by Lucinda Gosling, New York: Osprey Publishing in Association with The Illustrated London News Picture Library, 2008.

The First World War: A Photographic History by Laurence Stallings, New York: Simon & Schuster, 1933.

Handcuffed to a Corpse: German Intervention in the Balkans and on the Galician Front, 1914–17 by Michael P. Kihntopf, Shippensburg, PA: White Mane Books, 2002.

Prelude to Blitzkrieg: The 1916 Austro-German Campaign in Romania by Michael B. Barrett, Bloomington, IN: Indiana University Press, 2013.

The Zimmermann Telegram by Barbara W. Tuchman, New York: Dell Books, 1965.

Brest-Litovsk: The Forgotten Peace, March 1918 by John W. Wheeler-Bennett, New York: The Norton Library, 1971.

The Defeat of Imperial Germany, 1917–18 by Rod Paschall, New York: Da Capo Press, 1994.

1918: The Last Act by Barrie Pitt, New York: Ballantine Books, 1962.

No Man's Land: 1918—The Last Year of the Great War by John Toland, Garden City, NY: Doubleday & Co., Inc, 1980.

The Hundred Days: The Campaign That Ended World War I by Nick Lloyd, New York: Basic Books, 2014.

The Greatest Day in History: How, on the 11th Hour of the 11th Day of the 11th Month, the First World War Finally Came to an End by Nicholas Best, New York: Public Affairs, 2008.

The Great War in the Air: Military Aviation from 1909–21 by John H. Morrow, Jr., Washington, DC: Smithsonian Institution Press, 1993.

The Canvas Falcons: The Men and Planes of World War I by Stephen Longstreet, New York: Barnes & Noble Books, 1970.

The Zeppelin in Combat: A History of the German Naval Airship Division, 1912–18 by Douglas H. Robinson, Atglen, PA: Schiffer Military History, 1994.

Pictorial History of the German Army Air Service 1914–18 by Alex Imre, Chicago: Henry Regnery Co., 1973.

Jutland 1916: Death in the Grey Wastes by Nigel Steel & Peter Hart, London: Cassell, 2004.

The Kaiser's Merchant Ships in World War I by William Lowell Putnam, Jefferson, NC: McFarland & Co., Inc., 2001.

Seize the Trident: The Race for Superliner Supremacy and how it Altered the Great War by Douglas R. Burgess, Jr., New York: International Marine/McGraw, 2005.

The Overthrow of Kaiser Wilhelm II, 1918

The Kaiser and His Court: The Diaries of Admiral Georg von Müller, edited by Walter Gorlitz, New York: Harcourt, Brace, and World, 1961.
The Kings Depart/The Tragedy of Germany: Versailles and the German Revolution by Richard M. Watt, New York: Simon and Schuster, 1968.
The Fall of Eagles: The Death of the Great European Dynasties by C. L. Sulzberger, New York: Crown Publishers, Inc., 1977.
Eclipse of Kings: European Monarchies in the 20th Century by Denis Judd, New York: Stein & Day, 1974.
The Fall of the Kaiser by Maurice Baumont, New York: Alfred A. Knopf, 1931.

Selected Post-First World War Memoirs

Great Contemporaries by Winston S. Churchill, Wilmington, DE: Intercollegiate Studies Institute, 2012.
Daisy Princess of Pless by Herself, New York: E. P. Dutton & Co., Inc., 1923.
Better Left Unsaid by Daisy Princess of Pless, New York: E.P. Dutton & Co., Inc, 1931.
Memoirs of Prince von Bülow, Volume 1: From Secretary of State to Imperial Chancellor, 1897–1903 by Bernhard von Bülow, Boston: Little, Brown, and Company, 1931.
Memoirs of Prince von Bülow, Vol. 2: From the Morocco Crisis to Resignation, 1903–09 by Bernhard von Bülow, Boston: Little, Brown, and Company, 1931.
Memoirs of Prince von Bülow, Vol. 3: The World War and Germany's Collapse, 1909–19 by Bernhard von Bülow, Boston: Little, Brown, and Company, 1932.
Memoirs of Prince von Bülow, Vol. 4: Early Years and Diplomatic Service, 1849–97 by Bernhard von Bülow, Boston: Little, Brown, and Company, 1932.
Memoirs of the German Crown Prince Wilhelm, London: Thornton Butterworth, 1922.
The Memoirs of Crown Princess Cecilie, London: Victor Gollancz, Ltd., 1931.
The Kaiser's Daughter: Memoirs of HRH Victoria Luise, Princess of Prussia, New York: Prentice-Hall, Inc., 1965.

The Paris Peace Conference and Versailles Treaty, 1918–19

Paris 1919: Six Months That Changed the World by Margaret Macmillan, New York: Random House, 2003.

Kaiser Wilhelm in his Own Write

The German Emperor's Speeches: Being a Selection from the Speeches, Edicts, Letters, and Telegrams of the Emperor Wilhelm II translated by Louis Elkind, MD, London; Longmans, Green, and Co., 1904.
The War Lord: A Character Study of Kaiser Wilhelm II, by Means of His Speeches, Letters, and Telegrams compiled by J. M. Kennedy, New York: Duffield & Co., 1914.
The Kaiser's Letters to the Tsar copied from Government Archives in Petrograd and brought from Russia by Isaac Don Levine, London: Hodder and Stoughton Ltd., 1920.
The Kaiser's Memoirs by Wilhelm II, Emperor of Germany 1888–1918, New York: Harper & Brothers Publishers, 1922.
My Early Life by William II, ex-Emperor of Germany, New York: George H. Doran Company, 1926.
My Ancestors by William II, London: William Heinemann Ltd., 1929.

Biographies by American Authors

A View of the Spree by Alson J. Smith, New York: The John Day Company, 1962.
The Kaiser by Virginia Cowles, New York: Harper & Row, Publishers; 1963.
The Kaiser and His Times by Michael Balfour, Boston: Houghton Mifflin Co., 1964.
Wilhelm II: Prince and Emperor, 1859–1900 by Lamar Cecil, Chapel Hill: The University of North Carolina Press, 1989.
Wilhelm II: Emperor and Exile, 1900–41 by Lamar Cecil, Chapel Hill: The University of North Carolina, 1996.

Kaiser and Führer: A Comparative Study of Personality and Politics by Robert G. L. Waite, Toronto: University of Toronto Press, 1998.

Biographies by British Authors

The Kaiser and English Relations by E. F. Benson, London: Longmans, Green and Co., 1936.
The Last Kaiser: A Biography of Wilhelm II, German Emperor and King of Prussia by Tyler Whittle, New York: NY Times Books, 1978.
Kaiser Wilhelm II: Germany's Last Emperor by John van der Kiste, Phoenix Mill, UK: Sutton Publishing, 1999.
The Last Kaiser: The Life of Wilhelm II by Giles Macdonogh, New York: St Martin's Press, 2000.
King, Kaiser, Tsar: Three Royal Cousins Who Led the World to War by Catrine Clay, New York: Walker & Co., 2006.
George, Nicholas, and Wilhelm: Three Royal Cousins and the Road to World War I by Miranda Carter, New York: Alfred A. Knopf, Publisher; 2010.

Biographies by German Authors

Imperator et Rex: William II of Germany by Marguerite Cunliffe-Owens, New York: Harper & Brothers, Publishers, 1904.
The Kaiser: A Life of Wilhelm II, Last Emperor of Germany by Joachim von Kürenberg, New York: Simon & Schuster, 1955.
Wilhelm Hohenzollern: The Last of the Kaisers by Emil Ludwig Cohn, New York: G. P. Putnam's Sons, 1927.
Kaiser Wilhelm II: New Interpretations edited by John C. G. Röhl and Nicolaus Sombart, Cambridge: Cambridge University Press, 1982.
The Kaiser and His Court: Wilhelm II and the Government of Germany by John C. G. Röhl, Cambridge: Cambridge University Press, 1987.
Wilhelm II and the Germans: A Study in Leadership by Thomas A. Kohut, New York: Oxford University Press, 1991.
Young Wilhelm: The Kaiser's Early Life, 1859–88 by John C. G. Röhl, Cambridge: Cambridge University Press, 1998.
The Kaiser: New Research on Wilhelm II's Role in Imperial Germany edited by Annika Mombauer and Wilhelm Deist, Cambridge: Cambridge University Press, 2003.
Wilhelm II: The Kaiser's Personal Monarchy, 1888–1900 by John C. G. Röhl, Cambridge: Cambridge University Press, 2004.
Wilhelm II: Into the Abyss of War and Exile, 1900–41 by John C. G. Röhl, Cambridge: Cambridge University Press, 2014.

Other Biographies

Kaiser Wilhelm II: A Life in Power by Christopher Clark, New York, Penquin Books, 2009

Imperial Germany as World Power

The Pan-German League, 1890–1914 by Mildred S. Wertheimer, New York: Octagon Books, 1971.
Business and Politics in Imperial Germany, 1888–1918 by Lamar Alexander, Princeton: Princeton University Press, 1967.
Passenger Liners from Germany, 1816–1990 by Clas Brodrer Hansen, Atglen, PA: Schiffer Publishing Co., 1991.
The Lusitania by Colin Simpson, New York: Ballentine Books, 1972.
The Scramble for Africa: The White Man's Conquest of the Dark Continent from 1876 to 1912 by Thomas Pakenham, New York: Random House Publishing Co., 1991.
The German Colonial Empire, 1884–1919 by W. O. Henderson, London: Frank Cass & Co., Ltd., 1993.
The German Colonial Empire by Woodruff D. Smith, Chapel Hill: The University of North Carolina Press, 1978.

Germany's First Bid for Colonies, 1884–85: A Move in Bismarck's European Policy by A. J. P. Taylor, New York: Archon Books, 1967.

The German Presence in the Western Grassfields, 1891–1913: A German Colonial Account by Paul Nichoji Nkwi, Leiden, The Netherlands: African Studies Center, 1989.

Dream of Empire: German Colonialism, 1919–45 by Wolfe W. Schmokel, New Haven and London: Yale University Press, 1964.

Uniforms of the German Colonial Troops, 1884–1918 by Charles Woolley, Atglen, PA: Schiffer Military History Publishing, 2009.

Germany's Genocide of the Herero: The Kaiser's Holocaust: Germany's Forgotten Genocide and the Colonial Roots of Nazism by David Olusoga & Casper Erickson, London: Faber and Faber, 2011.

The Samoan Triangle: A Study in Anglo-German-American Relations, 1878–1900 by Paul M. Kennedy, New York: Harper & Row Publishers, Inc., 1974.

By Order of the Kaiser: Otto von Diederichs and the Rise of the Imperial German Navy, 1865–1902 by Terrell D. Gottshcall, Annapolis: Naval Institute Press, 2003.

Bismarck's Rival: A Political Biography of General and Admiral Albrecht von Stosch by Frederic B. M. Hollyday, Durham, NC: Duke University Press, 1960.

The German Naval Officer Corps: A Social and Political History, 1890–1918 by Holger H. Herwig, Oxford: The Clarendon Press, 1973.

The Great Naval Race: The Anglo-German Naval Rivalry, 1900–14 by Peter Padfield, New York: David McKay Co., Inc., 1974.

'Luxury' Fleet: The German Imperial Navy, 1888–1918 by Holger W. Herwig, London: The Ashfield Press, 1987.

The Great Naval Game: Britain & Germany in the Age of Empire by Jan Ruger, Cambridge, MA: Cambridge University Press, 2007.

Tirpitz: Architect of the German High Seas Fleet by Michael Epkenhans, Dulles, VA: Potomac Books, Inc., 2008.

Imperialism at Sea: Naval Strategic Thought, the Ideology of Sea Power, and the Tirpitz Plan, 1875–1914 by Rolf Hobson, Boston & Leiden: Brill Academic Publishers, Inc., 2002.

Yesterday's Deterrent: Tirpitz and the Birth of the German Battle Fleet by Jonathan Steinberg, New York: The Macmillan Co., 1965.

Building the Kaiser's Navy; The Imperial Navy Office and German Industry in the von Tirpitz Era, 1890–1919 by Gary E. Weir, Annapolis: Naval Institute Press, 1992.

My Memoirs Volumes 1 & 2 by Grand Admiral von Tirpitz, New York: Dodd, Mead, & Co., 1919.

Dreadnought: Britain, Germany, and the Coming of the Great War by Robert K. Massie, New York: Random House Publishing Co., 1991.

Castles of Steel: Britain, Germany, and the Winning of the Great War at Sea by Robert K. Massie, New York: Ballentine Books, 2003.

Heligoland: The True Story of German Bight and the Island That Britain Betrayed by George Brower, United Kingdom: Sutton Publishing, Ltd., 2002.

The Riddle of the Sands by Erskine Childers, Pleasantville, NY: The Reader's Digest, 1903 & 2008.

The Kaiser in Exile in Holland 1918–41

The Ex-Kaiser in Exile by Lady Norah Bentinck, New York: George H. Doran Company, 1921.

An Empress in Exile: My Days in Doorn by Empress Hermine, New York: J. H. Sears & Company, Inc, Publishers, 1928.

Knaves, Fools, and Heroes in Europe Between the Wars by Sir John W. Wheeler-Bennett, New York: St Martin's Press, 1974.

Novels

The Kaiser's Last Kiss by Alan Judd, London: Harper Perennial, 2003.

Articles

Benedict XV, Wilson, Michaelis, and German Socialism by John I. Snell, The Catholic Historical Review, Volume XXXVII, #2, July 1954, pp. 151–178.

The Kaiser and His Biographers by Blaine Taylor, Towson State College Modern Germany, 1871–1945 course, Dr Herbert Andrews, 1 March 1971.

Health in History: The Hohenzollern Kaisers by Blaine Taylor, Managing Editor, MD State Med. J., Baltimore: Medical & Chirurgical Faculty of the State of Maryland, June 1976.

Three Deliveries That Changed the History of the World: Kaiser Wilhelm II by Louis M. Hellman, MD, MD State Med. J., September 1972.

The German Emperor and England/Personal Interview/Frank Statement of World Policy/Proofs of Friendship, London: The Daily Telegraph, 28 October 1908.

Secrets of the Kaiser: "A battleship with steam up and screws going, but with no rudder," by Christopher Andrew, The Listener, 7 June 1984.

Kaiser Wilhelm II and the Cartoonists by W. A. Coupe, History Today, November 1980, pp. 16–22.

Empress Auguste Viktoria/(Dona) and the Fall of the German Monarchy by Andreas Dorpalen, American Historical Review, LVIII, 2 (1952), pp. 17-38.

Advent: The Rise of Wilhelm II, 1888–90, unpublished, unfinished manuscript by Blaine Taylor, Binh Chanh, former South Vietnam, 1 May 1967.

The Kaiser's Navy, Part 1 by Blaine Taylor, Canoga Park, CA: Sea Classics magazine, Challenge Publications, June 1993, Vol. 26, # 6 pp. 32-39, 72.

The Kaiser's Navy, Part 2 by Blaine Taylor, Canoga Park, CA: Sea Classics magazine, Challenge Publications, July 1993, Vol. 26, #7, pp. 48-56.

German World Power and the Alliance Negotiations with England, 1897–1900, by Paul M. Kennedy, Journal of Modern History, Vol. 45, #4, December 1973, pp. 605–25.

Gott, Kaiser, Vaterland/God, Emperor, Fatherland: Military and Patriotic Music of Imperial Germany, DVD, Brandenburg Historica, LLC, 2005, 2007.

Hoch Deutschlands Flotte/Hail Germany's Fleet! Music of the Imperial German Navy, Brandenburg Historica, LLC, 2006.

The Cult of Monarchy, Political Loyalty, and the Workers' Movement in Imperial Germany by Werner K. Blessing, SAGE, London & Beverly Hills, CA: *Journal of Contemporary History,* Vol. 13, 1978, pp. 357-75.

Government by Procrastination: Chancellor Hohenlohe and Kaiser Wilhelm II, 1894–1900 by J. David Fraley, *Central European History,* Vol. VII, #2, June 1974, pp. 159-83.

The Contemporary Colonial Movement in Germany, 1919–39, by Mary E. Townsend, Lancaster, PA: *Political Science Quarterly,* 1928, Vol. 43, pp. 64-75.

The German Colonies and the Third Reich by Mary E. Townsend, *Political Science Quarterly,* New York: Columbia University, 1938, Vol. 5, pp. 186-206.

A German Plan for the Invasion of Holland and Belgium, 1897 by Jonathan Steinberg, Cambridge, UK: *Historical Journal,* Vol. 6, #1, 1963, pp. 107-119.

"My Name is Ozymandias:" The Kaiser in Exile by Sally Marks, 2001. ("Ozymandias" is the title of a sonnet written by Percy Bysshe Shelley published in 1818, and was an alternate name for Egyptian Pharoah Ramses II that explores the fate of history and the ravages of time; that all prominent men, and the empires they build, are impermanent, and that their legacies fade to decay and oblivion, comparing that of Ramses II to that of Wilhelm II.)

Internet Sites

madmonarchist.blogspot.co.uk This is *the* very best site for *all* things monarchy, of *all* monarchists: articles, pictures, videos—not to be missed! I can't recommend this highly enough!